T0135862

Integration of Wireless Sensor Networks in Pervasive Computing Scenarios

Matthias Gauger

2010

Dissertation zur Erlangung des Doktorgrads (Dr. rer. nat.)

Angefertigt mit Genehmigung der Mathematisch-Naturwissenschaftlichen Fakultät
der Rheinischen Friedrich-Wilhelms-Universität Bonn.

Erstgutachter: Prof. Dr. rer. nat. habil. Pedro José Marrón, Rheinische Friedrich-
                   Wilhelms-Universität Bonn, Universität Duisburg-Essen
Zweitgutachter: Prof. Dr. rer. nat. Dr. h. c. Kurt Rothermel, Universität Stuttgart

Datum der mündlichen Prüfung: 22.03.2010

Bibliografische Information der Deutschen Nationalbibliothek

Die Deutsche Nationalbibliothek verzeichnet diese Publikation in der
Deutschen Nationalbibliografie; detaillierte bibliografische Daten sind
im Internet über http://dnb.d-nb.de abrufbar.

ISBN 978-3-8325-2469-2

Logos Verlag Berlin GmbH
Comeniushof, Gubener Str. 47,
10243 Berlin
Tel.: +49 (0)30 42 85 10 90
Fax: +49 (0)30 42 85 10 92
INTERNET: http://www.logos-verlag.de

Acknowledgments

My research work and this dissertation would not have been possible without the help and support by many people. I would like to take the opportunity to thank them here.

First of all, I would like to thank my advisor Prof. Dr. Pedro José Marrón for making the work on my thesis possible and for supporting me and my ideas. I am also grateful to Prof. Dr. Kurt Rothermel in whose department in Stuttgart I had the pleasure to begin my work and who continued supporting me as the co-advisor of my thesis. Special thanks also go to Prof. Dr. Michael Clausen and Prof. Dr. Peter Schulze Lammers who kindly accepted to be part of my dissertation committee.

I am very thankful for all the support I received during the last years from my colleagues both at the Universität Bonn and the Universität Stuttgart. My work would have been much more difficult without their contributions and a lot less fun without their companionship.

A special thank you goes to my colleague and very good friend Olga Saukh who I shared an office with both in Stuttgart and in Bonn. She was always available for fruitful discussions, for reviewing drafts of my work or just for providing another perspective on everything. Thanks, Olya!

I am lucky to have friends who greatly contributed to keeping me sane by providing for a lot of good times outside of the university. I really appreciate that they always remain good friends irrespective of which city I am currently moving to. You guys rock!

Finally, I want to give thanks to my family. I am very grateful for all the support and encouragement I received from my parents and my sisters during my studies and the work on my dissertation. I could not have done it without you!

Contents

Contents

List of Figures

List of Figures

List of Tables

List of Tables

Abstract

Wireless sensor networks consist of a large number of small, resource-constrained computing devices that are distributed in the environment and communicate over a wireless interface. The nodes use integrated sensors to monitor certain aspects of their environment and cooperate with each other in fulfilling a joint sensing task. The vision of pervasive computing is to integrate computers and computing technology in all kinds of everyday objects and to make services provided by these computers available to users at any place and at any time. The goal thereby is to integrate these services as seamlessly as possible with the user's environment and make interacting with them a natural task.

There exists a significant overlap between the two research areas of wireless sensor networks and pervasive computing both in the goals of their application scenarios and in the tasks and concepts of their system operations. One important aspect is the dependence of typical pervasive computing applications on many different types of environmental data and context information that might be provided by wireless sensor nodes and sensor networks. This motivates the integration of wireless sensor networks in pervasive computing scenarios.

Despite all similarities, using wireless sensor networks as part of pervasive computing scenarios is a difficult problem. It involves providing functionality and node behavior required by pervasive computing applications given the very limited capabilities and the constraints of wireless sensor nodes. Differences in the system model and the focus on specific research problems are also the main reason why the two research areas of wireless sensor networks and pervasive computing have been discussed largely separately from each other in different research communities so far.

The goal of the work presented in this thesis is to investigate the problem of integrating wireless sensor nodes and wireless sensor networks in pervasive computing scenarios and to develop solutions that facilitate such an integration. Based on an analysis of both research areas, of their specific properties and requirements as well as the similarities and differences of the two fields, we identify and discuss a set of five fundamental problem areas that complicate the integration of sensor networks and pervasive computing: communication, network setup and configuration, user experience, security and flexibility and adaptability.

The main part of this thesis introduces a total of six individual contributions that address different aspects of the problem of integrating wireless sensor networks into pervasive computing scenarios. The first solution approach deals with the routing of messages between mobile client devices and static, resource-constrained sensor nodes. The second and third solution approach consider the setup and configuration of wireless sensor nodes in typical pervasive computing scenarios and provide solutions to facilitate the configuration of a large number of nodes. Our fourth approach provides three different solutions to the problem of directly interacting with individual sensor nodes deployed in the environment. As part of our fifth solution approach we discuss a method for securing such interactions against malicious attacker nodes. In particular, we consider the assignment of secret key data to sensor nodes. The sixth and final solution approach contributes to the goal of supporting the flexibility and adaptability requirements of pervasive computing applications on resource-constrained wireless sensor nodes by providing an efficient code module exchange mechanism.

1 Introduction

Sensors have been integrated in different items of our everyday life for a long time, for example in thermometers, weather stations, motion detectors, smoke detectors or photoelectric barriers. A few years ago, researchers have begun to integrate different sensors together with a microcontroller, memory and a wireless communication interface into small embedded systems, the so-called wireless sensor nodes. Work on these small, resource-constrained devices has established a new branch of research which is primarily interested in the cooperation of many such nodes in wireless sensor networks.

The vision of pervasive computing (which is also often called ubiquitous computing) is to make information and services provided by computers available to users at any place and at any time. The idea is to enrich the environment of the user with a variety of novel applications and services by embedding intelligence in the form of a large number of computers, different types of sensors and diverse interaction mechanisms. At the same time, pervasive computing aims for an intuitive, natural interaction with the services and the environment. For this purpose, the computing devices providing these services have to work in an unobtrusive manner that does not interfere with the user's primary tasks and interests: The technology is supposed to disappear in the background [209].

Wireless sensor networks and pervasive computing share many goals and concepts and overlap in their areas of application. In particular, sensor nodes and sensor networks can play an important role in pervasive computing scenarios as providers of context data. However, an integration of the two types of systems is very difficult. This is mainly due to different assumptions concerning the system model, different capabilities of the devices involved and different application requirements.

The goal of the work presented in this thesis is to support the integration of wireless sensor networks in pervasive computing scenarios. Instead of treating both areas separately, we consider integrated systems consisting of both wireless sensor nodes and mobile pervasive computing devices. We aim to find solutions that facilitate the cooperation among the different types of devices in providing pervasive services to the users so that all participating nodes can contribute based on their respective capabilities and strengths and support each others' operation.

1.1 Motivation

To motivate our work on integrating wireless sensor networks in pervasive computing scenarios, it is helpful to take a short look at the main ideas and properties of the two types of systems.

Wireless sensor nodes are small, autonomous devices cooperating to achieve a common application goal. The small size of the nodes together with cost limitations and the need to operate wirelessly result in strong resource limitations being a fundamental property of individual sensor nodes and sensor networks as a whole. These limitations concern the available processing power, the capacity of the volatile and non-volatile memory, the transmission power of the wireless transceiver and the precision of the sensors. However, the most significant limitation of wireless sensor nodes lies in their limited energy supply.

Research in wireless sensor networks deals with a variety of topics, for example routing [4], localization [20], topology control [175], clustering [223] data aggregation [164] or security [159]. Common to all these research fields is that conserving resources in general and saving energy in particular must be one of the primary goals of the approaches developed for wireless sensor networks.

Sensor networks have the potential to be used in a variety of application areas and many promising application ideas have already been discussed in the literature. Some of these ideas have been realized in prototype deployments and a few sensor networks are already used in commercial systems. Popular examples of (future) application areas are the monitoring of flora and fauna [196, 39], precision agriculture [26, 224] or structural health monitoring [140, 132, 182, 124]. Another important application field for wireless sensor networks that we consider as part of this thesis lies in the area of pervasive computing.

The idea of pervasive computing is to integrate computing technology into a multitude of everyday objects and devices that together form an intelligent environment. Compared to wireless sensor networks, pervasive computing scenarios consist of a much more diverse set of devices ranging from mobile devices carried by the user over smart items deployed in the environment to high-performance computers operating as part of the infrastructure. All these devices cooperate in providing applications and services to their users.

Both the set of research topics and the set of application areas of pervasive computing are very diverse. Areas of research range from typical system topics like distributed systems and mobile computing to human-computer interaction and artificial intelligence. Examples of application scenarios for pervasive computing include healthcare [150], intelligent factories [214] or intelligent offices and smart homes.

The context of the user plays an essential role in pervasive computing, because many services rely on information about the current state of the user's environment and on the current situation of the user himself to fulfill their tasks. One important type of context information required in many cases is the position of the user. Depending on the type of application, a diverse set of other types of context information can play a role, including the temperature, the noise level, the number of persons present in the room or even the current mood of the user.

Sensor nodes and wireless sensor networks can play an important role in realizing the vision of pervasive computing by providing widely needed context data. Sensor nodes can record environmental data and support the operation of pervasive applications by providing this information to client devices in an appropriate manner. The task of a sensor network can thereby be limited to providing raw sensor data but can also involve the cooperative preprocessing and interpretation of data. In this case, the sensor nodes provide context information that can be directly used by the pervasive computing applications.

Despite the strong relationship between sensor networks and pervasive computing, the two research areas have been largely treated separately from each other so far. In sensor network scenarios, the focus usually lies on an efficient collection of data with resource-poor devices and the transport of this data to a sink node. In contrast, pervasive computing scenarios assume more powerful devices and solutions concentrate on problems in this area (e.g., mobility, interaction, user experience ...).

Combining the two types of systems with their different assumptions on the system models, device capabilities and application requirements is a hard challenge. It not only pertains to the question of how pervasive computing applications can access data of existing wireless sensor networks and how they can benefit of the provided information but also to the problem of having sensor networks play an active role in pervasive computing while not overburdening the individual sensor nodes. Answering these questions and solving problems related to such an integration is the focus of the work presented in this thesis.

1.2 Contributions

With the work described in this thesis, we address the problem of integrating wireless sensor networks in pervasive computing scenarios. Our work provides several contributions to this field that deal with different aspects of the problem. Many of these contributions are also relevant to the field of wireless sensor networks in general.

Our first contribution lies in a thorough discussion of the relationship of wireless sensor networks and pervasive computing and a motivation of the need for a better integration of the two areas. Based on this, we identify five fundamental problem areas that must be addressed to facilitate such an integration: Communication, network setup and configuration, user experience, security and flexibility and adaptability. We then introduce six different solution approaches that have been developed as part of this thesis each addressing one of the five problem fields and together contributing to an integration of wireless sensor networks and pervasive computing.

The first problem area that we deal with in this thesis is the communication among nodes and we propose a novel solution to the problem of routing messages between mobile devices and a wireless sensor network. Such a routing is difficult to do efficiently, because mobile devices contact the sensor network from different locations and need to be able to send queries to arbitrary areas in the network. We propose a solution that performs a source routing based on symbolic coordinates. It divides the routing overhead between the client device which has to specify a source route on the symbolic level and the wireless sensor nodes which are able to translate the symbolic route information into node-to-node routing decisions using purely local neighborhood information.

The second individual contribution of this thesis deals with the problem of configuring sensor networks that form a part of a pervasive computing scenario. More specifically, we are looking into simple ways of assigning symbolic coordinates to sensor nodes as are required by our routing based on symbolic coordinates. We specifically consider indoor scenarios and provide a solution that does a room-level assignment of symbolic coordinates. The idea is to send out symbolic coordinates by broadcast messages and filter on the receiver nodes based on sensor events.

We continue our work on the problem of configuring sensor nodes and sensor networks in pervasive computing scenarios with a discussion of how sensor nodes can autonomously learn about the context they are operating in. Such context information is important for interpreting the sensor data the nodes provide with respect to the environment and the context of the nodes. We consider a specific type of context information, namely the grouping of nodes based on real-world semantics. The idea is to group nodes together that are located in the same room. In our approach we do this grouping based on a statistical analysis of the sensor data that the various nodes collect. We then assign nodes that experience similar external conditions to the same group.

Another important problem that we deal with in this thesis is the interaction between users and devices of a pervasive computing scenario on the one hand and wireless sensor nodes deployed as part of such a scenario on the other hand. Users should be able to easily select sensor nodes for an interaction (for example to query the sensor readings of this node) based on criteria intuitive to the user. We introduce and discuss three different approaches to this problem that build upon different assumptions regarding the capabilities of the sensor nodes and the required actions by the user. One approach is based on gestures, one on interacting using light signals and the third approach allows the user to quickly browse through a list of nodes in order to select the correct destination node.

Related to the general problem of interacting with wireless sensor nodes is the problem of securing such interactions against external attacks. In the very dynamic context of pervasive computing scenarios, an important aspect of securing interactions and providing communication security in general is the availability of secret key information on the wireless sensor nodes. As part of this thesis, we provide a solution for the secure assignment of key information from mobile devices to wireless sensor nodes. The idea is to transmit the key information over a separate communication channel that cannot be accessed and tampered with from the outside. We achieve this by transmitting the key using a light signal that can be recorded by the sensor nodes using their integrated light sensors and transformed back to the original key sequence without requiring additional hardware.

Finally, this thesis also deals with the problem of customizing the behavior of sensor nodes in pervasive computing scenarios as part of solving the problem field of flexibility and adaptability. Due to the wide variety of devices, applications and user requirements, it can be necessary for a pervasive computing application to install custom code on the sensor nodes in the environment of its user to optimally support the application requirements. While executing different applications is usually trivial on more powerful devices, switching between applications is a challenge on wireless sensor nodes. Our contribution in this regard is a novel code update mechanism for wireless sensor nodes which provides for an efficient way of exchanging and integrating individual application code modules instead of exchanging the complete code image installed on a sensor node. This way, mobile pervasive computing devices can quickly distribute, install and execute custom application code on the sensor nodes in their vicinity.

Major contributions of this thesis have been published in international scientific workshops, conferences and journals [55, 57, 56, 61, 60, 62, 64, 59, 63, 58] including WSAN 2007 [57], COMSWARE 2008 [56], REALWSN 2008 [60], SECON 2008 [62], PerCom 2009 [64], INSS 2009 [59], MASS 2009 [63] and the Telecommunication Systems Journal [58].

1.3 Structure

The rest of this thesis is structured as follows. In chapter 2 we provide background information relevant to this thesis. It consists of a thorough description of the two research areas wireless sensor networks and pervasive computing including their main system properties and an overview of important application fields.

In chapter 3 we describe our approach of integrating wireless sensor networks in pervasive computing scenarios in more detail. We start with a detailed motivation of the problem and describe the general objectives of this work. We then describe our system model and introduce an example application that further motivates our work. In the main part of the chapter, we identify five different problem areas related to the integration of sensor networks and pervasive computing. We then provide an overview of our six solution approaches and classify them based on their contribution to solving the different problems.

After this general overview, the subsequent chapters describe the individual contributions of this thesis in more detail:

In chapter 4 we present our approach to the routing of messages between mobile devices and wireless sensor nodes that is based on symbolic coordinates. We continue in chapter 5 with the description of our approach to assigning symbolic coordinates to wireless sensor nodes in an efficient manner. Related to this is the topic of chapter 6 in which we discuss the self-configuration of sensor networks based on real-world criteria and introduce our solution to an automatic grouping of nodes based on the rooms the nodes are placed in.

Chapters 7 and 8 focus on the interaction of mobile users with wireless sensor nodes. Chapter 7 describes our three approaches to the problem of facilitating the interaction with specific nodes. In chapter 8 we deal with the problem of securing the interaction between users and wireless sensor nodes. More specifically, we describe our solution for assigning secret keys to wireless sensor nodes in a secure and efficient manner. The work in this chapter is also related to the problem of configuring wireless sensor nodes as discussed in chapters 5 and 6.

In chapter 9 we describe the final contribution of this thesis, a code module exchange mechanism that provides for efficient code updates in wireless sensor networks and that allows mobile users and devices to easily install and execute custom application modules on the wireless sensor nodes in their vicinity.

Finally, in chapter 10 we summarize the contributions of this work, provide an outlook to possible future research activities in this area and end this thesis with some concluding remarks.

2 Background

In this chapter we present background information relevant to the work of this thesis. We start with a more detailed description of the concept of wireless sensor networks including their main system properties, an overview of the state of the art in wireless sensor network systems and some exemplary application scenarios. We then continue with a similar description for the research field of pervasive computing and also discuss important differences between the two types of systems.

2.1 Wireless Sensor Networks

Wireless sensor networks are an active area of research with numerous research groups covering a large number of topics [5, 39, 220], for example routing [4], localization [20], topology control [175], clustering [223] data aggregation [164] or security [159]. The idea of wireless sensor networks is to instrument the environment with a large number of small, resource-constrained devices, the so-called wireless sensor nodes. These sensor nodes use integrated sensor chips to monitor specific properties of their environment and cooperate with each other by communicating messages over a wireless communication channel to achieve a common goal.

While each individual sensor node only records a small part of the relevant data and does only possess very limited resources for storing and processing it, the sensor network as a whole with all nodes contributing and cooperating is much more powerful and is able to monitor the complete application area and also support sophisticated applications.

A typical application example motivating the use of wireless sensor networks is the monitoring of natural habitats as it has been realized by the Great Duck Island project [196]. In this application, wireless sensor nodes were used to monitor the behavior of a breading colony of sea birds recording data like the temperature or the humidity in the burrows. Advantages of using wireless sensor networks in this setting included the possibility to distribute large numbers of nodes thus taking measurements at many locations, the small size of the sensor nodes which allowed placing the nodes near the monitored subjects without interfering with their normal behavior and the fact that no extensive infrastructure had to be installed for operating the sensor network.

An early vision that still inspires much research in the area of wireless sensor networks is the idea of having sensor nodes with the size of a single dust particle. Such sensor networks could not only be integrated in all kinds of everyday objects but could also be dispersed in a way similar to how dust moves with the wind. The Smart Dust project [89, 208] followed this goal and developed wireless sensor nodes with a size of

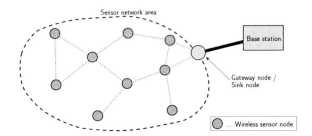

Figure 2.1: Overview of a typical sensor network architecture

only a few cubic millimeters. One solution approach they used to achieve such a small form factor was a passive optical communication where the sensor nodes communicate by either reflecting or not reflecting a beam of light sent by the base station.

Even if a node size in the range of the size of a dust particle is not required for most sensor network application scenarios, the node size is still one of the determining factors in the design of wireless sensor nodes. Only small sensor devices can be attached to a variety of real-world objects without interfering with the object's purpose or the experience of the user of an object.

Another important factor is the cost of the individual devices. This is mainly due to two reasons. Firstly, with the expected large number of nodes forming a wireless sensor network, node costs quickly add up to significant values. Secondly, sensor networks are envisioned to facilitate a whole new set of applications and services. While the user will likely find these services useful, many of them will not generate a huge monetary value by themselves and will therefore only be realized if their cost is low enough.

Fig. 2.1 shows an overview of a typical sensor network architecture. It consists of several wireless sensor nodes that are distributed to an application area where they monitor the environment and record sensor values. The nodes report their sensor readings to a *sink node* (also called *gateway node*) which connects the sensor network to an infrastructure and delivers the data to a *base station* PC for storage and analysis. Due to resource constraints, the transmission power of the individual nodes is strongly limited. Consequently, some sensor nodes have to communicate over multiple hops to reach the sink node making the sensor network a *multihop network*.

Relating Fig. 2.1 with the Great Duck Island application example mentioned above, the wireless sensor nodes were placed in the burrows of the sea birds distributed over the island forming a multihop network. The nodes collected various types of sensor data which they reported to a base station node were the data was recorded and transmitted to off-site clients using a wide area network link. The use of multihop communication was necessary to save transmission energy on the nodes in order to achieve the desired unattended lifetime of the overall network.

In parts, the ideas and concepts of wireless sensor networks have emerged from the research field of ad hoc networks. However, the differences in the system models of wireless sensor networks and ad hoc networks are significant and time showed that many of the solutions developed for ad hoc network scenarios are not applicable to sensor networks or require significant adjustments for being usable with wireless sensor nodes. The following description of characteristic system properties of wireless sensor networks illustrates some of these differences, like for example the larger number of nodes and the stricter resource constraints found in wireless sensor networks.

2.1.1 System Properties

There is a set of characteristic system properties of wireless sensor nodes and wireless sensor networks that are found in most typical deployments. We list and shortly describe these system properties in the following paragraphs.

Ad Hoc Deployment

One of the central elements of the vision of wireless sensor networks is the idea of deploying sensor networks in an ad hoc manner. This means that the placement of nodes and the resulting network structure do not have be planned in advance. Instead, it should be possible to distribute the sensor nodes spontaneously in the environment. This is important to make the sensor node deployment process cost effective.

To support an ad hoc deployment of sensor nodes, it is necessary that the sensor nodes organize themselves autonomously and form structures that support the operation of the network and allow the sensor network as a whole to fulfill its tasks.

Large Number of Nodes

Even though existing prototype deployments hardly consist of more than one hundred nodes, future wireless sensor networks are envisioned to consist of a very large number of nodes. For that reason, algorithms and protocols must be geared towards scalability and should simplify the process of setting up such large structures.

Autonomous Operation

Sensor nodes are independent computers that are able to operate autonomously. This has a number of positive as well as negative implications. One positive aspect is that sensor nodes are able to truly work in parallel, independently monitoring different parts or different aspects of the environment at the same time.

The sensor nodes usually need to cooperate with each other to achieve a common goal in the wireless sensor network. However, like in any real distributed system, there exists no global, omnipotent authority that would be able to perfectly coordinate and synchronize the operations of the individual nodes. Instead, nodes need to coordinate their behavior by exchanging messages. Such a distributed coordination can only approximate the optimal behavior and usually involves the use of heuristics.

Sensor nodes not only operate independently, they also fail independently. On the positive side, this means that the sensor network might be able to continue working even if some network elements have failed. However, this also implies that algorithms and protocols must be able to cope with such partial failures at any time of the network operation.

Strong Resource Constraints

One goal for wireless sensor networks is to minimize the size of the sensor nodes as well as their manufacturing costs. Both these size and cost limitations inevitably lead to strong constraints on the resources available on the individual nodes. This affects various parts of the node operation.

First and foremost, the available energy supply is severely limited. Sensor nodes are usually not connected to an external, unlimited power supply and can only use the amount of energy provided in the form of batteries. For that reason, conserving energy is one of the primary tasks in every part of the design of sensor node systems.

Secondly, sensor nodes only provide limited processing power and a small memory capacity. Algorithms and protocols running on the sensor nodes must be specifically designed to cope with these limitations and have to find suitable compromises between processing and storing data inside or outside the sensor network.

A third resource constraint relates to the limitations of the wireless interface. It is only possible to use cheap, low-power transceiver chips which limits both the data transmission rate and the transmission range of the node communication.

Finally, the resource constraints also affect the actual task of the nodes – the sensing of their environment. The utilized sensor chips together with the processing capabilities of the node can only support a limited sampling rate and in many cases also a limited accuracy in monitoring the environment.

Wireless Communication

Since most sensor nodes do not have access to a (wired) infrastructure, all communication between the nodes has to be done using their wireless communication interfaces. This entails several complicating factors for the communication among network nodes.

Firstly, as the wireless medium is subject to many external influences and interfering signals, data loss and data retransmissions must be considered a normal part of the system operation.

Secondly, the wireless medium is shared among all nodes lying within each other's transmission range and multiple nodes trying to send data at the same time leads to contention for accessing the wireless medium.

Related to the first two properties are the inherent variations in the message transmission times. Since the transmission of a message might be delayed by the channel being blocked by other senders or the transmission might have to be repeated due to message loss, it is very hard to provide upper bounds on the message transmission times. This affects, in particular, applications with real-time requirements.

Finally, as the sender and the receiver of a message might not lie in each other's transmission range, there often exists the need for multihop communication.

Limited Reliability

The strong resource constraints and the largely unsupervised operation of most system components implicate a limited reliability of individual system parts and even the overall system. Typical errors occurring during the lifetime of a wireless sensor network are (temporary) failures of sensor nodes and disruptions or disturbances of the wireless communication.

Sensor network applications and protocols need to be able to deal with the effects of the unreliability of its network components, because errors and failures are a natural part of the system operation. One popular way of keeping the overall system running despite of failures of individual components is the use of redundancy.

Application Specific Solutions

The setup of a wireless sensor network and the configuration of individual sensor nodes is often tailored to a single specific application. The reason for this lies in the need to optimize the behavior of the sensor nodes to conserve scarce resources.

The focus on specific applications manifests itself in several directions. Most fundamentally, the sensor node hardware limits the set of applications that can be executed on the node (e.g., based on which type of sensor chip is available). While today's prototype platforms are still quite generic, we expect more specialized hardware in future commercial deployments.

A specialization based on the application can also be found in many sensor network operating systems. Instead of providing general purpose services, they are optimized for the typical tasks of wireless sensor nodes. The popular operating system TinyOS goes beyond that and only integrates the set of operating system components into the code image that are actually needed by the application.

On the application level, the specialization shows in that sensor nodes are usually programmed to execute a single application. The operating systems are also not well-suited for running multiple independent applications in parallel. For example, they only provide limited resource arbitration support like for deciding which application should get access to a sensor.

The application specific focus of typical sensor network deployments can be problematic if sensor nodes are used as part of pervasive computing scenarios where different clients moving through the network might have different goals and might set different requirements on the nodes. This motivates our work on providing an efficient mechanism for exchanging application modules in TinyOS that we present in chapter 9 of this thesis.

Table 2.1: Key hardware properties of sensor node platforms

	TelosB	MICAz	IRIS	eyesIFX v2.1	Fleck 3
Processor	MSP430	ATmega128L	ATmega1281	MSP430	ATmega1281
Processor speed	8 MHz	8 MHz	8 MHz	4 MHz	8 MHz
Main memory	10 kB	4 kB	8 kB	10 kB	8 kB
Program memory	48 kB	128 kB	128 kB	48 kB	128 kB
Data memory	1024 kB	528 kB	528 kB	528 kB	1024 kB
Radio chip	Chipcon CC2420	Chipcon CC2420	Atmel RF230	Infineon TDA5250	Nordic 905
Radio speed	250 kbps	250 kbps	250 kbps	19.2 kbps	50 kbps
Number of LEDs	3	3	3	3	3

2.1.2 State of the Art of Wireless Sensor Network Systems

The capabilities of the sensor node hardware and the functionality of the system software running on the nodes play an important role for the work presented in this thesis. For that reason, in the following paragraphs we provide a short overview of the state of the art both in sensor node hardware and in sensor node operating systems.

Hardware Platforms

In recent years, a variety of sensor node hardware platforms have been developed that all follow the concept of integrating sensor chips with a microcontroller, memory and a wireless communication module. While the platforms differ in their emphasis on certain aspects of the hardware design, the overall properties of the sensor node hardware are relatively similar and the platforms also share many hardware components. To illustrate this, Table 2.1 compares important hardware properties of five representative sensor node hardware platforms: The TelosB [162], the MICAz as a representative of the MICA family of nodes [78], the IRIS node [38], the eyesIFX as a representative of the EYES sensor node platform [74] and the Fleck 3 sensor node [186].

A comparison of the properties of the different sensor node platforms in Table 2.1 confirms our statements regarding the strong resource constraints of wireless sensor nodes. For example, the processing power is very limited with microcontrollers running with a clock rate of only a few megahertz. The typical size of the main memory lies in the range of a few kilobytes which can be a strong limitation for some algorithms executing on these nodes.

While some resource limitations might be alleviated in the future (e.g., Crossbow introduced the IRIS node as a successor of the MICAz which doubled the amount of main memory available), we primarily expect that future improvements to the technology will be used to decrease the size of the nodes, to reduce their power consumption or to make them cheaper rather than making the nodes much more powerful. Moreover, more powerful devices often also translate into a higher energy consumption which is undesirable as battery technology does not evolve at the same high pace as other

(a) TelosB   (b) MICAz

Figure 2.2: Sensor node platforms

hardware technologies.

There is also some trend recognizable with respect to a common communication standard based on the physical layer of IEEE 802.15.4 [84]. Among our representative sensor node platforms in Table 2.1, the radio chips of the TelosB, the MICAz and the IRIS nodes are IEEE 802.15.4 compliant RF transceivers which allows these nodes to interoperate if the radio protocol stack implemented on top of the physical layer is compatible.

In the practical experiments and measurements performed as part of this thesis, we worked with TelosB [162] and MICAz [78, 38] sensor nodes. The original designs of both sensor node platforms were developed at the University of California, Berkeley and are now commercially available from Crossbow Technology Inc. [38]. Fig. 2.2 shows images of both a MICAz and a TelosB sensor node. We are going to describe the hardware of these two sensor node platforms in more detail in the following paragraphs.

TelosB The central element of the TelosB sensor node is a MSP430 microcontroller from Texas Instruments, a 16 bit RISC processor with ten kilobytes of RAM and 48 kilobytes of program memory. The TelosB also provides 1024 kilobytes of serial flash memory for the storage of data and the CC2420 radio chip for wireless communication. As mentioned above, the CC2420 is IEEE 802.15.4 compliant, operates at a frequency of between 2.4 GHz and 2.4835 GHz and transmits with a maximum data rate of 250 kilobits per second.

The TelosB board includes one sensor chip for measuring temperature and humidity as well as two light sensor chips that capture the photosynthetically active radiation (PAR) and the total solar radiation (TSR) respectively. Additional sensors or actuators can be connected to a TelosB node using a 6 pin and a 10 pin expansion connector on the board. The TelosB also provides three programmable LEDs that allow providing simple feedback to the user.

Each TelosB sensor node provides an USB connector (visible on the right side of the node in Fig. 2.2 (a)) which can be used for programming the node, for a direct, wired communication with the node and also for powering the node. However, the normal power supply of the TelosB consists of two AA batteries attached to the bottom of the board in a battery pack.

MICAz The MICA family of sensor nodes, to which the MICAz belongs, is based on AVR-RISC processors from Atmel. The MICAz uses the ATmega128L, an eight bit processor running at 7.37 MHz with four kilobytes of internal SRAM and an integrated EEPROM memory for configuration data also with a size of four kilobytes. The program memory of the processor has a size of 128 kilobytes. Like the TelosB sensor node, the MICAz uses the Chipcon CC2420 radio chip for the wireless communication. For the storage of data, the MICAz possesses 512 kilobytes of serial flash memory. It also provides three user-programmable LEDs.

Unlike the TelosB, the MICAz does not include any sensor chips in its basic setup. Instead, each sensor node features a 51 pin I/O connector that allows attaching a variety of external sensor boards. In our experiments we used two different sensor boards which are both available from Crossbow Technology Inc. [38]. The MTS300 provides a light sensor, a temperature sensor, a microphone and a sounder element. The MTS310 additionally provides a dual-axis accelerometer and a dual-axis magnetometer. Fig. 2.2 (b) shows a MICAz node with a MTS310 sensor board attached to the I/O connector.

The MICAz sensor node is powered by two AA batteries and can be programmed with the help of an external programming board attached through the I/O connector. Such a programming board is also required to connect a MICAz sensor node to a base station PC for wired communication.

Operating Systems

An operating system for wireless sensor networks should have a small memory footprint and should work in an energy efficient manner. At the same time, it needs to support certain real-time requirements and a high degree of parallelism. It is very difficult to provide such features and cope with the resource constraints of sensor nodes when using a general purpose operating systems that has to support a large set of functions and interfaces. Moreover, classical operating system concepts like the separation of kernel and applications, a multithreading architecture or virtual memory are also difficult to transfer to wireless sensor nodes and require special solutions.

Several operating systems have been proposed specifically for wireless sensor nodes in recent years. Popular examples include TinyOS [79], Contiki [43], SOS [72] and MANTIS [3]. We provide a short overview of the key ideas of these four systems in the following paragraphs.

TinyOS TinyOS [79] is an operating system that has been developed specifically for resource-constrained embedded systems. Originally developed by the University of California in Berkeley, TinyOS is now used and supported by a large number of research groups worldwide. It supports a large number of sensor node platforms including most of the example platforms mentioned above.

The architecture of TinyOS builds on the concept of components with both the operating system and the applications consisting of a set of components wired together to provide the desired functionality. TinyOS uses a special programming language called nesC [65] to support this component architecture. A program written in nesC consists of modules, interfaces and configurations. A module implements a specific part of the application logic and expresses its outside dependencies with the help of interfaces. A configuration wires modules (and other configurations) together so that a module requiring a certain functionality is matched with a module providing it.

TinyOS does not really differentiate between the operating system and the application software and does not separate the two parts. Instead of having a fixed operating system part that applications can build on, TinyOS integrates the operating system components required by an application with the application components at compile time. This generates a single executable which contains both operating system and application functionality.

We are going to discuss the component model of TinyOS in a little more detail in chapter 9 of this thesis when we introduce TinyModules, our approach to efficient, modularized code updates for TinyOS. TinyModules preserves some of the component structure of the source code in the binary code image to provide for an efficient exchange of application modules.

Contiki The Contiki operating system has been developed specifically for resource-constrained devices like wireless sensor nodes. It aims to support a sufficiently powerful and flexible execution environment for applications despite the limitations of the underlying hardware. Together with TinyOS, Contiki probably forms the group of the most active and widely-used operating system projects for sensor networks.

One of the core features of Contiki is support for dynamic loading and replacement of individual programs and services. For this purpose, the Contiki system consists of a system kernel and multiple application processes and service processes. While the system kernel is static, applications and service processes can be dynamically exchanged at runtime. Service processes define their services in a service interface and offer it to other processes through a service layer in the kernel. This service layer as a level of indirection together with a dynamic linking mechanism provides for the dynamic exchangeability of services and applications.

The kernel of Contiki is event-driven which provides for very low memory requirements. However, to facilitate programming on top of this kernel, applications and services can use a special threading library called Protothreads [44] which supports blocking operations at a very small memory cost.

SOS The development of the SOS operating system was motivated by the need for reconfiguring and reprogramming wireless sensor nodes and SOS sets a special focus on facilitating this. Thereby, SOS was explicitly positioned as an alternative to TinyOS. However, the active development of SOS has stopped recently and the operating system is not officially supported anymore.

SOS consists of a static kernel and dynamically loadable modules that can communicate with each other through the kernel. This communication can be done either by asynchronously exchanging messages or using direct function calls. For the second option, the provider needs to register the function with the kernel so that other modules can retrieve a so-called function handler block to access the function. Like TinyOS and the Contiki kernel, both the SOS kernel and the modules building on top operate in an event-based fashion.

Compared to TinyOS, the use of SOS is more costly during the normal system operation due to its modularized operation. However, it provides significant advantages during the reconfiguration and update of code modules which the developers consider important for typical sensor network applications, especially in the prototyping phase.

MANTIS Among the operating systems discussed here, MANTIS OS is most closely oriented on classic operating systems for standard computer hardware. It provides a kernel with a traditional priority scheduler and supports preemptable threads and semaphores. One major goal in the development of MANTIS was the ease of use to provide for rapid prototyping of sensor network applications. The authors argue that traditional operating system abstractions optimally support this.

Like for Contiki and SOS, the dynamic reprogramming of sensor nodes is a core feature of MANTIS and it allows to exchange the complete code image, individual threads or even single variables. Another interesting feature supported by MANTIS is the mixed operation of deployed sensor nodes and simulated parts of the sensor networks which also supports the rapid prototyping.

Despite its feature set, MANTIS is optimized for a small memory footprint and fits kernel, scheduler and network stack in only 500 bytes of memory. Nevertheless, the focus of MANTIS seems to be rather on ease of use than on resource efficiency which makes it more of a prototyping system than an operating system for real-world deployments.

2.1.3 Application Fields

The use of wireless sensor networks has been proposed for a variety of application fields. A classic application example is habitat monitoring [197, 147], or expressed more generally the **monitoring of flora and fauna** [196, 39]. A special strength of wireless sensor networks in this context lies in the possibility of ad hoc deployments and the fact that no extensive infrastructure installation is required. This allows for an unobtrusive monitoring with minimal interferences with the subjects of interest.

Related to the monitoring of flora and fauna is the application field **environmental monitoring** [212, 48] that deals, for example, with the observation of volcanic activity [212] or the monitoring of noise pollution [48].

A practical application of environmental data collected by wireless sensor networks lies in **precision agriculture** [26, 224, 135]. Data provided by sensor nodes can help in optimizing the growing conditions of plants but also to monitor the behavior of farm animals. Again, the low deployment overhead and the adaptability of wireless sensor networks plays an essential role in these scenarios.

Another popular type of monitoring applications involving wireless sensor networks is **structural health monitoring** [140, 132, 182, 124]. It deals with monitoring the structural integrity of civil engineering structures like large buildings or bridges and aims to detect faults and damages in these structures as early as possible. One significant cost benefit of using wireless sensor networks for this purpose is that no extensive and costly cabling of the sensors is required.

In a few examples, wireless sensor networks are already used as part of **industry applications** [101, 6]. Specific usage examples in this area include inventory systems and machine monitoring [6]. Another application field with growing importance where wireless sensor networks are used in are **healthcare applications** [8, 80]. Here, one application example is to continuously monitor the state of health of patients at home or in a hospital.

Finally, there are also several examples of wireless sensor networks used as part of particularly dynamic application scenarios. The most notable application field is **disaster recovery** [200, 7] where sensor networks provide information and support in areas where currently no infrastructure is available. Another dynamic application field is **target tracking** [16, 75] where the sensor network observes persons or objects moving through the application area.

As part of this thesis, we aim to support applications of wireless sensor networks in a more general setting, as part of pervasive computing scenarios.

Characteristics of Sensor Network Applications

If we compare the application fields described above with respect to how they use the sensor nodes and the sensor networks, we can identify three characteristic approaches: Sensor data collection, event-based systems and sensor networks integrating actuators.

As mentioned above, the classic application area of wireless sensor networks is the monitoring of properties of the environment and the **collection of sensor data** at a central base station for analysis. Such data collections are performed periodically to get information on the behavior of the relevant criteria over time or on demand triggered by the user, for example with the help of a query support system like TinyDB [126].

In **event-based systems**, the sensor nodes not only collect sensor data but also perform analyses to detect certain events that in turn trigger actions in the sensor network (e.g., activating additional nodes, notifying the user). This way, the sensor network is able to automatically adapt its operation to the requirements of the current situation.

Integrating actuators with a wireless sensor network is another step in the direction of operating sensor networks independently of an outside infrastructure. Instead of delivering sensor data to an external base station where it can be stored and interpreted, such systems use actuators to directly perform operations in the environment where the data is collected.

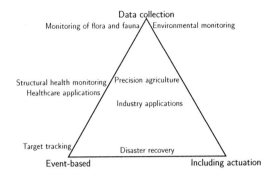

Figure 2.3: Classification of wireless sensor network applications

Fig. 2.3 provides a coarse classification of the sensor network application fields based on whether typical representatives focus on data collection, work based on events or integrate actuation capabilities. Note that individual representatives of the groups can have a different focus. We will discuss later how pervasive computing applications fit into this classification.

2.2 Pervasive Computing

The term pervasive computing represents the idea of computing technology being integrated into a multitude of everyday objects and devices that together form an intelligent environment that is able to provide a variety of services to the user at any place and at any time. Mark Weiser was one of the earliest researchers to write on this subject in his very influential article "The computer for the 21st century" [209]. By now, research on pervasive computing has been picked up by numerous research groups around the world leading to contributions in a wide variety of areas [210, 174, 176].

While computers and computing technology are expected to become pervasive, they are also supposed to disappear, becoming gracefully integrated with their environment. The individual computer with its hardware and software should lose much of its importance to the user who is only interested in using certain services instead of interacting with specific devices. These services are to be offered in an unobtrusive manner that minimizes interferences with other tasks of the user.

Pervasive computing builds upon many concepts from the areas of distributed systems and mobile computing. However, for realizing the vision of pervasive computing, a larger number of research fields are relevant. Besides many classic computer systems research topics, human-computer interaction research plays a significant role. Moreover, research on expert systems and software agents can also provide important contributions [176].

There are two different terms commonly used by researchers and practitioners to denote the ideas and concepts introduced above: "Pervasive computing" and "ubiquitous computing" which was coined by Mark Weiser in his work on the subject. While sometimes the term "pervasive computing" is used to emphasize the industry perspective and "ubiquitous computing" is used for the academic perspective [134], most researchers do not make this distinction and use the expressions interchangeably. We consistently use the term "pervasive computing" in the remainder of this thesis.

2.2.1 System Properties

The characteristic system properties of pervasive computing systems and devices are much more difficult to define than for wireless sensor networks. One reason is that the participating set of devices can be extremely heterogeneous, ranging from simple smart tags to full-fledged personal computers. Moreover, the provided set of applications and services can also be quite diverse. For that reason, we mainly discuss some key concepts and fundamental properties of pervasive computing and pervasive computing systems in the paragraphs below. We also discuss challenges and highlight a few differences of pervasive computing devices to typical wireless sensor nodes.

Key Concepts

Depending on the focus of the work, people argue for different basic concepts as characteristic for pervasive computing systems. Below, we concentrate on context awareness, proactivity, invisibility and mobility.

Context Awareness   Pervasive computing applications are aware of the context they are operating in or rather of the context of their user. This way, pervasive computing applications are able to adapt their behavior to the current situation of their user and thereby respond to the user's current needs and preferences.

It is difficult to define what constitutes context and which types of context information are relevant to pervasive computing applications. Dey [41] speaks of context as "implicit situational information" and notes that not only environmental parameters are relevant. Besides the state of the environment, the situation of the user but also factors like the social environment of the user, the user preferences or his habits can be relevant context information.

A particularly important type of context is the spatial context, i.e., information on the current location of the user or the location of objects that are of interest to the user. Many pervasive computing applications rely on such information and adapt their behavior based on the current user location.

Context awareness as a key concept of pervasive computing is also interesting from the viewpoint of integrating sensor nodes and sensor networks in pervasive computing scenarios. Sensor nodes can provide data on the state of the environment either in the form of raw sensor data or preprocessed and interpreted in the form of more complex context information. This way, wireless sensor networks can play an important role in pervasive computing scenarios.

Proactivity   Another key concept of pervasive computing is proactivity [176]. Pervasive computing devices and applications not only act when explicitly triggered by the user but rather constantly operate in the background. Instead of reacting to tasks given by the user, the goal is to act anticipatory and to actively prepare for (potential) future situations.

For being able to proactively operate in the background and to provide services to the user without being requested, it is necessary for the pervasive computing system to track and anticipate the user intent. A major challenge is to design such proactive behavior in a way that it is considered helpful and does not annoy the user.

Invisibility   As mentioned above, pervasive computing technology is supposed to operate in the background requiring only minimal attention from the user and minimizing user distraction. The developer of a pervasive computing application needs to be aware of the fact that the application does not and should not lie within the main focus of the user most of the time and is also not important to the user in itself. It rather should provide its service when needed without consciously being noticed by the user. This key concept of pervasive computing is best described by the term invisibility.

Providing for invisibility not only involves a careful design of the user interface and the user interaction operations, it also requires masking the details of the operations executed and of the systems currently involved. The user should not have to worry about what devices have to execute which operations to provide him with the desired service. Optimally, a constant service quality should be provided irrespective of variations in the available resources.

Mobility   Finally, another typical concept of pervasive computing is mobility. Both the users of pervasive computing services and some of the devices move within the application area and dynamically enter or leave the application area. The result of these movements is an inherent dynamics in the scenario. One cannot assume a fixed set of resources in the neighborhood of a pervasive computing device and needs to be prepared for disruptions of the connections between cooperating devices.

Mobility in pervasive computing is not only a complicating factor that needs to be considered in the design of applications and services, it is also an important motivation for many applications that provide services that accompany the user while he moves around.

Challenges

In addition to many challenges that pervasive computing systems share with other distributed systems (e.g., distributed control) or that are common to typical mobile computing systems, there are also challenges considered specific to pervasive computing or challenges that require special consideration in these scenarios. Among those, we discuss the important challenges privacy and security, heterogeneity and adaptation.

Privacy and Security In pervasive computing scenarios, the individual user relies on services provided by the surrounding infrastructure. However, using this infrastructure often entails providing sensitive data to cooperating devices. It also implies a constant monitoring of the user by the pervasive computing technology. The privacy of such user data is one of the main challenges in pervasive computing [110]. One problem is that the data collected by pervasive computing devices is usually particularly privacy sensitive, as it is used to tailor the service to the specific user needs. Examples of such data are the user location, user movement profiles or user preference data. Moreover, the invisibility of systems makes it hard for the user to understand and control who has access to his data and what exactly happens with his data.

Appropriate security mechanisms are an important precondition for ensuring the privacy of user data. In particular, user data stored in the infrastructure or on pervasive computing devices must be protected against unauthorized access and the communication among pervasive computing devices must be protected against eavesdropping. The main security goals for securing user privacy in these scenarios are confidentiality, integrity and authenticity.

Addressing privacy and security issues is of primary importance to the success of pervasive computing as privacy concerns might severely impede the acceptance of the technology.

Heterogeneity Another challenge in realizing the vision of pervasive computing lies in coping with the heterogeneity of devices. Different users operate with various types of devices providing different capabilities. Moreover, they also operate in different situations at locations with a variety of infrastructure services available.

One specific challenge resulting from the heterogeneity is providing for the interoperability and cooperation among devices. One aspect of this relates to basic communication capabilities of the network nodes. However, more difficult to solve is the problem of cooperation on the application level: How can nodes with different capabilities provide meaningful information and services to each other without overburdening the resource-constrained participants?

Another important problem is to provide the user with a stable service quality despite changes in the set of available devices and resources when the user is moving or when the set of available resources in his environment changes. Applications and services should be able to work in a variety of scenarios and should manage the transition between different situations without negatively affecting the user experience.

Related to the challenge of heterogeneity is the problem of long system lifetimes. Since pervasive computing aims to integrate computing technology in a variety of everyday items, this technology must also adopt the typical lifetimes of these items. For example, one cannot expect that a washing machine is exchanged every two years just to accommodate for the newest pervasive computing technology. Consequently, the challenge is to design systems in a way that anticipates future uses not available at design time and the overall pervasive computing system must be able to deal with several different generations of hardware operating together.

Adaptation   The final challenge for pervasive computing discussed here is the need for adaptation which is related to the challenge of dealing with heterogeneity as discussed above. Adaptation is required to overcome the inherent dynamics of pervasive computing scenarios where the environment of the users and the devices underlies constant changes. Moreover, the requirements of the user can also change over time. Applications and services should be able to adapt themselves to such changes with minimal service disruptions for the user.

Differences to Wireless Sensor Nodes

Since sensor nodes can also be considered as pervasive computing devices with specialized tasks and capabilities, it is difficult to draw a clear dividing line between the properties of sensor nodes and pervasive computing devices. We expect that there will exist devices that possess both typical properties of sensor nodes and properties of pervasive computing devices. Nevertheless, we see three characteristic differences of pervasive computing systems to sensor nodes related to resource constraints, mobility and infrastructure support.

Availability of Resources   Similar to wireless sensor nodes, pervasive computing devices are also subject to size and cost limitations. Consequently, pervasive computing applications also have to deal with resource constraints. However, compared to wireless sensor nodes, one can usually assume that these constraints are less stringent. For example, it is reasonable to expect that the user regularly reloads the batteries of a PDA (that acts as a mobile client device) so that the energy consumption of the applications is a smaller problem on the PDA than on typical sensor nodes.

Mobility of Devices   A significant fraction of the computing devices in pervasive computing scenarios is mobile whereas we often expect sensor nodes to be placed at a fixed location. An important consequence of this mobility is that devices can neither be attributed to a constant location nor to a fixed set of communication partners. This requires a large amount of flexibility in the algorithms involved.

Infrastructure Support   Unlike wireless sensor nodes, at least some of the pervasive computing devices possess the resources required to communicate with an infrastructure and to receive support by the infrastructure. One possible example is the access to data from the Internet over a wireless LAN or a cellular phone network. However, it is important to note that such infrastructure support will not be available in all pervasive computing scenarios or might only be available temporarily at certain places in specific situations.

Figure 2.4: Sharp Zaurus SL-3200

2.2.2 Hardware

As mentioned above, pervasive computing scenarios can be composed of a very diverse set of devices with very different properties. Consequently, there do not exist representative hardware examples like we have discussed for sensor networks with the TelosB nodes and the MICAz nodes. However, with the personal digital assistant (PDA) (or nowadays also often called smartphone if integrating telephone functionality), a small handheld computer running on batteries, we have a widely used type of device which is a good example of a device that can be used as part of a pervasive computing application. Even though it does not yet fulfill the ideal of disappearing technology (i.e., the user still has to explicitly interact with the PDA), a PDA can provide the user with flexible and mobile access to various pervasive computing services. We are going to refer to the PDA as a client device interacting with wireless sensor nodes throughout this thesis.

For some of the practical experiments performed as part of this thesis, we worked with Linux PDAs from Sharp (Sharp Zaurus SL-3200), a relatively powerful hardware platform featuring a 416 MHz processor, 64 MB of RAM, 128 MB flash memory and a 6 GB hard disk, a 3.7 inch display and a small fold-out keyboard. Fig. 2.4 shows an image of the Zaurus PDA.

To allow the Zaurus PDA to directly communicate with wireless sensor nodes in its vicinity, we need to attach a TelosB sensor node to the PDA over USB. This sensor node then acts as a communication bridge to the sensor network, because the PDA itself would only be able to communicate with 802.11 networks. We expect this limitation to go away in the future when mobile devices are able to directly communicate with wireless sensor nodes, for example using a technology like 802.15.4.

2.2.3 Application Fields

To illustrate the wide variety of applications that could benefit from pervasive computing technology and the many types of new applications that could be created, the following paragraphs describe several exemplary application fields that pervasive computing researchers are working on.

We start with the application area of **smart environments** [36] and **smart homes** which play a significant role in pervasive computing research and are the main target scenarios for our work. The idea is to make buildings, rooms or, in general, the environment aware of its occupants, their goals and their activities and to provide intelligent services to the people living or working in these environments. The goal of these services it to support users in their everyday activities and to enrich their lives with new types of experiences while not distracting or annoying the user.

Many research initiatives have established special prototype installations for long-term experiments and evaluations of smart environment and smart home approaches in a realistic and natural setting. Popular examples include the Georgia Tech Aware Home [94], the Gator Tech Smart House [77], the UC Boulder Adaptive House [143] or the MIT Intelligent Room [22].

The Georgia Tech Aware Home and the Gator Tech Smart House initiatives both set a strong focus on technologies for supporting elderly and disabled people. Their goal is both to support aging people in retaining an independent life and to support and disburden caretakers assisting relatives in their homes. The special user group in these scenarios sets very high demands on the usability and accessibility of these systems. The main goal of the UC Boulder Adaptive House was to take the wide variety of existing and emerging home automation solutions and create a home that essentially programs itself by learning about the user preferences and predicting future needs and desires without the user having to explicitly express them. Consequently, a strong focus of this work lay on machine learning. An important focus of projects conducted in the context of the MIT Intelligent Room initiative lay on the workplace, for example developing an intelligent private workspace and an intelligent conference room. This allows for the use of different kinds of technology than in home settings.

The many projects working on smart homes or smart environments have developed a wide variety of smart devices and smart appliances with examples including smart mailboxes, smart floors, smart bathrooms, smart plugs, smart mirrors or smart refrigerators [77]. Almost all of these examples require some type of sensing – ranging from very simple sensors like a touch sensor to sophisticated sensing infrastructures like object recognition and tracking system with cameras. As an example, the UC Boulder Adaptive House project mentions 75 sensors being integrated in their prototype installation in a residential home.

The large demand on sensor information of various kinds provides a strong motivation for the integration of sensor node technology and sensor networks into smart environment scenarios. This is one of the reasons why we have picked smart buildings and smart environments as the main target scenario for the work presented in this thesis.

Let us now shortly mention a few other examples of pervasive computing application fields to illustrate the diversity and wide applicability of pervasive computing solutions.

Like for wireless sensor networks, **healthcare** is also an important application field for pervasive computing [202, 11]. The set of possible applications is very wide ranging from patient monitoring systems over hospital information systems to emergency intervention applications or full-fledged telemedicine systems. One critical factor for the success of these systems is the consideration of the security and privacy aspects [189].

The activities of pervasive computing research related to healthcare go beyond hospital scenarios or medical practices and also deal with **domiciliary care** in general and **elderly care** in particular [192]. This is an important work area considering the aging societies around the world.

As a final example, **transportation** is another application field for pervasive computing. On the one hand, pervasive computing technology can be used as part of general driver assistance systems, to support emergency assistance or to support the driver with a smart parking system [68, 113]. On the other hand, it can be applied on a more global level aiming to improve the transportation and traffic of all vehicles moving within an area [136].

If we consider the application fields of pervasive computing together with the application fields of wireless sensor networks discussed in Section 2.1.3, we can detect detect some clear overlap (e.g., in healthcare applications) which hints on sensor networks and pervasive computing growing together. If we consider pervasive computing (and indirectly the pervasive computing applications) as an application field of wireless sensor networks and want to use our coarse classification from Fig. 2.3, then pervasive computing would have to be added in the middle as different applications involve the collection of data, are often event-based and definitely include actuation. One might have to add a fourth dimension expressing the proactivity of pervasive computing systems.

3 Sensor Networks and Pervasive Computing

An integration of wireless sensor networks in pervasive computing scenarios can be beneficial to many types of applications but it also involves a variety of new problems and challenges. After having introduced the two research fields in the previous chapter, let us now concentrate on the various aspects of integrating wireless sensor networks and pervasive computing which is the main topic of this thesis. We start with a motivation of our work and then describe the objectives and the general system model of our work. In the main part of this chapter, we introduce smart environments as the main target scenario of our work and motivate why sensor networks can play an important role here. Finally, we use this scenario to identify and elaborate five fundamental problem areas of the integration of sensor networks and pervasive computing. We then introduce the individual approaches developed as part of this thesis in a little more detail and discuss their roles with respect to solving these problem fields and achieving the overall goal of integrating sensor networks in pervasive computing scenarios.

3.1 Motivation

Pervasive computing applications rely on a variety of contextual information for providing services to their users including information on the state of the user's environment. Wireless sensor nodes and networks of sensor nodes can play a very important role in pervasive computing scenarios as providers of such context data: Sensor nodes are specialized in recording environmental data and in cooperating with nodes in their neighborhood to provide a coherent view on the state of the monitored environment. Sensor networks are particularly attractive for pervasive computing, because they provide a comparatively low-cost and low-overhead solution to capturing context information.

While a combination of pervasive computing and wireless sensor networks appears natural, sensor network research originally aimed in another direction and focused on monitoring applications where sensor nodes record and report environmental data in largely static settings. This allows many optimizations that help saving the scarce resources available on the individual sensor nodes. For pervasive computing applications, sensor networks need to support much more dynamic scenarios with changing sets of clients, tasks and external requirements. Some of the established sensor network solutions are not transferable to these different scenarios and novel problems need to be solved that are not important in classic sensor network settings.

Besides the differences in the original focus of pervasive computing and wireless sensor networks, there is a variety of other challenges associated with an integration of the two types of systems. Many of these challenges result from the different system models of sensor networks and pervasive computing – the first group concentrating on small, extremely resource-constrained devices whereas the focus of the second group lies on dynamic settings with more powerful, mobile devices.

The motivation for the work presented in this thesis results from the conflict between sensor networks potentially being useful building blocks of pervasive computing on the one hand and the problems of integrating sensor networks into these scenarios on the other hand. We aim to tackle the various challenges associated with the integration of pervasive computing and wireless sensor networks and to provide solutions for various problems resulting from such a combination.

An important part of the vision of pervasive computing is that in the future all kinds of everyday items will have integrated computing technology and possibly also sensing technology that transforms these items into intelligent devices. However, for this to become a reality, these items must remain as easy to install and use as they are today, because we can neither expect ordinary users to go through complicated installation procedures nor to hire external support staff for each new item they buy and place in their smart homes.

We envision the following future development for pervasive computing in general and sensing technology integrated in pervasive computing scenarios in particular: People go and buy smart devices, items and appliances in single line stores, department stores or supermarkets without worrying about the integrated technology just like they buy washing machines, TV sets or toasters today. Installing, configuring and starting to use these items requires only minimal effort. In the optimal case, most required configuration is done by the devices automatically in the background. Everybody is able to do this and no help by special administrators is required. This aspired ease of configuration and, more general, the ease of use is another important goal that is motivating our work.

3.2 Objectives

The fundamental objective of this thesis is to facilitate the integration of wireless sensor nodes and wireless sensor networks in pervasive computing scenarios. We thereby aim to combine the individual strengths of wireless sensor nodes and pervasive computing devices to achieve the common goal of providing a variety of services to the user in a truly pervasive manner. Wireless sensor nodes can contribute in the perception of the world with their sensors whereas the more powerful mobile devices can provide more resources for actually delivering services to the user.

We argue that an integration of such a diverse set of devices can only succeed if we take advantage of their complementary capabilities and have both sensor nodes support pervasive computing devices and pervasive computing devices support sensor nodes. Such cooperation and mutual assistance is a recurring theme found in the different approaches throughout this thesis.

3.3 System Model

For the following description of the general system model that we build on in this thesis, we concentrate on two aspects: The types of devices found in the system and the properties of the scenario they operate in.

3.3.1 Devices

We assume that there exist two basic types of devices in our system, a large number of small and extremely resource-constrained wireless sensor nodes and a smaller number of mobile, more powerful pervasive computing devices.

The wireless sensor nodes and the networks formed by these nodes are expected to possess typical properties of wireless sensor networks as detailed in section 2.1 including a lack of reliability and the need for low-power operation. We expect most of these nodes to be statically deployed in the environment while a much smaller number of nodes might also be carried around by users or attached to mobile objects.

The mobile pervasive computing devices can be carried around by the user. These devices are typically less resource-constrained than wireless sensor nodes. Reasons for this are less stringent limitations concerning the cost and the size of these devices. Moreover, the user is often able (and also willing) to reload the batteries of these devices in regular intervals.

We assume that the two types of devices share a common communication interface that allows the mobile devices to communicate with any sensor node in their direct neighborhood. To account for the resource limitations of the wireless sensor nodes, it is likely that a communication standard aimed at low-power operation like 802.15.4 is used. The mobile devices might additionally have an interface to a high-bandwidth network like 802.11 or UMTS for the communication among mobile devices or for occasionally communicating with an infrastructure.

3.3.2 Scenario

We assume that the wireless sensor networks and other static devices are deployed in indoor scenarios. On the one hand, we are thinking of typical homes or apartments with a few small to medium-sized rooms. However, we also want to target office buildings where the number of rooms included in a deployment can be significantly larger which motivates the need for solutions that scale beyond a small number of nodes.

A particular limitation of the operation in indoor scenarios lies in the difficulty to provide precise location information to the nodes, because neither the satellite-based localization technology GPS nor typical sensor network localization methods work well indoors (We will discuss this problem in more detail later in this thesis). For that reason, we do not assume that the wireless sensor nodes deployed in our scenarios initially possess information on their respective locations.

We assume that the infrastructure support available to the individual devices, in particular to the wireless sensor nodes, is limited. As mentioned above, the mobile devices might have (limited) access to a high-bandwidth network which they can use to access infrastructure services. The wireless sensor nodes, however, can only use a low-power communication. Some base station nodes connecting the sensor network to an infrastructure might be available in the network. However, we do not require such base station nodes or assume that they might be far away and costly to reach from some of the nodes.

3.4 Smart Environments using Wireless Sensor Networks

As explained in the previous chapter, smart environments are a very important application area of pervasive computing. Since embedding intelligence in the environment of the user is also one of the core ideas of pervasive computing, smart environments are a natural choice as the motivating scenario for our work. More specifically, we consider smart homes and smart offices equipped with pervasive computing technology as the target scenario for our efforts of integrating wireless sensor nodes and sensor networks in pervasive computing scenarios.

In this section we want to elaborate on the idea of using wireless sensor networks as part of smart environment scenarios. We start by introducing a concrete application example that we have developed as part of this thesis. It deals with the control of the lighting in a smart environment. Coming from this specific application, we then sketch a complete smart environment scenario with a user named Bob who is using and interacting with services in a smart home and a smart office building that heavily rely on support by wireless sensor networks. This scenario motivates the integration of sensor networks and pervasive computing scenarios and will later help us in identifying and illustrating problems related to such an integration.

3.4.1 Light Control with Wireless Sensor Networks

The focus of our first smart environment application using wireless sensor networks is the automatic control of the lighting in a building. We aim to provide for constant, predefined light levels in the different parts of a smart environment by reacting to changes in the external conditions (e.g., the light coming through the window) and controlling the light sources in these areas accordingly. One motivation for doing this is to provide the users with an optimal experience while at the same time saving electricity.

As part of the work on this thesis, we have developed a simple prototype implementation of a light control system that takes advantage of wireless sensor nodes for

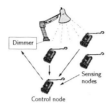

Figure 3.1: Light control application components

performing its task [60]. The main goal in developing this very application was to explore the combination of sensor networks and home automation systems and to learn more about the integration of wireless sensor networks with actuators in general.

Our light control system consists of three types of components: Sensing nodes, control nodes and dimmers attached to the light sources in the application area. We assume that the set of light sources is static. The sensing nodes that are distributed in the application periodically record the light level in their surroundings and report this data to a controller node in their vicinity. The spheres of influence of the light sources can overlap and multiple sensor nodes can lie in the light cone of the same light source. The control nodes are responsible for managing the light level at the measuring points and keeping it within the specified target ranges. For this purpose, the controller node converts the reported light level information into light control commands which it sends to the dimmers. Fig. 3.1 gives an overview of the system components showing a single control loop.

A very interesting aspect of our system is the automatic calibration process that we use to let the network determine parts of the configuration autonomously (self-organization). It has two tasks: Firstly, it matches sensor nodes to actuators (the light sources) in whose sphere of influence they lie. Secondly, it determines the level of influence each actuator has on the behavior of a node to help in coordinating the control operations during the system operation. The calibration process works by turning on one light source at a time, going through the different dimming levels of the light source and measuring and analyzing the resulting light levels at the sensor nodes.

The user is able to interact with the system in multiple ways. Firstly, a simple user interface running on a base station PC both provides information on the state of the sensor nodes and allows the user to control their behavior, i.e., to set the target light level of each node. As an alternative, the user button on the TelosB sensor nodes can be used to gradually increase or decrease the target light level directly at the node. An interaction between mobile devices and the wireless sensor network has not been realized in our prototype system.

For our prototype, we have achieved the interoperability of the sensor nodes and the home automation system controlling the lamps by implementing the controller nodes

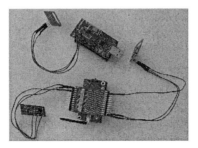

Figure 3.2: Control node prototypes

as bridge nodes that are able to communicate both in the wireless sensor network and with the home automation devices. Fig. 3.2 shows a TelosB control node and a MICAz control node with separate sender and receiver chips of the home automation platform attached to the external pins of the nodes.

While the prototype application discussed here only implements a small set of functionality, it hints at the potential of wireless sensor nodes as part of smart environment application scenarios. One can easily imagine implementing a similar system where sensor nodes are used for heat or air conditioning control in a building. Here, the distributed nature of a wireless sensor network could be particularly helpful in monitoring the application area as a whole and optimizing the behavior of the systems accordingly.

3.4.2 Bob's World

Let us now continue with a description of a fictitious, but more complete smart environment scenario where the control of the lighting in the rooms of a building is only a small aspect: Bob's smart home and his smart office.

Bob is a modern person who enjoys the amenities of technology although he is not very technology-savvy himself. He lives in a smart home equipped with a multitude of smart devices and smart appliances and works in a smart office building where pervasive computing technology is used to manage the building and to support the employees in performing their day-to-day tasks.

Bob uses the smart technology in his home for a variety of purposes[1]. For example, smart blinds and smart lamps automatically adjust the ambient light level in a room based on the preferences of the people present whereas the smart air conditioning regulates temperature and humidity. Bob's smart kitchen automatically checks the availability and freshness of food supplies and creates shopping lists based on that

---

[1]Most examples of pervasive services mentioned here have been taken from literature describing ideas or implementations of smart environments [77, 198, 143, 95, 22, 141, 108].

information. It also supports Bob with hints and reminders while he is preparing food. His smart entertainment system suggests music based on Bob's mood and the music or videos follow Bob from room to room. A smart alarm system protects Bob and his home from intruders. His smart home also makes sure that Bob is reminded at the right time and in the appropriate context of important tasks that Bob needs to perform.

The list of smart environment applications in Bob's office environment is also large and diverse. First of all, the building also provides basic automation functionality like regulating the blinds, the room lighting or the air conditioning with a specific focus on adapting the behavior to the needs and preferences of the people present in the rooms. The system takes also care of the plants in the office building and monitors whether they are watered correctly. Beyond that, the smart office building supports the employees in their daily tasks. For example, it provides computational resources throughout the building that adapt to the users current physical location and situation, it detects and supports meetings and it provides office-wide smart communication systems.

While the list of possible smart environment applications used by Bob in his office and at home could be continued much longer, it is more important for us to illustrate the pervasive need of sensors and sensing data in these applications. For the application examples sketched above, the system needs to monitor the light level, the temperature, the humidity or the ambient noise in the rooms. It also needs to be able to detect the presence of Bob and other building occupants and track both them and relevant objects within the application area. Another important task is the detection and interpretation of various kinds of activities (e.g., "Bob is sitting at his desk taking a nap") to adapt the application behavior to the context of the users.

Different kinds of sensors are required to fulfill the diverse set of sensing tasks in Bob's smart environment scenarios. On the one hand, basic sensors like light sensors, temperature sensors or humidity sensors but also microphones, accelerometers, magnetometers, pressure sensors or motion detectors are required to provide both raw sensor information (e.g., the temperature in a room) and basic context data (e.g., a pressure sensor detecting whether a chair is occupied). On the other hand, more sophisticated sensing facilities like cameras together with image recognition software are required for other, more complex tasks.

We expect that some sensing technology will have to be tightly integrated in the building infrastructure and installed and serviced by experts (e.g., cameras or sensors integrated in the floor to track the movement of persons). However, we also see the need for a large number of small, resource-constrained sensing devices that can only communicate wirelessly and are often integrated with certain appliances in the building. While probably not looking like today's wireless sensor nodes, these small sensing devices will still have the typical properties and limitations of wireless sensor nodes.

There are several reasons why we perceive small, wireless sensing devices useful in smart environments like Bob's home or Bob's office. Firstly, wireless sensors save much of the cost and effort required for installing a sensing infrastructure. Otherwise, the more sensing devices the smart environment contains, the more cables would have to be laid to provide for communication and power supply. In some locations it might also be highly undesirable to have cables running to an object (e.g., a picture frame on the wall). Secondly, we expect the installation of such devices and appliances to be simpler than for solutions integrated in the infrastructure of the building. In the optimal case, Bob does not have to install a new smart appliance integrating wireless sensing functionality at all but instead simply starts using it like he would do with the equivalent appliance not containing smart functionality. Thirdly, using wireless sensing devices makes it very easy to dynamically add and remove appliances from a smart environment. Finally, in some cases the mobility of the objects mandates the integrated smart device to operate wirelessly. This does not have to be due to objects being carried by users all the time but can also be movable items in general, like a pressure sensor in a chair or a water sensor in a flower vase.

A Typical Day in Bob's Life

Let us conclude this section by looking at a typical day in the life of Bob. This will help us in the next section to identify and to illustrate the different problem fields that Bob (or rather the developers of the pervasive computing services Bob uses) might face in his smart home and in the smart office building.

In the morning, the smart bedroom gently wakes up Bob based on the schedule in his calendar by regulating the light in the bedroom and by playing some of Bob's favorite music. At this time, it has already preheated the bathroom and has warmed up the breakfast buns Bob put in the oven the evening before. After getting up, taking a quick shower and grabbing some breakfast, Bob sets off to the office. On the way out of his home, he checks on his PDA whether he remembered to water the plants in the living room and is satisfied that this is the case.

Bob's day at the office is full of meetings and Bob hardly spends time at his desk. For incoming phone calls, the smart office decides based on the type and importance of the meeting, the current activity of Bob in the meeting and the importance of the caller whether to forward the call to the answering machine or directly to Bob or whether Bob needs to be notified of the call.

On the way back to this home, Bob stops at a department store and buys a new television set. He directly installs it in his living room, prepares some food and spends the rest of the day watching his favorite television show. Once the television show starts, the lighting in the living room is automatically tuned down exactly the way Bob likes it.

3.5 Problem Fields and Solution Approaches

In chapter 2 we have described the system properties both of wireless sensor networks and of pervasive computing systems and have extracted typical challenges and problems in realizing applications with these systems. For wireless sensor networks, the main challenges and problems discussed were the strong resource constraints of the nodes, their limited reliability, the largely autonomous operation and the large scale of the networks. For pervasive computing systems, we identified privacy and security, the heterogeneity of devices and the need for adaptation as important challenges.

An integration of wireless sensor networks and pervasive computing systems not only combines the challenges of both types of systems but also raises new kinds of problems or sets a special emphasis on known challenges. In this section, we elaborate on these kinds of challenges and identify five important problem fields that are characteristic for the integration of wireless sensor networks in pervasive computing scenarios. We then introduce six approaches that we have developed as part of this thesis that address important aspects of these problems.

3.5.1 Problem Fields

For illustrating the fundamental problem fields that we have identified for the integration of sensor networks in pervasive computing scenarios, we look again at Bob's smart environment scenario and specifically at the exemplary description of Bob's daily routine in the previous section.

Bob's smart home and the smart office building both integrate a wide variety of different devices ranging from tiny sensor nodes over mobile devices carried by persons to appliances and devices integrated with the building infrastructure. Despite their differences in properties and capabilities, the devices need to cooperate for providing their services to Bob. A basic precondition for such a cooperation is the ability to communicate. In the example scenario given above, Bob's PDA needs to communicate (directly or indirectly) with the moisture sensors of his plants to figure out whether Bob needs to water his plants or not. Another example is the smart office monitoring Bob's meeting where devices carried by Bob (e.g., his mobile phone) and sensors in Bob's environment need to exchange information to cooperatively determine the current meeting status. Providing for **communication** in such heterogeneous environments involving both mobile and static nodes and powerful as well as very resource-constrained devices is the first problem field that we have identified as part of our work.

Bob's smart environments deal with a diverse set of applications that involve a large set of smart devices and build on a multitude of different sensor criteria. With a growing number of devices involved in the system operation (e.g., with a large number of sensor nodes deployed), not only the complexity of the system operation grows but also the complexity of setting up and configuring the complete system. Tiny sensor nodes that do not possess a traditional user interface further complicate such a network configuration. At the same time, smart environments appeal to users like Bob who do not want to be bothered with the details of system operation. Moreover, the example of Bob buying a new television set that needs to integrate itself in the smart living room illustrates that the network configuration in pervasive computing environments is not a one-time activity but might have to be repeated with each new smart appliance being added to the system. This is particularly critical in home environments where one cannot assume that professional administrators are available in a regular fashion.

Managing the **network setup and configuration** is the second problem field that we deal with in this thesis.

The description of Bob's day-to-day activities hardly mentioned the devices involved in providing the services to Bob. This reflects the way Bob uses the system: While Bob likes to use advanced technology, he is not very interested in the inner workings of the system. He does not want to know about issues like the resource constraints of wireless nodes or the limited communication capabilities of these nodes. He just wants the services and applications to run as expected and provide him with a pleasant use. Providing such a **user experience** given the limited capabilities of wireless sensor nodes is the third problem field that we consider.

Many of the pervasive computing applications Bob uses in his smart home concern his private life and some of the data exchanged between the devices is very privacy sensitive. For example, data about the presence or the activities of people in the smart home should not be accessible to outside entities under any circumstances. Another example is Bob's smart alarm system for which it is essential that no outside entity is able to manipulate or even deactivate the system. Securing the privacy of the user and the security of the user data are core challenges of pervasive computing. In our contexts integrating wireless sensor networks, the additional challenge is to provide the required levels of security in a very dynamic environment given the limited capabilities of wireless sensor nodes. This makes **security** the fourth problem field of our discussion.

Finally, the diversity of applications and devices in Bob's scenarios requires a high level of flexibility and adaptability of the nodes participating in providing services to Bob. One has to expect that new users, new applications and new nodes (e.g., the television set) will be added every now and then throughout the lifetime of the overall system. Other nodes need to adapt to such changing requirements and changing environments. This is particularly difficult for the very specialized wireless sensor nodes making **flexibility and adaptability** the fifth and final problem field that we consider in this thesis.

We are going to discuss the five problem fields *communication, network setup and configuration, user experience, security* and *flexibility and adaptability* in more detail below further motivating why they are critical in systems integrating sensor networks and pervasive computing. As will become clear in this discussion, a common element found in all five problems is the challenge of fulfilling the requirements of pervasive computing scenarios and applications given the capabilities and constraints of individual wireless sensor nodes and wireless sensor networks as a whole.

Communication

The communication among nodes is a basic building block of both wireless sensor networks and pervasive computing. Our experience with the light control application has shown that communication is a central problem field in the integration of sensor networks and pervasive computing. In our application, central problems were the integration of different basic communication technologies and proprietary protocols. To limit the complexity of the application, we did not support mobile client nodes and also assumed that each sensor node can reach a control node in its direct neighborhood using one-hop communication. However, in more complex pervasive computing scenarios, the ability to route data over multiple hops from different endpoints as well as to communicate with mobile client devices will be indispensable.

If we generalize from our light control application to our target scenarios in general, the problem of communication pertains to several aspects, namely the communication hardware, the basic connectivity among nodes and node-to-node communication abstractions.

On the hardware level, the main obstacles to an integration are different communication technologies used in pervasive computing systems and sensor networks. While the first group usually builds on powerful communication technologies like wireless LANs or even data communication over cellular telephony networks, sensor nodes usually rely on low-cost and low-power solutions like IEEE 802.15.4. However, we do not see a conceptual problem here but rather expect that many future pervasive computing devices will also integrate a low-power communication technology like many of today's PDAs and smartphones include Bluetooth to communicate with devices in their vicinity.

More challenging than the problem of using a common communication hardware are different assumptions regarding the basic communication capabilities of the participating devices. The basic connectivity among nodes is usually not considered a problem in pervasive computing systems and nodes are assumed to be able to communicate with each other. The communication among sensor nodes, however, uses low-power technology and cannot rely on extensive infrastructure support. For that reason, direct communication is inherently unreliable and also limited to nearby nodes. In larger scenarios this mandates the use of multihop communication which creates a whole set of new challenges. In particular, a routing solution is required that supports transporting data among the communication partners.

Most communication in wireless sensor networks is many-to-one and one-to-many between the sensor nodes and a base station which can be supported with simple, relatively static routing structures. Pervasive computing scenarios, however, require support for a many-to-many communication between any pair of nodes. Moreover, the mobility of devices in these scenarios requires the routing structures to dynamically adapt to changing network topologies. Supporting such many-to-many communication in dynamic scenarios is challenging considering the strong resource constraints of the wireless sensor nodes.

In summary, the main problem regarding communication in scenarios including both mobile pervasive computing devices and wireless sensor nodes is to provide the communication services required by pervasive computing applications while taking the special capabilities and resource constraints of the sensor nodes into account.

Network Setup and Configuration

The setup and configuration of a wireless sensor network can be a time-consuming and tedious task, particularly due to the large number of nodes involved. One major approach in sensor networks research for addressing this problem is self-organization. The goal is for the nodes in the network to autonomously learn about their environment and to form structures that support an efficient network operation and optimally support the application requirements.

Self-organization in wireless sensor networks alone is a very challenging problem and an area of active research [42]. In the context of pervasive computing scenarios, an additional challenge is the focus of applications on the user context. While many self-organization mechanisms in sensor networks are network-centric (e.g., topology control mechanisms), in pervasive computing scenarios sensor nodes also need to learn about the context they are operating in and their tasks within the application setting. Some of this information is difficult or impossible to "learn" autonomously but rather has to be provided to the nodes.

To facilitate the application of sensor nodes and sensor networks in pervasive computing scenarios, it is on the one hand necessary to advance self-organization approaches and develop self-organization mechanisms specifically for the application scenarios at hand. On the other hand, it is essential to provide mechanisms that simplify and alleviate the burden of manually configuring nodes at deployment time.

User Experience

The user experience is a core element of pervasive computing systems. In addition to providing valuable services, pervasive computing systems also need to ensure that these services are convenient to use and do not distract the user from his other tasks. A central element here is the interaction of users with pervasive computing devices and with their environment enriched with pervasive computing capabilities.

In pervasive computing systems integrating wireless sensor networks, the focus on services and user experience can be problematic, because the strong resource limitations of wireless sensor nodes make it very difficult to implement services that are both resource-efficient and convenient to use. So far, usability has not been in the focus of sensor network research as researchers still concentrate on fulfilling application requirements with the given resources or optimizing the resource requirements of applications. Moreover, direct interactions with the sensor nodes are rather uncommon in most sensor network applications that rather concentrate on an external data analysis.

The problem to solve with respect to user experience is to provide the expected level of service and usability in a way that does not overburden the wireless sensor nodes involved. Once again, this can only be achieved by an intelligent cooperation of the different types of devices participating in an interaction.

Security

The security of the systems and applications is an important goal both in pervasive computing and in wireless sensor networks. For pervasive computing, another essential factor related to security is the privacy of the user data, because users will only accept pervasive computing systems if they have sufficient trust that their private, sensitive data is well protected from unauthorized access.

While the basic goal of security is the same for pervasive computing and for wireless sensor networks, the specific requirements are different. Most importantly, pervasive computing systems have to deal with a higher level of dynamics like client devices joining or leaving the system or nodes moving around the application area. Sensor networks are usually more concerned with securely delivering data collected within the network to an outside entity (e.g., a base station computer) in a relatively static setting.

For the integration of sensor networks in pervasive computing scenarios, we need to solve the problem of providing for security with wireless sensor nodes both in static and in dynamic scenarios with varying sets of clients. A special problem novel to wireless sensor networks are secure interactions between mobile devices and individual sensor nodes or groups of nodes in the vicinity of the user.

Flexibility and Adaptability

Sensor nodes are usually very specialized devices that are programmed to execute a single application performing one specific task. This is not a limitation for traditional sensor network applications as the application goals and requirements are well-defined and only change infrequently. An adaptation of the sensor node behavior is mostly necessary within an application to adapt to changing environmental conditions or to changing structures within the sensor network. The sensor node operating system TinyOS takes advantage of this and only installs the operating system components and application-level components actually needed by the application. This in turn helps in saving resources on the sensor nodes.

The situation is different in pervasive computing scenarios where the sets of clients and client applications together with their requirements underlie continuous changes. For sensor networks to play an active role in these scenarios, we need to go beyond the basic approach where sensor nodes are solely providers of raw sensor values. Instead, the sensor nodes should cooperate in providing higher-level context data but also directly participate in the provision of services to the user. As a consequence, we expect the tasks of wireless sensor nodes to be much less static in pervasive computing scenarios than in classic sensor network applications: The sensor nodes now also have to deal with varying sets of clients with different priorities and interests and need to adapt their behavior to optimally support the current situation. Flexibility and adaptability of the sensor node behavior become core requirements. In some cases, it will be necessary to execute special code specified by the client device requesting services from the node or the network of nodes.

Sensor nodes need to provide for the flexibility and adaptability required in pervasive computing scenarios as described above while at the same time keeping their resource consumption under control. In particular, it is necessary to optimize the energy consumption of their operation.

3.5.2 Solution Approaches

The five problem areas discussed above have been the starting point for our work on solutions for the integration of sensor networks and pervasive computing. We have developed six approaches as part of this work that all contribute to the solution of one of the problem areas.

Addressing and Communicating with Wireless Sensor Nodes

The first problem that we address is the communication among mobile pervasive computing devices and wireless sensor nodes. Since we do not see fundamental issues in the basic communication among neighboring nodes, we concentrate on the problem of how mobile client devices can initiate a communication with arbitrary sensor nodes even if these nodes are several hops away and investigate how messages can be routed between those entities.

To select and address wireless sensor nodes for communication, we work with symbolic location information and assume that the sensor nodes know the symbolic coordinate of the area they are located in. Mobile devices then use symbolic coordinates to specify the destination area for their communication requests. This way, symbolic areas instead of individual nodes are addressed which is the desired resolution for many types of queries. For other cases our approach supports a simple mechanism for forwarding messages to individual nodes once the destination area has been reached.

Traditionally, the addressing of nodes in wireless sensor networks is either done based on node identifiers or on the exact geographic location of nodes. However, the first approach does not scale well to large networks and does not support mobile clients whereas the second approach requires detailed location information and complex geographic routing solutions. Our use of symbolic coordinates for addressing nodes in wireless sensor networks is a novel solution that aims to avoid these limitations.

The idea of our routing solution based on symbolic coordinates is to let the mobile client devices specify a symbolic source route from the current location of the mobile device to the destination area. This symbolic source route is included in the request message and allows the wireless sensor nodes to forward the message in the direction of the destination area using purely local routing information. This way, the routing task is divided between the client device and the wireless sensor network in a way that optimally utilizes their respective capabilities: The client device can easily manage and apply the symbolic location model whereas the wireless sensor nodes have an up-to-date view of the network connectivity in their local neighborhood and can translate symbolic route information into node-to-node routing decisions.

Room-level Configuration of Wireless Sensor Networks

For the problem of simplifying the setup and configuration of wireless sensor networks, we have developed two approaches, one aiming to facilitate the manual configuration of sensor nodes and one providing for a special type of self-organization in our target scenarios.

Our first approach is motivated by the need for distributing symbolic coordinate information to a wireless sensor network for being able to support our symbolic routing mechanism described before. In indoor scenarios, the main target scenarios of our work, this means that wireless sensor nodes need to learn about the identifier of the room in the building they are deployed in. Since symbolic location information is very hard to determine autonomously, we aim for a mechanism facilitating a fast and simple assignment of such symbolic coordinates. Abstracting from the specific goal of assigning symbolic coordinates, we are looking for a mechanism for a room-level configuration of wireless sensor networks.

The main idea of our approach is to have an administrator visit the individual rooms of the building which corresponds to visiting the symbolic areas of the application area. In each room he sends out radio messages containing the symbolic coordinate information of the area. Sensor nodes learn about the symbolic coordinate they should assign from these radio messages. We use several techniques for preventing the assignment of symbolic coordinates received in radio messages coming from neighboring areas. The most sophisticated one filters coordinate assignment messages based on sensor events triggered by the administrator.

Sensor Network Structures based on Real-World Semantics

While solutions facilitating the manual configuration of sensor networks are essential for practical pervasive computing applications, the desired optimum is a self-organization and self-configuration of the sensor network. We work in this direction with our second approach in the area of network setup and configuration which provides a self-organization solution aimed specifically at our target scenarios.

The goal is for the sensor network to autonomously determine a grouping (or clustering) of nodes where the groups represent the individual areas in the scenario. This means that nodes located in the same symbolic area should be member of the same group and vice versa. Again, we are targeting indoor scenarios which means that each group is supposed to contain sensor nodes placed together within one room.

The idea of our approach is to collect time series of sensor values on the individual nodes using the different sensor criteria available in the system. The time series of neighboring nodes are then compared in a statistical analysis process to determine correlation values. Sensor nodes exhibiting a high degree of correlation in the behavior of their sensor values are then grouped together as they experience similar external conditions.

Using appropriate sensor criteria and collecting sensor values over a sufficiently long period of time, a sensor network is able to learn about the real-world structure of the application area it is deployed in.

Support for Interactions with Wireless Sensor Nodes

With the fourth solution approach of this thesis, we work on the problem area of providing a satisfying user experience in pervasive computing systems integrating wireless sensor networks. For our contribution to this field, we have selected the specific problem of supporting interactions with wireless sensor nodes.

The ability of the user to select and interact with devices and objects in his vicinity is a common requirement in pervasive computing scenarios, for example to retrieve data from a specific device or to control the behavior of selected parts of the environment. With wireless sensor networks integrated into pervasive computing scenarios, it is necessary that sensor nodes also provide such interaction support and our goal is to provide this with the given capabilities and limitations of sensor nodes and sensor networks.

The main difficulty of interactions between mobile clients and sensor nodes deployed in the environment is the initiation of the interaction or, more specifically, the selection of nodes that the user wants to interact with. We explore different ways of initiating an interaction between a user carrying a mobile client device and one specific sensor node or a group of sensor nodes. Thereby, an important condition is that the user is able to select the nodes he wants to interact with based on criteria that pertain to the real world and that are relevant and intuitive for the user (e.g., selecting a node that he sees placed on the wall) instead of purely network-centric criteria like the connectivity among nodes.

We introduce three different possible solutions that allow the user to select a wireless sensor node for interaction. The three solutions build on different assumptions regarding the capabilities of the nodes and set different requirements on the user action to initiate an interaction. Our first solution detects gestures performed by the user in front of the light sensor of the nodes whereas our second solution uses the light sensors to detect a coded light signal sent by a special client device to initiate an interaction. Our third solution provides visual hints to the user with the help of LEDs integrated on the nodes and lets the user quickly browse through the list of candidate nodes for an interaction. These three solutions allow us to provide adequate interaction capabilities for a wide range of scenarios.

Securing Interactions / Key Assignment for Wireless Sensor Nodes

The problem of security in pervasive computing and wireless sensor networks is a very diverse field of research. Many of the existing solution approaches are also applicable to systems integrating pervasive computing and wireless sensor networks but might have to be adapted to support the heterogeneity of the device capabilities found here. In our contribution to the field, we concentrate on a specific problem found in our types of scenarios, namely on secure interactions with wireless sensor nodes.

To secure the interactions between mobile client devices and wireless sensor nodes, it is necessary to secure the message exchange between the two types of devices. Since basic cryptographic mechanisms for encrypting messages and for authenticating communication partners are already available, we deal with the problem of providing secret key information to the nodes. Such secret key information shared by the communication partners is a precondition for most security protocols.

Given the two different types of devices in our scenarios – resource-poor wireless sensor nodes on the one hand and more powerful mobile client devices on the other hand – with widely differing capabilities, we do not aim for a symmetric exchange of key data between any pair of nodes. Instead, the goal of our approach is to let the mobile client device assign secret key information to wireless sensor nodes in its vicinity. Several existing mechanisms then support the exchange of key information among any pair of nodes based on such initial key data assigned to the nodes.

The goal of our key assignment solution is to avoid transporting the key data over the radio communication channel which can easily be intercepted by external attackers. Instead, the idea is to use a separate communication channel based on a light signal generated at the client device and recorded on the wireless sensor nodes using their integrated light sensor. Two different types of devices can be used to generate the light signal.

Unlike for radio communication, the propagation of a light signal can be easily controlled and it is possible to prevent eavesdroppers from recording the transmitted secret key data.

Customizing Sensor Node Behavior with Code Module Exchanges

Our final solution approach to the problem of integrating sensor networks and pervasive computing scenarios deals with the problem field of flexibility and adaptability. We provide a special code update mechanism for sensor nodes using the TinyOS operating systems that aims to facilitate the adaptability of the sensor node behavior and to support pervasive computing devices in installing small, application-specific modules on nodes they are requesting services from.

The idea of our approach is to divide the code image installed on the sensor nodes in two parts, a static module frame and an exchangeable application module. Instead of exchanging the complete code image or using sophisticated update mechanisms that aim to minimize the code update size, our approach is able to exchange the application module separately from the rest of the code image with very little overhead. The programmer is able to freely define the border between the static part and the exchangeable part of the code image which provides for the applicability in a wide range of scenarios. Nevertheless, the exchangeable module is very small compared to the size of the overall code image in most cases so that code updates using our mechanism are both saving transmission time and energy.

A special characteristic of our approach is the low integration overhead on the sensor nodes. While other code update solutions that aim to minimize the transmission overhead require extensive computations on the nodes to integrate the code update into the existing code image, our solution mainly requires copying the new code module to the program memory.

4 Symbolic Routing in Sensor Networks

The communication among nodes is one of the main challenges in integrating sensor networks and pervasive computing. In particular, it is difficult to support one-to-one communications between mobile client devices and wireless sensor nodes: On the one hand, the changing positions of the client devices as well as the inherent dynamics of the sensor network topology prevent the use of simple static routing structures. On the other hand, the strong resource constraints of the wireless sensor nodes limit the amount of routing state that the nodes are able to maintain and the amount of recalculations of routing information that can be performed.

In this chapter we present a novel solution to the routing problem between mobile devices and wireless sensor networks that is based on the concept of symbolic coordinates. Our approach splits the routing task between the mobile client device and the wireless sensor network with the client device specifying a symbolic source route and the sensor nodes translating this into node-to-node routing decisions using purely local topology information.

4.1 Preliminaries

Combining wireless sensor networks with mobile pervasive computing devices creates new challenges for the communication among nodes that result from the differences in the capabilities of the devices and the different communication models typically used. The routing of messages between mobile client devices and wireless sensor nodes deployed in the application area is the most fundamental communication problem to solve and is the focus of this chapter: If the sender and the designated receiver of a message do not lie within each other's transmission range, then the message must be forwarded over multiple hops and it is the task of the routing algorithm to find and select the nodes for this forwarding.

Sensor networks usually operate in a relatively static setting with the nodes placed at fixed locations and the data being delivered to a single sink node. Consequently, most sensor network routing algorithms are tailored to this kind of scenario and are optimized for efficiently collecting data or events from the network while limiting the amount of traffic and the amount of state on the nodes required for their operation [4]. Many of these algorithms use tree structures for this purpose. The main limitation of this class of routing algorithms and protocols is that they can neither easily support multiple independent client nodes at different locations nor mobile client nodes that frequently change their position within the network.

In pervasive computing scenarios, routing is often not considered to be a challenging problem. This is due to the fact that most pervasive computing devices can use a powerful communication technology that provides for a direct node-to-node communication or they can rely on infrastructure support for the routing and forwarding of messages (e.g., WLAN or cellular telephony networks). This allows for a communication among different nodes despite the mobility of devices. Consequently, while communication and data exchange are important issues in pervasive computing, solution approaches typically address problems on a higher level than raw node-to-node communication, like for example the reconfiguration of services in reaction to varying node availabilities.

When sensor networks and pervasive computing scenarios are combined, then new aspects become relevant in considering the problem of routing messages between nodes in the network. Now, on the one hand, there are mobile client devices that request data from nodes in the environment for providing services to their users. On the other hand, there are sensor nodes that need to find a way of servicing the requests from a multitude of clients contacting the network at different positions. The challenge is to create suitable routing structures and routing mechanisms for this task that provide the necessary flexibility, do not overwhelm the resource-constrained sensor nodes and – within reasonable limits – scale with the size of the network.

One possible solution for the data exchange between mobile devices and wireless sensor nodes could be the use of infrastructure support. Like in the original, static sensor network communication model, sensor nodes would send all their data to a central sink node and would also receive requests solely through this sink node. The sink node, attached to a more powerful base station device, would act as a bridge or gateway to an infrastructure network used by the mobile pervasive computing devices. All communication requests between mobile client devices and wireless sensor nodes would then be serviced by two separate network parts: A high-performance network connecting powerful mobile pervasive computing devices with each other and with an infrastructure and a static, low-power wireless sensor network answering requests received over one or multiple gateway nodes.

One important disadvantage of separating the sensor network and the high-performance network is the high cost of installing the required infrastructure in all areas where wireless sensor nodes are deployed in. The need for an extensive infrastructure would negate many of the advantages wireless sensor networks are used for. One might trade off the amount of infrastructure deployed (i.e., the number of sink nodes in the network) against the cost of reaching a node and communicating data with these nodes. However, going large detours from the client node to the destination node costs both the energy of all nodes involved and greatly increases the response time. Moreover, we expect a significant amount of locality in the communication between mobile devices and wireless sensor networks (i.e., many requests sent to nodes located close to the requesting device) which further motivates preferring a direct communication path.

Another possible solution approach might be to resort to routing solutions from the area of ad hoc networks where the basic requirement is to route data between mobile devices without relying on infrastructure support. However, the applicability of ad hoc routing solutions to our types of scenarios is very limited due to the special properties of wireless sensor networks [216, 4]. The main problems are the scarce availability of resources, the instability of nodes and the communication links between nodes and the expected larger scale of sensor networks. We will discuss the drawbacks of different classes of ad hoc routing algorithms in a little more detail in the related work section of this chapter.

Finally, another existing routing solution that might be applicable to our scenarios is geographic routing, the routing of messages based on the position information of the nodes in the network. Geographic routing is well-established both in the ad hoc network and sensor network communities due the following advantageous properties: It supports the routing of messages between any pair of nodes while requiring only a small amount of state information on the individual nodes that does not grow with the size of the network. This makes geographic routing scalable – an important property in wireless sensor networks. Unfortunately, using geographic routing in our scenarios is very hard to do as the precise location information of all nodes would be required. Such location information is very difficult to acquire in wireless sensor networks in general and even more difficult in the indoor scenarios that we concentrate on. Moreover, recent work has shown that applying geographic routing in realistic settings is significantly more difficult and costly than in idealized scenarios [97, 96]. This is mainly due to irregularities in the radio communication which is another factor common in our indoor scenarios.

The obvious limitations of existing routing solutions like infrastructure-based routing, ad hoc network routing and geographic routing in our application scenarios motivate the need for a novel routing solution that better supports the routing of messages between mobile pervasive computing devices and resource-constrained wireless sensor nodes. The goal of the work presented in this chapter is to provide such a solution that offers the flexibility to send different types of queries to a network, is able to deal with the mobility of client nodes and is considerate of the resource constraints of the wireless sensor nodes participating in the communication.

4.1.1 Problem Definition

Let us now provide a formal definition of the routing problem between mobile devices and static nodes in our scenarios. We start by introducing some important terminology and then provide a definition of the general any-to-any routing problem. Based on this basic definition, we add two restrictions specific to our scenarios that allow us to solve the routing problem in a more efficient and scalable manner.

Terminology

In the target scenarios of our work, we assume that we have a set of wireless sensor nodes $S_{sensors} = \{sensor_1, sensor_2, \ldots, sensor_n\}$ and a set of mobile client devices

$S_{clients} = \{client_1, client_2, \ldots, client_o\}$. Let us use $S_{nodes} = S_{sensors} \cup S_{clients}$ to identify the union of the set of sensor nodes and the set of client nodes.

We assume that the sensor nodes are placed at fixed locations in the environment whereas the client devices might be carried around by users and therefore operate at changing locations within the application area. We also assume that both sensor nodes and client nodes possess unambiguous node identifiers $Id_{sensors} = \{id_{sensor_1}, id_{sensor_2}, \ldots, id_{sensor_n}\}$ and $Id_{clients} = \{id_{client_1}, id_{client_2}, \ldots, id_{client_o}\}$. Note that we do not assume any relation between the node identifier of a node and its position in the network communication graph or in the application area.

Considering the network communication graph with the sensor nodes and client devices acting as vertices and edges representing direct communication links between nodes, one can define the neighborhood $Neigh(x) \subset S_{nodes}$ of node $x \in S_{nodes}$ as the set of nodes x shares a direct communication link with.

For the second restriction of our routing problem, we need to define some more terminology related to the concept of symbolic coordinates (which will be introduced in detail in Section 4.3): The application area A consists of m symbolic areas $A_1 \ldots A_m$ with symbolic coordinates $C_{areas} = \{c_1, c_2, \ldots, c_m\}$. The partitioning of A into the symbolic areas is given by the symbolic location model. Each wireless sensor node lies inside of one symbolic area and we assume that the sensor nodes are aware of their respective symbolic coordinates. How this can be achieved will be discussed in the next chapter.

Basic Routing Problem

The basic routing problem in wireless networks relates to providing for a message exchange between any two network nodes x and y with $x, y \in S_{nodes}$. x is the source node of the route request and y is the destination node x wants to send messages to. How the destination node y is specified (e.g., using the node identifier id_y) and what kind of information about y must be provided as input depends on the respective routing algorithms used.

The task of the routing algorithm is to find a connected path of nodes in the network starting at node x and ending at node y. Expressed more formally, the routing mechanism needs to find a path $P_{(x,y)} = \{p_1, p_2, \ldots, p_q\}$ with $p_1 = x$ and $p_q = y$ that fulfills the following condition[1]:

$$\forall a \in \{1 \ldots q - 1\} : p_a \in Neigh(p_{a+1}) \wedge p_{a+1} \in Neigh(p_a) \qquad (4.1)$$

In our target scenarios, only the routing of messages within the wireless sensor network is of interest, because we assumed in our general system model that the client devices possess their own, more powerful communication technology for exchanging messages with each other. Consequently, we can assume that either the sender of a message or the message receiver is a sensor node: $x \in S_{sensors}$ or $y \in S_{sensors}$.

---

[1]Note that we are only considering bidirectional communication links here – a reasonable restriction required by many communication mechanisms and protocols in wireless networks.

Moreover, it is reasonable to assume that only sensor nodes lie on the path between x and y: $\forall a \in \{p_2, \ldots, p_{q-1}\} : p_a \in S_{sensors}$.

Routing Problem in Our Scenarios

Our first restriction to the general any-to-any routing problem for wireless networks described above is that we require every communication to be initiated by a client device and never by a wireless sensor node. We do not support any-to-any communication between pairs of wireless sensor nodes and sensor nodes cannot initiate a communication with a mobile client device by themselves. With respect to our formulation of the routing problem above, this means that $x \in S_{clients}$ and $y \in S_{sensors}$.

The motivation for requiring the involvement of a client node and only letting client nodes initiate a communication lies in the less stringent constraints on the resources of these devices compared to wireless sensor nodes. As we will show in the discussion of our solution approach, the client node can take over a significant part of the route discovery process thereby reducing the burden on the wireless sensor nodes involved.

From the viewpoint of our application scenarios, requiring client nodes to initiate all communications is not a serious limitation. This can be justified as follows: The client device of a user usually plays the active role in a communication with the nodes deployed in its environment: It requests data by sending queries to the network, sends commands to influence the behavior of the nodes or, in general, requests support in providing services to its user. Even in the publish/subscribe paradigm, the client device actively subscribes to data channels provided by wireless sensor nodes before any data is delivered in the other direction. Sensor nodes and sensor networks, in contrast, do not have their own agenda and either deliver data in a periodic fashion, in reaction to events or the nodes react to requests and queries sent to them.

It is important to note in that context that our restriction only affects the setup of a communication. After a route has been established between client and sensor nodes, the sensor nodes are able to send multiple consecutive messages over extended periods of time back to the client node. Only when the client node moves or when the topology of the network changes, the route between client node and sensor nodes needs to be refreshed. The client node is able to detect such changes without problems (e.g., based on changes to its set of neighbors) and is able to initiate an update or a recalculation of the route if necessary. This is an important property for being able to support communication paradigms like publish/subscribe.

In summary, our first restriction defines that mobile client devices are responsible for the setup and maintenance of routes whereas wireless sensor nodes participate in these route setups but are not able to initiate them independently.

The second restriction that we apply with respect to the original routing problem is more fundamental and defines the way in which a client node addresses the destination node or the set of destination nodes. Instead of specifying the node identifier of the destination node, we require the client node to specify the destination area of the communication in the form of a symbolic coordinate like one would specify a geographic destination coordinate for geographic routing. We will only give some basic definitions here and will discuss the concept of symbolic coordinates in some more detail in section 4.3.

For our routing problem, using symbolic coordinates means that we have a mobile client device x which specifies the symbolic coordinate c_y of an area A_y as the destination coordinate for the routing of a message. We also require the client device to specify the symbolic coordinate c_{start} of the area it currently resides in. The client device can easily determine this information by querying the symbolic coordinate of the neighboring sensor node it will pass the message to.

The task of the routing algorithm is to find a connected path of nodes in the network starting at node x and ending at a node lying within A_y. As in the general problem described above, we need to find path $P_{(x,A_y)} = \{p_1, p_2, \ldots, p_q\}$ with $p_1 = x$ and $p_q \in A_y$ that again fulfills the condition specified in Equation 4.1.

Let us now shortly explain why it is reasonable to use symbolic coordinates for the addressing of nodes in our scenarios instead of directly using node identifiers. Firstly, the importance of individual nodes is traditionally very low in wireless sensor networks. Applications and their users are usually not interested in the sensor node itself but rather in the data of the environment it monitors. In many cases, multiple sensor nodes cooperate to provide a meaningful view of this environment. Secondly, in most cases node identifiers have no meaning to the user of a pervasive computing application and they also should have no importance as this would require a detailed view of the deployment of nodes in the application area. Symbolic coordinates, in contrast, have a semantic meaning that is valuable to the user and that can often directly be used in formulating queries. Thirdly, we expect that symbolic areas will be a natural unit for querying the network providing the right resolution for information required by pervasive computing systems, for example when an application needs to determine the temperature in a given room identified by a symbolic coordinate. Finally, as we are going to show in the description of our approach, it is still possible to address individual nodes with the help of a two step routing process: The client device specifies both the node identifier of the destination node and the symbolic coordinate of the area it is located in. In the first step, the message is routed to the correct symbolic area. Once this area has been reached, the node identifier is used to forward the message to the correct destination node.

To summarize, the problem that we need to solve is to find a mechanism that is able to find a route starting at a client node $x \in S_{clients}$ and ending at a node lying within a specified symbolic area A_y. In the following paragraphs, we will detail the main requirements such a routing solution needs to fulfill in our scenarios.

4.1.2 Requirements

The first requirement on any routing algorithm is the **correctness** of the routing result: Messages addressed to a destination node y or a destination area A_y should only be delivered to y or A_y. Directly related to that is the **completeness** of the routing approach: It should be possible to determine routes to any destination in the network given that the communication graph between source and destination is connected.

Note that while a 100% correctness and completeness of message routing is definitely desirable, we do not set such a strict requirement on our routing approach. In wireless networks, it is quite common that a certain fraction of messages is lost or that nodes are temporarily unreachable. Consequently, we aim for a high success rate in the routing of messages but do not require a 100% reliability. We will discuss these restrictions in more detail later in this chapter.

While the **efficiency of routing** is another important requirement, it is important to be aware of the different aspects of efficiency in the context of routing. On the one hand, there is the efficiency of computing the route. One important criterion for that is the total number of messages that need to be sent between nodes as part of the route computation process. On the other hand, the quality of the route itself and the resulting efficiency of forwarding messages along this route needs to be considered.

Clearly, there often exists a tradeoff between the efficiency of the route computation and the efficiency of forwarding messages between source node and destination node based on this route. One extreme case of this is to use flooding to distribute messages in the network thereby also reaching the destination node. While this generates zero routing overhead, it constitutes the worst case in terms of nodes involved and messages sent for forwarding the message to the destination node. The other extreme is to determine the shortest path based on global topology information which minimizes the forwarding cost but requires maximum effort in determining the route.

Which compromise between routing effort and forwarding cost is optimal heavily depends on the properties of the scenario and the application (e.g, packet send rate, topology change rate). It is therefore very difficult to formulate clear efficiency requirements for our routing approach. In general, our routing solution should aim for low message forwarding overhead based on reasonable costs for the route calculation. Since communication links are rather unstable in wireless sensor networks, the solution should avoid high investments for route calculations that might become invalid after a short time period.

Irrespective of the compromise between routing effort and message forwarding cost, one of the most important requirements is to **limit the resource requirements and the overhead on the wireless sensor nodes** involved in the routing and the forwarding of messages. Sensor nodes are limited in the amount of processing power, storage space and energy that they can commit to the routing of messages. In particular, our routing approach should avoid maintaining large routing data structures that grow with the size of the network and that need regular updates.

When developing algorithms for wireless sensor networks, the **scalability** of the procedure is always a critical factor, because many deployments are expected to comprise a very large number of nodes. Scalability considerations are particularly important for tasks like routing that refer to the sensor network as a whole and cannot be computed and executed in a fully localized fashion. For our routing approach presented in this chapter, the main requirement is that it is able to operate in scenarios with a large number of nodes and, more importantly, that the cost for determining routes and for forwarding messages along these routes does not grow with the size of the network.

Note that – despite all efforts on achieving scalability – we cannot avoid longer path lengths when increasing the size of the network, because source node and destination node might be farther away from each other.

Regarding the **support of communication models**, the main requirement is to provide for *one-to-one communication* between mobile client devices and wireless sensor nodes. As discussed above, the basic idea of our approach is not to address individual sensor nodes by their node identifier but to initiate a communication to a specific part of the application area (a symbolic area) identified by a symbolic coordinate. The routing method should support reaching an arbitrary representative node lying within the destination area (*anycast*) or a specific node within that area (*unicast*), if a node identifier is provided as additional information. Moreover, going beyond one-to-one communication, it should also be possible to distribute a message to all nodes lying within a symbolic area (*multicast*).

4.1.3 Application Scenarios

The main goal of our routing solution is to better support the communication in heterogeneous pervasive computing scenarios comprising both mobile devices and resource-constrained nodes deployed in the environment. Therefore, our main application scenarios consist of a large set of static wireless sensor nodes or other static devices with similar constraints distributed in the application area of a pervasive computing environment and a set of mobile client devices that move around these areas and use the data of the sensor nodes to provide pervasive services to their users.

Since our approach is based on the concept of symbolic coordinates, our target scenarios must provide a symbolic location model. This means that the application area must be partitioned into a set of symbolic areas and the network nodes should be aware of the symbolic coordinate of the area they are deployed in. In the optimal case, a meaningful partitioning can be directly deduced from the scenario description (e.g., the floorplan).

In this thesis, we concentrate on pervasive computing applications in smart environments with a focus on smart buildings like smart homes or smart offices. Such indoor scenarios are particularly well suited as application scenarios for our routing approach, because the definition and use of symbolic areas comes naturally there: Identifiers of floors, hallways and rooms can often directly be used as symbolic coordinates. Our routing approach also supports the deployment of a large number of nodes in these scenarios without the need for extensive infrastructure support.

In addition to our pervasive computing scenarios, the routing solution could also be used in other large-scale sensor network scenarios that need to support mobile data access. Examples include agricultural applications or habitat monitoring in outdoor scenarios.

4.1.4 Overview of Approach

The basic idea of the routing approach introduced in this chapter is to split the routing task between the mobile client device initiating the routing request and the static wireless sensor nodes forwarding the messages. The client device specifies a symbolic source route from its current position to the destination area and the sensor nodes use this symbolic route information to infer node-to-node routing decisions based on purely local route information exchanged with neighboring nodes.

Mobile client devices and wireless sensor nodes maintain routing information on different levels. The client devices manage a global routing table at the symbolic level whereas the sensor nodes maintain a local routing table providing routing information to neighboring areas on a node level. The advantage of such a splitting is that the client nodes do not need to manage a detailed view of the current sensor network topology and the sensor nodes can correctly forward messages using purely local information that is independent of the network as a whole.

To initiate the routing process, a mobile client device calculates a symbolic source route to the destination area and embeds this route information into the message. A sensor node forwarding such a message investigates the symbolic source route and determines the next symbolic area on the route to the destination. It then forwards the message in direction of this neighboring area using its local routing table. This is repeated by all nodes on the path until the destination area is reached.

One important challenge discussed in this chapter is how to route around holes in the routing structure that occur when neighboring symbolic areas are not connected by communication links on the node level.

4.2 Related Work

In this section we review relevant related work from the general area of routing in wireless networks. As part of this discussion, we cover the various types of routing approaches coming from the areas of wireless ad hoc networks and wireless sensor networks. We also introduce the concept of geographic routing which is used both in ad hoc networks and in sensor networks. An important aspect of this review is a discussion of the respective shortcomings of the different approaches in the context of our scenarios with pervasive computing scenarios integrating wireless sensor networks.

4.2.1 Ad Hoc Network Routing Protocols

The idea of wireless ad hoc networks is to create spontaneous, self-configuring networks of nodes operating in the same area using their wireless communication interfaces. The goal is to create a connected network of nodes covering one or multiple hops without the need for infrastructure support. The main classes of ad hoc network routing protocols realizing such multihop networks are proactive routing protocols, reactive routing protocols, hybrid routing protocols and overlay routing protocols.

Proactive Routing Protocols

Proactive routing protocols continuously maintain lists of destination nodes and information on how to reach them in routing tables on the individual nodes in the network. Keeping this route information up-to-date requires that the nodes distribute their local connectivity information in the network either periodically or triggered by changes. Destination-Sequenced Distance Vector (DSDV) [157] routing and Optimized Link State Routing (OLSR) [35] are two classic proactive routing protocols that also represent the two basic approaches of distributing and calculating routing information in the ad hoc network. DSDV belongs to the family of distance vector routing protocols whose idea it is to exchange distance vectors among neighboring nodes which specify distances to all other nodes in the network. Based on these received distances, a node can update its local distance information and is also able to select the best forwarding link for each message destination. OLSR belongs to the family of link state routing protocols. Here, the basic idea is to let each network node periodically distribute information about its communication links to the complete network. By collecting these link state messages from all other nodes, each node has a global view of the network topology and is able to calculate optimal routes based on this.

The main advantage of proactive routing protocols in ad hoc networks is the constant availability of routes. Since each node proactively maintains its routing table, messages can be sent and forwarded with minimum delay. However, this constant effort on maintaining the routes is also an important disadvantage as the maintenance overhead is generated even during periods when and in areas where no communication occurs.

From the point of view of wireless sensor networks, an additional major disadvantage of proactive routing protocols is their lack of scalability concerning the number of nodes in the network. As each node receives, forwards and manages routing information from all other nodes in the network, the overhead for each node grows with the size of the network. Due to their particularly limited resources concerning memory, sensor nodes have problems storing and processing the required state (e.g., the distance vector information) when the number of nodes in the network grows beyond a certain point. Moreover, the inherent instability of communication links in wireless sensor networks entails a constant high overhead for updating route information.

Reactive Routing Protocols

Reactive routing protocols do not continuously maintain routes between all nodes in the network but only calculate routes on demand. When a node needs to send a message to another node, the first step of the routing protocol is to initiate a route discovery procedure. Once a route to the destination has been found, the message and subsequent messages to the same destination can be forwarded using this route information. Different reactive routing protocols mainly differ in the methods they use for caching and reusing discovered route information in order to increase the efficiency of the routing procedure. Dynamic Source Routing (DSR) [88, 87], Ad hoc On-demand Distance Vector (AODV) routing [158, 156] and the Temporally-

Ordered Routing Algorithm (TORA) [152] are three classic representatives of the class of reactive routing protocols.

Compared to proactive routing protocols, the main advantage of the reactive approaches is that the overhead for route discovery is only generated when a route is actually needed by a source node. Moreover, the protocols do not calculate and maintain routes that are never used which limits the amount of state that the individual nodes need to manage. However, the on-demand calculation of the required routes also causes a delay before the actual payload message can be sent in direction of the destination node. Which solution – a proactive or a reactive approach – is better suited therefore depends on the requirements of the application and the characteristics of the message traffic in the network.

Reactive routing protocols share their main disadvantage with the proactive routing protocols: the lack of scalability. The problem here is the overhead generated by the route discovery process which in many cases entails flooding the complete network.

Hybrid Routing Protocols

Hybrid routing protocols combine the concepts of proactive routing and reactive routing by actively maintaining routes for a limited set of nodes (e.g., the nodes in the local neighborhood) while using reactive routing for destinations outside of this set. An intelligent combination of the concepts allows a good routing performance with small delays while effectively limiting the continuous overhead for maintaining routing tables.

Examples of hybrid routing protocols include the Zone Routing Protocol (ZRP) [70] and the Self Organized Terminode Routing [17] protocol. With ZRP, each node actively maintains a routing table for all nodes lying within a specified maximum hop distance. A route discovery is only required for nodes lying outside of this zone and only needs to discover a node having the destination node in its routing table. Self Organized Terminode Routing combines the active maintenance of a routing table for the local neighborhood (Terminode Local Routing) with a geographic routing approach for routing messages on a global scale (Terminode Remote Routing).

Overlay Routing Protocols

A relatively new class of routing protocols that aim to improve the scalability of one-to-one routing in ad hoc networks are formed by the overlay routing protocols. They operate without position information and avoid the flooding of messages both for the setup of routing tables and the sending of payload messages. To illustrate the concept of overlay routing protocols, we discuss two representative examples in the following paragraphs: Virtual Ring Routing (VRR) [27] and Scalable Source Routing (SSR) [52, 53].

VRR organizes the nodes of a network in a virtual ring and routes messages along this ring. For each network node, the virtual neighbors are the node with the smallest identifier larger than the identifier of this node and the node with the largest identifier smaller than the identifier of this node. Each node actively maintains routes to its virtual neighbor nodes and optionally to the next x neighbors in both directions. The required next-hop information is stored on the nodes on the path to the virtual neighbor. Messages are now always forwarded to the neighbor whose identifier lies nearest to the identifier of the destination node. As each node stores routing information of many paths (for connecting virtual neighbors), a message forwarded along the virtual ring quickly finds shortcuts in direction of the real destination.

The basic idea of SRR is similar to the concept of VRR. However, SRR lets nodes maintain source routes to their virtual neighbors. Consequently, when messages are routed in direction of the next virtual neighbor this is done by inserting the source route in the header of the message and using this route to forward the packet.

Overlay routing protocols address several issues of other ad hoc routing protocols. In particular, they avoid the overhead of flooding the network for route discovery and route maintenance and do not need to distribute a global view of the network topology to all nodes in the network. From the viewpoint of resource-constrained sensor networks, however, the scalability of the algorithms remains a serious issue: The main drawback of both approaches is that the required amount of state at each node grows with the size of the network. Together with the instability of links in sensor networks this can make the management of routes to the virtual neighbor nodes a complex and expensive task. The limited memory size of typical sensor nodes also strictly limits the number (or the length) of virtual routes that each node is able to manage.

Summary

Ad hoc network routing protocols deal with a problem similar to the one addressed in this chapter: the routing of messages between nodes in dynamic network topologies. However, in the context of wireless sensor nodes and sensor networks, major limitations of ad hoc routing solutions are the scalability to very large numbers of nodes, the instability of the communication links and the very strong resource constraints of the sensor nodes involved in the routing process.

4.2.2 Sensor Network Routing Protocols

As we have discussed in chapter 2, the requirements on the communication and routing capabilities of the network are fundamentally different in wireless sensor networks compared to mobile ad hoc networks. Consequently, different classes of routing protocols have been developed specifically for wireless sensor networks. Their mechanisms deal with the different typical routing tasks occurring in sensor networks: Data dissemination, data collection and one-to-one routing.

Data Dissemination

One important type of communication that is required in most sensor network scenarios is data dissemination. A single node – in most cases the base station of the sensor network – needs to distribute one message or multiple messages to all other nodes in the network. Examples of applications for this kind of communication include the dissemination of queries or the distribution of code updates to all nodes in the network.

The most basic data dissemination mechanism in a sensor network is flooding. Here, each node forwards each message to all of its neighbors by broadcasting the message which repeat this process until every node in the network has received the flooded message. Since basic flooding generates a huge message overhead, several improvements have been developed to reduce the number of messages sent, for example gossiping [71] and polite gossiping [118]. With gossiping, nodes only forward messages with a given probability p that typically depends on the density of the network or the number of neighbors of a node. Polite gossiping additionally takes into account how often it has received the message from neighbors in a given time interval in order not to forward messages that have already been seen multiple times in the neighborhood.

Data Collection

The second important communication task in wireless sensor networks is the collection of data in a many-to-one communication model. Again, it is typically a single base station that needs to collect sensor data from the nodes in the network.

The most common solution to the data collection problem in sensor networks that combines the distribution of queries to all nodes with the collection of reply data is tree-based routing (e.g., [216, 183]). Each node has a parent node as well as a set of child nodes and routes messages in direction of the sink by forwarding them to its parent node. The selection of the parent node is done with the help of a routing metric that determines the costs (and path properties) of reaching the sink through the different neighbor nodes. Routing metrics range from very simple approaches like counting the number of hops to sophisticated approaches that take both the gain and the energy costs of paths into account [177].

While tree-based routing is an efficient solution for data collection and also data dissemination, it is not well suited for our routing scenarios with multiple mobile client nodes as tree structures neither adapt well to mobility nor do they support multiple sink nodes.

Another common approach to collecting data in sensor networks are cluster-based solutions [76, 222]. The nodes of the sensor network first organize themselves into clusters whose cluster heads are then responsible for forwarding data coming from cluster members. This effectively creates a hierarchical routing solution. However, regarding the properties in our dynamic scenarios, cluster-based routing has the same limitations as tree-based routing.

One-to-One Routing

In most classic sensor network scenarios, one-to-many and many-to-one communication between the base station and the wireless sensor nodes is sufficient to fulfill the communication needs of the applications. However, if it is necessary to support the routing of messages between any pair of nodes, then a one-to-one routing approach (also called any-to-any routing) is required. Clearly, this more powerful communication abstraction asks for more sophisticated routing solutions than, for example, a tree structure. In the following paragraphs, we are going to discuss two specific routing solutions implementing different flavors of such a one-to-one routing: Rumor routing and Beacon Vector routing.

Rumor routing [21] aims for a compromise between flooding queries in the network when some specific information is needed and flooding event notifications whenever a sensor node generates a sensor event of some type. The basic idea is that each event source generates a so-called agent which then travels for a specified number of hops on an approximately straight line through the network. On each node the agent visits, it stores routing information pointing back to the event source. When a client node is requesting information from the sensor network it generates a similar agent that also travels a straight line through the network and that also sets up a route back to the requesting node. When the agent sent by the client node meets a node visited by a matching event agent it can create a route from the event source to the client node using the data stored by the two agents. If no intersection can be found by the client agent, then flooding the query can be used as a fallback solution.

Rumor routing uses a simple heuristic to approximate straight lines in forwarding messages. The agent stores the sets of neighbor nodes of its previously visited nodes. When selecting the next step among the set of neighbors of the current node the agent tries to avoid nodes already in the list. This simple heuristic effectively prevents the formation of loops in a large fraction of cases.

Rumor routing is a very simple protocol that allows the addressing of individual event sources. The main disadvantage of the approach is that routes from the event source to the sink are only found probabilistically and flooding as the fallback solution is rather expensive. Additional problems are the potentially long delay for the discovery of routes and the length of the routes created between source and destination which can be significantly higher than the length of the shortest path.

The Beacon Vector Routing (BVR) [50] protocol implements a greedy geographic routing (which is explained below in Section 4.2.3) that allows addressing individual nodes. However, instead of using geographic coordinates, a limited set of predefined beacon nodes are used to define the coordinates of the nodes. The idea is to let each node determine its hop distances to all beacon nodes and uses this collection of distances as its coordinate vector. Given a good distribution of the beacon nodes over the network area, the calculated coordinates are a relatively good approximation of a geographic coordinate system and allow a successful greedy geographic routing in many cases. The beacon nodes also play a central role as the location directory of the network to allow nodes to determine the coordinate vector of a node they want to communicate with. Beacon nodes managing the location of a node can be determined with the help of a simple hash function.

One major downside of BVR is the overhead of setting up and managing beacon nodes in the network. For the algorithm to work, it is important that the nodes are relatively evenly distributed in the network. Moreover, the number of beacons required is relatively high. Another problem is the need for managing a location directory on the beacon nodes which limits the scalability of the approach.

Summary

There exist a variety of routing protocols for wireless sensor networks that focus on different application scenarios and support different communication models. However, the any-to-any communication between arbitrary pairs of nodes is difficult due to the size of the network and the resource limitations of the nodes. A flexible communication between mobile client devices and static wireless sensor nodes is not supported by these protocols.

4.2.3 Geographic Routing

Routing based on geographic coordinates is used both in wireless ad hoc networks and in wireless sensor networks to implement any-to-any routing between arbitrary pairs of nodes. The basic idea of this geographic routing is to use a geographic coordinate as the destination address of a message and let each node forward this message in the direction of this destination. For being able to do this, it is necessary that all participating network nodes are aware of their respective positions in the form of geographic coordinates. Each node also needs to periodically send out its geographic coordinate by broadcast so that all nodes learn about the geographic coordinates of their 1-hop neighborhood.

In the basic forwarding mechanism, called *greedy forwarding*, a node inspects the geographic destination coordinate of a message it receives and calculates which of its neighboring nodes lies closest to this destination coordinate. It then forwards the message to this neighbor. An alternative to selecting the neighbor closest to the destination node is to take routing metrics into account and to select the neighbor node that provides the desired compromise between progress in direction of the destination coordinate and expected link cost [114].

The greedy forwarding of a message fails if a node cannot find a neighbor whose geographic distance to the destination coordinate is smaller than the geographic distance of the current node to the destination. This situation is called a void or a hole in the network. A common mechanism to recover from such holes is called face routing [19, 93, 103]. The basic idea of face routing is to circumvent a hole by following the perimeter of the face that constitutes the current routing hole until the network structure allows to continue based on greedy routing. The various geographic routing approaches differ in how they follow the perimeter of a face, where they switch from one face to the next face and based on which condition they return to greedy geographic routing.

For face routing to work, the underlying graph must be planar. Greedy Perimeter Stateless Routing (GPSR) [93], a very popular representative of the class of geographic routing protocols, calculates a planar subgraph of the network connectivity graph for this purpose either based on the Gabriel Graph (GG) or the Relative Neighborhood Graph (RNG).

While the basic geographic routing using greedy forwarding and face routing works well in simulations, more recent work [97] has shown serious limitations of the various approaches for the planarization of network graphs in real-world deployments. The reason for this is that the planarization algorithms only reliably work with the idealized unit disk graph (UDG) radio model. In realistic settings, it can happen that links between nodes are wrongly removed, crossing links can be left active and unidirectional links can be part of the resulting network graph [97].

More sophisticated and significantly more costly approaches are required to address the problem of planarizing a network graph in the presence of radio model irregularities and imprecise position information. The Cross-Link Detection Protocol (CLDP) [96] and the Lazy Cross-Link Removal (LCR) [98] protocol do this by letting nodes check each of their links with the help of probe messages to detect whether a crossing of links exists. A sophisticated mechanism then decides which links to deactivate based on the information collected by these probe messages.

GDSTR [115] takes another approach and recovers from local distance minima without requiring to calculate a planarization of the underlying connectivity graph. Instead, GDSTR calculates one or more so-called hull trees in which each node stores and maintains information about the convex hull of the coordinates of all its descendant nodes in the tree. A node which needs to forward a message as part of recovering from a hole is then able to determine a a set of candidate convex hulls the destination coordinate potentially lies in and can forward the message in direction of these nodes. While GDSTR avoids the complex and costly planarization done by CLDP and LCR, storing the convex hull information can be very memory intensive. Moreover, when nodes join or leave the network, the required maintenance of the hull trees can involve a very large number of messages sent and forwarded inside of the network.

Summary

Compared to other routing approaches for wireless sensor networks, geographic routing provides several advantages. Firstly, it supports the routing between any pair of nodes. Secondly, it limits the amount of state each node has to manage to purely local neighborhood information which provides for the scalability of the approach. Finally, geographic routing is able to deal with both (temporary) node or link failures as well as reasonable levels of node mobility without requiring global recalculations of the routing structures.

From the viewpoint of our scenarios, the major downside of geographic routing is the need for a precise knowledge of node coordinates. Presetting such information manually entails an excessive configuration effort at deployment time. Adding a localization system like GPS to every node is costly in terms of node size, energy consumption and node costs and does not work scenarios without a clear line of sight to the sky (e.g., in our indoor scenarios). While many localization algorithms and systems have been developed for wireless sensor networks, most of them fall short in terms of accuracy in realistic settings. We will discuss the problem of localization of wireless sensor nodes in more detail in chapter 5 of this thesis when we discuss the assignment of symbolic coordinates.

Another disadvantage of geographic routing is that the destination of a communication must be specified as a geographic coordinate. If a specific node and not an area or a coordinate must be reached, then a location service is required that performs this mapping. Maintaining such a location service generates additional overhead. This is less of a problem for our routing based on symbolic coordinates as only group (area) membership must be maintained. Moreover, unlike geographic coordinates, symbolic coordinates typically have a direct semantic meaning for many applications.

Finally, a serious disadvantage of geographic routing is the problem of dealing with irregular radio models as discussed above. The costs on the individual nodes for maintaining a routable topology with solutions like LCR or GDSTR can be considerable, particularly in degenerated topologies, and might negate some of the cost and scalability advantages of geographic routing compared to other routing solutions.

4.3 Symbolic Coordinates

The concept of symbolic coordinates plays a very important role for the routing approach presented in this chapter and also appears in the description of our other solution approaches throughout this thesis. After already hinting on the ideas of symbolic coordinates before, let us now introduce the motivation and the concept of symbolic coordinates in some more detail.

As discussed before, information on the location of objects is essential both in wireless sensor networks and in the field of pervasive computing. Working with such location information in applications not only requires methods for capturing location data but also an appropriate representation of the location information in memory that allows applications to query, interpret and process this data and reason on the acquired information. There exist several different representations of location information that are used by different applications. Most of these representations belong to one of two main classes: geographic location information and the symbolic location information discussed in this chapter.

4.3.1 Geographic Location Information

Geographic coordinates allow to express the location of an object relative to a two-dimensional or three-dimensional coordinate system that is either defined for a certain area or even the entire earth. The location of an object is then provided by specifying its latitude, its longitude and optionally its height. WGS 84 [2] is a popular example of a geographic coordinate system that covers the entire earth. It is, for example, used by the Global Positioning System (GPS).

One important advantage of geographic coordinate systems and geographic location information is that arbitrary types of location can be represented – both individual points and also areas of any shape and any size. Another clear advantage is that geographic coordinates allow calculating distances between coordinates and the size of areas.

For many applications of pervasive computing or wireless sensor networks, it is sufficient to use a limited local coordinate system that only covers the target area of the respective application instead of a global coordinate system like WGS 84. In this case, the location of objects is specified with respect to a reference point and a local coordinate system originating at this point. If the local coordinate system is well-defined, it is generally possible to translate from the local to a global coordinate system or the other way round.

Geographic coordinates are commonly used in pervasive computing and wireless sensor networks and a multitude of localization methods have been developed in recent years [66, 128]. However, due to the limited precision of common distance and position estimation techniques in realistic scenarios, the node localization problem can by no means be considered solved, particularly for wireless sensor networks. We are going to discuss the node localization problem in some more detail in the related work section of Chapter 5 when we motivate our work on the assignment of symbolic coordinates.

4.3.2 Symbolic Location Information

Symbolic coordinates are an alternative way of expressing location information that is in many cases more intuitive to use for the human user of a localization system than the raw coordinate data of a geographic coordinate system: A symbolic coordinate expresses location information in the form of a symbolic identifier rather than a numerical coordinate. How this symbolic identifier is to be interpreted depends on the application scenario and is usually specified in a symbolic location model. Typical real-world examples of symbolic coordinates are street names, street numbers or the room numbers in a building. As these examples illustrate, symbolic coordinates usually do not represent individual geographic points but rather areas of different shapes and different sizes.

While we speak of symbolic coordinates and symbolic location models in this thesis, there are also other terms used to describe the same or similar concepts. Brummit and Shafer [23] speak of **topological models** to emphasize that the model describes the containment and connectedness of spaces in a hierarchy without necessarily providing exact information on the size or the shape of these spaces. Another popular term is **semantic location** [163] which emphasizes the semantic meaning symbolic coordinates have for their user.

Compared to geographic coordinates, symbolic coordinates typically provide less information, because complete areas or regions might be represented by the same symbolic coordinate. The granularity of the location information is defined by the symbolic location model. At the same time, on the semantic level, symbolic coordinates can provide more information to the user as the symbolic coordinate itself can have a semantic meaning directly relevant to the application.

Symbolic Location Models

A symbolic coordinate by itself does not provide any location information as it is only an identifier. It has to be interpreted in the context of a symbolic location model much like geographic coordinates must be interpreted relative to their coordinate system. To the user, such location models can be either implicit (e.g., the user directly understands and interprets the meaning of a room number) or explicit (e.g., the user refers to a floor plan to identify the location of a room based on its room number). When using symbolic coordinates in computing, there exist various types of symbolic location models that are tailored to different application requirements and set different requirements on the input information for initializing the model.

One basic type of symbolic location models are **set-based location models**. The base of these models is a large set comprising all symbolic coordinates of the scenario. Subsets of this overall set can be used to denote larger areas, for example a set "First floor" which consists of all symbolic coordinates of the offices lying on this floor.

Hierarchical location models organize symbolic locations based on their spatial containment relation in a hierarchy. As an example, the symbolic location "Office 121" might be contained in the location "First floor" which in turn is part of the symbolic location "Office building A". Since it is often not possible to organize all locations in a strict hierarchy, an alternative is to arrange them in lattice-based location models.

Graph-based location models are more general than hierarchical models. They represent individual symbolic locations as vertices of a graph. An edge between two vertices then expresses a connection between the locations, either a direct connection resembling the "neighbor of" relationship or a weighted edge expressing a distance between locations.

Finally, **hybrid location models** aim to combine the advantages of geographic and symbolic location models. For this purpose, hybrid location models add some geometric information to a symbolic location model, like the area size or the orientation and position of the symbolic area with respect to a geographic coordinate system.

The type of information the nodes require in our approach is not the typical symbolic location model data, as addressed in the literature, but rather a symbolic topology graph expressing the neighborhood relationship between individual symbolic areas. Such a topology graph can be extracted from different types of location models using simple tools.

Since our applications of symbolic coordinates are largely independent of the specific type of symbolic location model used, we do not go into more detail on symbolic location models here here. A more complete classification is provided by Becker and Dürr [13] who also discuss how well the different models support basic queries and tasks (e.g., position queries, nearest neighbor queries, . . .) in pervasive computing scenarios.

Advantages and Disadvantages

Compared to geographic coordinates, the use of symbolic coordinates and symbolic location models provides both advantages and disadvantages. One definite advantage in many scenarios is the direct relation between the symbolic coordinate and the semantics of the location it represents. A classic example from outside the computer science domain that helps illustrating this is the addressing of a letter. Writing the street address on the letter is more natural and also easier for the mailman compared to specifying the WGS 84 coordinate of the destination. While a geographic coordinate would allow to express the destination of a letter more precisely, the symbolic information is actually sufficient and more intuitive to use. At least for human users, it is usually easier to determine and specify the symbolic coordinate of a location they are referring to than the exact geographic coordinate.

Another advantage of using symbolic coordinates is that they are easier to assign manually to individual nodes or devices which is mainly due to their lower requirements on the resolution of available location information. For example, it is often simple to assign the correct symbolic coordinate of a sensor node manually at deployment time whereas a GPS device or something similar would be required to identify precise geographic coordinate information. We take advantage of this property and describe several solutions for a simple and efficient assignment of symbolic coordinates in Chapter 5.

Symbolic coordinates are at a disadvantage when it comes to performing an autonomic localization of nodes as is often done in wireless sensor networks (Although the use of localization is also limited for geographic coordinates due to many unresolved issues regarding precision in realistic scenarios). For symbolic coordinates, there is no measurable criterion such as distance or connectivity like for geographic coordinates that cooperating nodes could use together with the symbolic locations of anchor nodes to infer their symbolic location information. The existence of room-level localization services in mobile and pervasive computing scenarios is no contradiction to this statement as these localization services for mobile devices heavily rely on infrastructure support (e.g., a large number of beacon nodes distributed to the different symbolic areas) – a role that the nodes of a wireless sensor network could play once configured with their correct symbolic coordinates.

In principle, one could use standard geographic localization methods for the nodes in the sensor networks and then infer their respective symbolic coordinates based on their geographic coordinate and an appropriate mapping function translating geographic coordinates into symbolic location information. However, this approach would negate many of the advantages of using symbolic coordinates. Moreover, localization errors from the localization based on geographic coordinates would translate to localization errors on the symbolic level – resulting in some nodes being assigned to the wrong area.

Another disadvantage of symbolic coordinates for certain applications is that the calculation of distances between objects or between areas is not supported. For example, this does not allow nearest neighbor queries based on symbolic location information. This is one of the motivations for using hybrid location models that combine symbolic and geographic location information and can use the geographic information for calculating distances or size values.

Symbolic Coordinates in Wireless Sensor Networks

So far, symbolic coordinates play a bigger role in pervasive computing scenarios than in wireless sensor networks. One reason is that the users of pervasive computing applications can directly profit from the semantic information delivered as part of a symbolic coordinate. Moreover, the more powerful pervasive computing devices are more likely able to deal with the processing and interpretation of symbolic location models than the resource-poor wireless sensor nodes.

One of our contributions in this thesis is to show how symbolic coordinates can be used in wireless sensor networks and how the use of symbolic coordinates can help in integrating sensor networks in pervasive computing scenarios.

One exemplary field where symbolic coordinates can be used is the retrieval of sensor data from specific areas of a sensor network. As symbolic coordinates often directly represent the semantics of a location, data retrieval operations can be implemented very easily without having to map from user-defined areas to sensor node coordinates or vice versa first. For this to work effectively, it should be possible to directly address specific areas and efficiently route query and reply messages between a client device and the sensor nodes operating in the target area.

In the following sections, we introduce our solution for a cost-effective many-to-many routing between mobile devices and wireless sensor nodes. We are going to demonstrate how symbolic coordinates can be used for this purpose and how this provides for an efficient routing solution that does not overburden the wireless sensor nodes.

4.4 Symbolic Source Routing

Let us start the description of our routing protocol with an overview of the concept and an illustration of the individual steps of the protocol. Then we describe a set of challenges that handicap the routing in real-world scenarios. Finally, we describe several extensions to our basic approach that address these challenges.

4.4.1 Basic Approach

The idea of our approach is to perform symbolic routing between mobile pervasive computing devices and static wireless sensor nodes by letting the mobile client nodes specify a symbolic source route from their current position in the network to the destination area they want to communicate with. The sensor nodes lying on the route

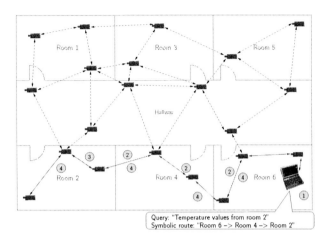

Figure 4.1: Example query in an office scenario

then use this source route information to make node-to-node routing decisions and to forward the messages accordingly.

Fig. 4.1 illustrates this idea using a simple example with a mobile client device querying the sensor network in an office scenario. The mobile client currently is in room 6 and aims to retrieve temperature values from room 2. In addition to the query itself, the client device also provides the symbolic route ("Room 6 - Room 4 - Room 2") as part of the query message that it passes to a neighboring node. The sensor nodes have learned about their local neighborhood using a beaconing mechanism. They now use this information to forward the message along the specified route until the destination area "Room 2" is reached. In the following paragraphs, we describe the individual parts of the algorithm in detail.

Beaconing mechanism

Like many other communication and routing protocols for wireless networks, our mechanism requires that the sensor nodes periodically send out beacon messages to inform neighboring nodes about their presence. As part of the beacon message, the nodes advertise their own symbolic coordinates and neighboring symbolic coordinates they have already heard of. For these neighboring symbolic coordinates, the beacon messages also contain a distance field that represents the number of hops on the node level to the respective neighboring symbolic coordinate.

In a local routing table, each node manages distance information about directly neighboring symbolic coordinates, i.e., symbolic coordinates the node's own symbolic coordinate can directly communicate with. This local approach limits the amount of state each sensor node has to manage.

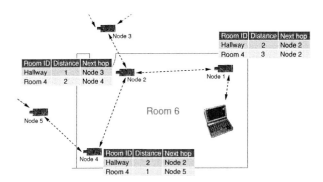

Figure 4.2: Example of local routing tables

Fig. 4.2 illustrates the result of the beaconing process with the help of an example. It shows room 6 from our example scenario in Fig. 4.1 and displays the local routing tables of the three nodes located in room 6. Since room 6 has two neighboring areas, the routing tables of the nodes contain only two entries. Each entry consists of the identifier of the symbolic area, the node identifier of the next hop in direction of this area and the hop distance to this area. Note that the list of neighboring areas does not have to be preconfigured on the nodes but is discovered dynamically when the nodes in room 6 start to receive beacon messages from nodes in neighboring areas.

Like all protocols that store distance vectors in nodes, our beaconing mechanism is vulnerable to the count-to-infinity problem when a connection breaks down. However, since we only work with local distances to neighboring symbolic coordinates, it is possible to prevent this by defining a reasonable maximum distance value. For example, we often assume that all nodes within a room (a symbolic area) can directly communicate with each other. Neighboring areas should then be reachable within two hops. Even if this assumption does not hold, it should not take more than 4-5 hops to reach a neighboring symbolic area in most realistic scenarios.

Mobile client nodes only participate passively in the beaconing process – learning from received beacon messages about their current symbolic coordinate and about sensor nodes they can forward their queries to. In our example shown in Fig. 4.1 and Fig. 4.2, the mobile client device only receives beacon messages from node 1 advertising the symbolic coordinate of room 6. Based on this fact, the client device can infer that it is likely to be currently located in room 6. Node 1 then also acts as the direct communication partner for queries sent by the mobile client device.

Query preparation

When a mobile client node wants to send a query message to a specific area of the sensor network, it first needs to determine a symbolic route from its current location to the symbolic coordinate of the destination area. This is shown as step 1 in the example in Fig. 4.1 with the client device providing the symbolic route "Room 6 - Room 4 - Room 2".

Since we generally assume that a client device is more powerful than typical sensor nodes, it should have the capabilities to compute a symbolic route from source to destination using the symbolic topology graph information contained in the location model. This query preparation step is the main reason why we require that only mobile client devices can initiate a communication with nodes in a symbolic area of the network. If wireless sensor nodes were to initiate such a communication themselves, they would also have to provide symbolic route information and would have to have access to the underlying symbolic location model – a requirement clearly overburdening typical sensor node hardware.

An important property of our routing solution is that symbolic routes can be computed without the client device possessing detailed information on the sensor network topology (the network communication graph) and without having to perform a route discovery procedure at the node level. This way, we achieve a clear separation of concerns: The client devices deal with the routing on the global, symbolic level whereas the wireless sensor nodes are responsible for the local routing on the node level.

Node-to-node routing

Once the client has passed its request message to one of the sensor nodes in its neighborhood, it is the task of the sensor network to perform the node-to-node routing (shown as step 2 in Fig. 4.1). For doing this, the sensor nodes use the symbolic route contained in the request message as well as their local routing tables calculated based on the beacon messages received from neighboring nodes.

When a node receives a message it needs to forward, it first inspects the symbolic route included in the message and looks for the symbolic coordinate following the symbolic coordinate of its own area. The node then looks up this next-hop symbolic coordinate in its local routing table and retrieves the next node in direction of this coordinate. It then forwards the message to this node.

One simple optimization that achieves shorter communication paths is to check the source route beyond the next-hop symbolic coordinate to see whether a symbolic coordinate further down the path can be directly reached. We call this optimization **path look-ahead**. As we will see in the evaluation, path look-ahead is an effective method to reduce the path length overhead of our routing paths compared to the shortest paths connecting source and destination node.

Message delivery

Following our node-to-node forwarding procedure from area to area, the message finally arrives at the destination area A_y. Once the first node inside of A_y is reached, the system provides different semantics for delivering the message to the sensor nodes (Step 3 in Fig. 4.1): delivering to an arbitrary node in the area (**area anycast**), delivering to all nodes in the area (**area broadcast**), or delivering to a specific node (**area unicast**) specified by the sender. Depending on the scenario, it could also make sense to support semantic criteria for delivering messages (**semantic multicast**). For example, it could be possible to send a query to all temperature sensors or to any temperature sensor within A_y.

The implementation of area anycasts is very simple: The message is delivered to the first node on the route that lies inside of the destination area. We have implemented area broadcasts and area unicasts by broadcasting the message inside of the destination area and delivering the message to all nodes or the unicast destination node. Note that the costs of forwarding and processing such a broadcast are limited to the nodes belonging to the destination area, because nodes of neighboring areas do not forward the broadcast.

Reply routing

There are two possibilities for routing reply messages from a sensor node back to the original sender of a request: by reversing the symbolic route or by explicitly setting up routes between sender and receiver (Step 4 in Fig. 4.1).

Sending a reply message by reversing the symbolic route is simple. The responding sensor node takes the symbolic route received with the query message, reverses its entries so the the source area of the original message is now the destination area and uses this as the symbolic source route for the reply message. Note that this does not require any model knowledge stored on the sensor nodes. As the sensor node wants to reach the original sender of the request, the reply message is always sent as an area unicast with the node identifier of the request sender as the unicast destination address of the reply.

The alternative method for routing replies back to the original request sender is to interpret the routing of the request message as a route setup procedure and establish explicit forward and backward forwarding paths. This way, further messages between sender and receiver can be forwarded in both directions without consulting the symbolic routes again. This alternative method is advantageous if multiple messages have to be transmitted between the mobile client device and the symbolic destination area. A disadvantage is the requirement to store state on the intermediate nodes for each connection established this way. In contrast, routing replies by reversing symbolic routes does not require any additional state on the intermediate nodes.

Irrespective of the reply method used, a reply message can only be delivered to the mobile client device if it stays within the transmission range of the symbolic area it sent the request from for the short time period between sending the request and receiving the reply. Note that this should be the common case for individual request-reply pairs as we expect the speed of nodes to be rather small compared to the speed of message transmission. If, however, the mobile node moves to another symbolic area, it is able to detect this situation based on the beacon messages it receives from its new neighbor nodes and can resend the request or initiate a new route setup.

We imagine that a more sophisticated solution could be useful in scenarios where higher node mobility is a critical factor: The mobile node could explicitly store for-

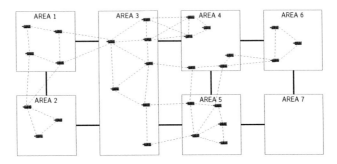

Figure 4.3: Example of a symbolic area graph and a node connection graph

warding information at one of the sensor nodes before leaving the symbolic area it sent a request from.

4.4.2 Challenges

The basic routing approach described above will always work as long as the symbolic routing path specified in a message is covered by the sensor network. In this case, message loss is only caused by transmission errors – for example due to collisions – and can be dealt with at the MAC layer on a hop-by-hop basis or end-to-end at the application level between the sender and the receiver of the message.

Unfortunately, in real-world settings there exists another reason why a certain fraction of the routing attempts fails even though the client device specified a perfectly valid symbolic source route: discrepancies between the symbolic topology graph formed by symbolic coordinates and their neighborhood relationships and the network communication graph of the wireless sensor network. Our basic routing approach works based on the assumption that a neighborhood relationship between two symbolic coordinates implies that nodes in these two areas are able to communicate with each other. In most cases, this is a helpful heuristic, because the adjacency of areas provides for comparatively small distances among the nodes located in the areas. Consequently, there is a high probability that there also exist communication links between the nodes in adjacent areas. However, this clearly does not have to hold in general as we illustrate with the help of another example topology in Fig. 4.3. We have identified three different types of problems caused by the limitations of our heuristic that we are going to discuss in the following paragraphs: Communication holes, coverage holes and area partitionings.

A sensor network deployment contains a **communication hole** if sensor nodes deployed in two neighboring symbolic areas cannot communicate with each other without going through nodes in other symbolic areas. In Fig. 4.3 this problem appears between area 2 and area 3. Even though area 2 lies next to area 3, there is no communication link from a node in area 2 to a node in area 3. A message coming from a node in area

2 must go through area 1 to reach area 3 even though the symbolic path might specify area 3 directly following area 2.

We speak of a **coverage hole** when the area belonging to a symbolic coordinate does not contain any sensor nodes. In Fig. 4.3 area 7 shows an example of this. Coverage holes cause the same problems as communication holes which means that routing over symbolic paths including the uncovered coordinate fails. As an additional problem, messages addressed to the uncovered symbolic area cannot be delivered at all. However, this second problem does not constitute a routing problem and cannot be solved by the routing algorithm – coverage of all relevant areas in a smart environment based on wireless sensor networks must be ensured at deployment time.

More subtle than the communication and coverage hole problems is the problem of having **area partitionings**. We consider a symbolic area to be partitioned if two nodes of the same symbolic coordinate are not connected through a communication path that only consists of nodes lying in the same symbolic area. Fig. 4.3 again illustrates this problem: While the sensor network as a whole is connected, the nodes in the upper half of area 4 can only communicate with the nodes in the lower half of the same area by going through nodes located in area 3.

Area partitions cause two types of problems in the routing of messages based on symbolic coordinates. Firstly, the success of routing through a partitioned area can depend on which partition is used. In the example in Fig. 4.3, a message coming from area 3 can only be successfully forwarded to area 6 through area 4 if the partition in the lower half of area 4 is used. Secondly, partitioned areas also interfere with the delivery of messages: Area broadcasts can only reach nodes in the partition the broadcast is started in. An area unicast only completes successfully if the destination node lies in the partition reached by the symbolic routing.

4.4.3 Extensions to the Basic Approach

We have developed several extensions to our basic symbolic routing approach that address the three types of challenges described above. Our extensions can be classified along whether they aim to prevent problems (*preventing holes*), whether they are used to react to problems (*recovering from holes, recovering from partitionings*) or a mixture of both (*collecting connectivity information*). In the following paragraphs, we describe our extensions and also discuss assumptions on the network topology or on available knowledge of the topology that help in dealing with the routing challenges.

Preventing Holes

It would be desirable to completely avoid the occurrence of communication and coverage holes on symbolic paths used for routing in the first place. While avoiding or even eliminating all holes might not be possible in practice, control over the topology and the use of some model knowledge – where available – can help reducing the number of routing failures experienced by the clients.

The canonical way of preventing communication holes, coverage holes and area partitionings is to provide for a sufficiently **dense deployment** of sensor nodes over the network area. The more nodes are deployed, the larger is the average number of neighbors and the less likely are both communication and coverage holes (assuming a random deployment of nodes). However, a network topology with these properties usually cannot be guaranteed over the complete network area due to both cost and deployment reasons.

Another way of avoiding the appearance of communication holes on symbolic paths is to **store knowledge about holes in the location model** used by the client nodes for calculating symbolic routes. Clients can then remove the affected neighborhood relations from their symbolic location graph. However, this approach assumes a very detailed knowledge about the topology of the sensor network.

A slightly less demanding alternative for incorporating communication model knowledge is to store a **weight factor based on the (expected) node density** for each symbolic area. The reasoning behind this approach is that two neighboring areas with high node densities are connected with a higher probability than two neighboring areas with low node densities. By avoiding areas with a low node density, a node can select a comparatively safe path from the source area to the destination area.

Recovering from Holes

In spite of the different possible approaches for avoiding communication and coverage holes that we described above, nodes still must be able to deal with such holes, because none of the approaches can guarantee the prevention of holes in all cases. Moreover, the required model information might be imprecise or not available at all. We have developed two approaches to recover from holes: **local symbolic broadcasts** and **feedback messages**.

The goal of **local symbolic broadcasts** is to recover locally from a communication hole in the symbolic area it occurred. If a node is not able to forward a message to the specified next-hop symbolic coordinate, because the coordinate is not included in its current list of neighboring coordinates (i.e., it detects a hole), then the node forwards the message to all neighboring symbolic coordinates and asks them to check whether they can find a way back onto the original symbolic route specified in the message. If the nodes in one of the neighboring symbolic areas have the next-hop symbolic coordinate (or one of its successors) in their neighborhood list, they can continue the normal symbolic routing thereby successfully recovering from the communication hole.

If the one-hop symbolic neighbor coordinates are not able to forward the message back to the original route, local symbolic broadcasts can also be sent over two or more symbolic hops. The maximum depth of the symbolic broadcast is configurable in our implementation. Note, however, that the forwarding costs grow considerably when going beyond a broadcasting depth of one or two.

As part of a local symbolic broadcast, the neighboring coordinates can be contacted in parallel or one after the other waiting for feedback stating whether the neighboring coordinate was able to forward the message. Such sequential broadcasts offer the advantage that they avoid creating multiple copies of the message that might have to be filtered out later on. The downside is an increased latency for the delivery of the message.

Note that broadcasting the message to neighboring symbolic coordinates of the node does not require any flooding, because each neighboring coordinate can be reached using unicast messages following the entries in the node's routing tables.

Our alternative to using local symbolic broadcasts for hole recovery is to send a **feedback message to the original message sender** in order to inform the client device about the routing failure and to provide information about where the routing failed. Such feedback messages can travel the same backwards path normally used by reply messages. Based on the received feedback, the client node is then able to calculate a new symbolic route that is not using this connection and is also able to buffer this information for later use. Even in the presence of multiple communication holes, it should always be possible to send messages to the desired destination area after a sufficient number of such message send and feedback cycles – provided the sensor network is not partitioned. Although not part of our implementation, we also imagine that mobile client devices could share this feedback information by exchanging messages when meeting each other or pushing it back to infrastructure. Over time, the mobile client devices would get a good picture of the connectivity situation in the network and could optimize their queries accordingly.

Which of the two solutions – broadcasting the message or sending feedback to the original sender – is preferable might not only depend on the properties of the scenario but also on the amount of symbolic hops the message has already travelled. A message that has almost reached the destination coordinate should probably be recovered using local symbolic broadcasts whereas it might be more efficient to send back a feedback message when the message has only covered a few symbolic steps.

The two mechanisms for reacting to holes can also be useful when dealing with area partitionings. Using these mechanisms, routing over partitioned areas can be performed successfully in many cases. However, irregularities in the reachability of neighboring coordinates can lower the efficiency of routing as some routing attempts report a failure although the symbolic path could be followed successfully when routing over a different partition.

Recovering from Partitionings

While the symbolic routing over partitioned areas is possible in most cases with the help of hole prevention and hole recovery techniques, it is more difficult to find a solution for the second type of problems caused by area partitionings – the delivery of broadcast and unicast messages within a partitioned area. Guaranteeing the delivery of a message to all partitions of a symbolic area can become arbitrarily complex: While the two partitions in our example in area 4 of Fig. 4.3 are connected through the neighboring area 3, it is also possible that the shortest connecting path between two partitions traverses multiple symbolic areas. Connecting all partitions through routing paths for the general case would thus require searching and storing complex

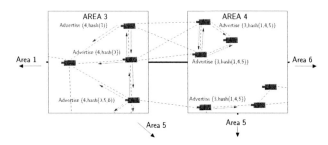

Figure 4.4: Example of advertisement messages for a partitioned symbolic area (Extract from Fig. 4.3)

routing structures that are not necessarily limited to the local neighborhood.

In our solution approach for the recovery from partitionings, we only consider the common case where only one neighboring symbolic area must be traversed to connect two partitions of a symbolic area. The idea is that a node receiving a beacon message from a neighboring symbolic area not only stores the information that it can directly reach this coordinate but also calculates a hash value over the set of neighboring coordinates this node advertises. In regular time intervals, it advertises this hash value to the other nodes in its own symbolic area. Let us illustrate this idea with the help of an example. In Fig. 4.4, which shows a small part of the example scenario from Fig. 4.3, the upper most node in area 4 would advertise its connectivity to area 3 together with the hash value $hash(1, 4, 5)$ which represents the symbolic neighbors of area 3.

If the neighboring symbolic area is partitioned and both partitions are connected to nodes of this symbolic area, two different hash values will be advertised. Note that the hash values of the two partitions should differ since it is extremely unlikely that two partitioned sets of nodes of a symbolic area are connected to exactly the same set of neighboring coordinates. In the example in Fig. 4.4, two different hash values are distributed in area 3 for the partitioned area 4: $hash(3, 5, 6)$ and $hash(3)$. In area 4, in contrast, only one hash value exists for representing the unpartitioned area 3.

If the nodes in a symbolic area receive more than one hash value advertised for a neighboring coordinate over a longer period of time, then they assume that a partitioning exists in this area and treat the partitions like separate neighboring symbolic areas. Treating partitions separately can help solving both problems caused by area partitionings. Firstly, the nodes forward messages addressed to the partitioned area to all known partitions. This way, messages are delivered to all partitions reachable from that area which supports the correct delivery of area broadcasts and area unicasts. In principle, one could forward all messages routed through the partitioned area to all known partitions to avoid communication holes. Secondly, the nodes forward broadcast or unicast deliveries overheard from one partition to all other known partitions of the area. This supports the delivery of area broadcasts and area unicasts in cases where not all partitions could be reached by the neighboring area initiating the message delivery.

Collecting Connectivity Information

Our final solution to deal with holes in the network deployment, the **collection of connectivity information** over time, takes advantage of the mobility of client devices in typical pervasive computing scenarios. The idea is to let the client devices collect information about available and missing connections in the network while they move through the network.

The mobile client devices can take advantage of the beacon messages the sensor nodes periodically exchange as part of the routing mechanism. Since these beacon messages contain information about the source coordinate of the sending node as well as the neighboring areas this node knows of, this information can be used to validate or invalidate connections between symbolic areas in the internal model of the deployment area stored by the client device. Together with the information from feedback messages received after failed routing attempts, this data can provide an up-to-date view of the sensor network and is able to support the client in communicating successfully with the network.

In principle, by visiting large parts of the area of the sensor network, a mobile client device could also learn the complete map information it needs for sending queries to the sensor network without ever loading a symbolic topology graph from the external location model.

4.5 Evaluation

Let us now provide an evaluation of our symbolic routing mechanism. We start with a theoretical analysis of the properties of our approach and then, in the second part of the evaluation, provide an experimental analysis using simulations.

4.5.1 Theoretical Analysis

As a first part of the evaluation of our routing approach based on symbolic coordinates, let us now analyze some of the basic properties of our approach and compare them to the properties of related approaches. In addition to our symbolic routing, we consider proactive and reactive ad hoc network routing protocols and geographic routing as these three approaches are similar to our approach in the type of routing they support.

In the following discussions, we assume a network consisting of n static wireless sensor nodes deployed in an area consisting of m symbolic areas.

Configuration Costs

Our symbolic routing approach requires all network nodes to know the symbolic coordinate of the area they are deployed in. This coordinate information must be provided to the nodes during the network setup and configuration. As we will show in the next chapter, there exist efficient methods for doing such a coordinate assignment using operations executed once per area instead of requiring individual assignments once per node. The configuration costs are therefore in $O(m)$.

Unlike symbolic coordinates, geographic coordinates must be assigned on a per-node basis which generates configuration costs in $O(n)$. Alternatively, automatic node localization techniques can be used that determine the coordinates of nodes without human intervention. However, as we will discuss in the following chapter, these localization techniques are very costly in terms of message overhead, computational overhead and required hardware and do not perform well in indoor scenarios.

In terms of configuration costs, proactive and reactive ad hoc routing protocols are at advantage. Given unique node identifiers at all nodes, no additional configuration information must be provided to the individual nodes or to clients using the network.

Beaconing Mechanism

As part of our routing mechanism, the wireless sensor nodes need to exchange beacon messages for building the local routing tables containing the routing information to neighboring symbolic areas. These beacon messages need to be resent periodically in order to account for changes in the network topology. The beacon send interval $t_{beaconInterval}$ should be selected based on the expected variability of the sensor network topology.

In real-world topologies, one can assume that a reasonable upper bound can be found on the number of neighboring areas a symbolic area can have (if we assume reasonable minimum and maximum sizes of areas). This provides both for a fixed maximum size of the local routing tables that have to be maintained in the main memory of the nodes and for a fixed maximum size of the beacon messages sent to neighboring nodes. Consequently, the costs of the beaconing mechanism for individual nodes does not grow with the network size. Given a constant beacon message size, the beaconing mechanism generates a base message load of $\frac{n}{t_{beaconInterval}}$ messages per time unit.

Proactive routing approaches also require a beaconing mechanism for distributing route information. The difference to our approach is that route information needs to be distributed in the complete network as each node needs to be able to calculate routes to each other node in the network. For protocols following the distance vector approach, this means that the size of the beacon messages depends on n, the number of nodes in the network. For link state messages, each beacon message needs to be sent up to n times to ensure its distribution to all network nodes. In both cases, the resulting base message load of the beaconing mechanism is $\frac{n^2}{t_{beaconInterval}}$: The overhead grows quadratically with the number of nodes in the network.

As the name suggests, reactive routing protocols only operate in reaction to user requests and do not actively maintain routing structures. Consequently, no costs for a beaconing mechanism are generated.

Geographic routing shares the basic properties of the beaconing mechanism of our symbolic routing approach. In both cases, nodes need to periodically inform their neighbors about their existence and some local routing information with the help of a beacon message. Since the beaconing information of geographic routing is of constant size and does not have to be distributed within the complete network, the base message load is $\frac{n}{t_{beaconInterval}}$ messages per time unit.

Route Discovery Costs

For our symbolic routing, the discovery of routes is only done on the symbolic level: The mobile client device calculates the symbolic route from the source area to the destination area based on symbolic topology information. Note, however, that this does not require any communication as we assume that the client device possesses a local copy of the symbolic topology model. The route discovery calculation itself can be implemented using a simple breadth-first search whose computational complexity is not considered critical to the system performance (It is a purely local operation on the client device whose cost only grows with the number of areas and not the number of nodes).

No route discovery is required for proactive routing, because routing tables are maintained at all times and messages can directly be forwarded without requiring any preparatory communication or computation initiated by the client device.

While reactive routing does not incur any continuous costs for a beaconing mechanism, it generates a large overhead for route discovery. In the worst case, setting up a route from the source node to a destination node requires flooding the complete network resulting in a message complexity of $O(n)$ per route request.

In principle, geographic routing does not entail any costs for route discovery, because the geographic destination coordinate can directly be used for the node-to-node forwarding of messages. However, this assumes that the geographic coordinate of the destination node is already known when starting the routing process. If this is not the case, then a query to a location directory must be sent first to determine the current geographic location of the destination node.

Message Forwarding Costs

There are two main factors that influence the costs of forwarding a message from a source to a destination node: The protocol overhead per message and the length of the path this message needs to be forwarded along. The cost of converting the symbolic route information into node-to-node routing decisions is minimal (a simple lookup) and involves purely local operations.

Messages forwarded by our symbolic routing approach need to include the symbolic source route to the destination area. The length of this source route depends on the path length on the symbolic level. While the maximum symbolic path length does not grow with the number of nodes in the network, it does grow with the number of symbolic areas in the deployment area (which usually relates to the size of the deployment area). This can become critical in very large deployments due to the limited maximum size of messages sent between wireless sensor nodes.

To avoid the per-message overhead for the symbolic route, we can use the route setup mechanisms described before. In this case, the first message is used to setup a route from the client device to the destination area buffered on the intermediate nodes which is then used to efficiently forwarding messages between client device and destination area without any protocol overhead in each message. The additional cost for this is one additional message pair sent at the beginning of each communication.

Regarding the second aspect, the length of the path taken between source and destination, symbolic routing cannot guarantee taking the shortest path, because the client selects the shortest path only on the symbolic level whereas the individual nodes only know the shortest paths for reaching neighboring symbolic areas and not global shortest paths to any symbolic area in the network. We are going to analyze this path length overhead in the practical experiments discussed below.

Both proactive and reactive routing (except source routing) represent the optimal case in terms of message forwarding costs. Ignoring small (short-term) inconsistencies due to topology changes, messages are always forwarded along the shortest path so that the number of forwarding steps is optimal. Moreover, each message only needs to contain the node identifier of the destination node – a small data value of constant size – to provide sufficient information for forwarding the message along the route.

Geographic routing only requires protocol data of constant size in each message forwarded between source and destination as each message needs to contain the destination coordinate of the message. Like our symbolic routing, geographic routing also does not guarantee to follow the shortest possible path between source and destination resulting in a path length overhead that we will evaluate later in this section.

Summary

Table 4.1 summarizes our analysis results for the various cost factors that we considered above. At first view, both proactive and reactive ad hoc routing seem to be quite competitive with good results for most criteria. However, the costs of the beaconing mechanism for proactive routing and the costs of route discovery for reactive routing are clear deal breakers that impede the scalability of the approaches. This is particularly critical if wireless sensor nodes are involved that cannot store large amounts of routing data (proactive routing) and are quickly overwhelmed by repeated floodings of the network for each routing request also involving the maintenance of significant amounts of routing state (reactive routing).

Despite its strong limitations regarding scalability, reactive routing can be preferable to both symbolic routing and geographic routing in specific cases: If only extremely few messages are sent between mobile client devices and wireless sensor nodes, then the cost of flooding the network for route discovery a few times can be lower than the costs for the periodic sending of beacon messages required for symbolic and geographic routing. Which volume of messages forms the border of these cases depends on a variety of factors including the network topology and its stability, the traffic distribution and the

Table 4.1: Comparison of routing approaches

	Symbolic routing	Proactive routing	Reactive routing	Geographic routing
Configuration costs	+	++	++	-
Beaconing mechanism costs	+	–	++	+
Route discovery costs	+	++	–	+
Message forwarding costs	0	++	++	+
Scalability	+	-	-	+

route caching mechanism used. Note, however, that a beaconing mechanism is also required by other types of protocols running in wireless networks (e.g., node clustering) so that the beaconing costs cannot be fully allocated to routing in all cases.

Geographic routing and our symbolic routing approach are comparable in their costs for the beaconing mechanism and both approaches incur low costs for route discovery. Geographic routing provides advantages in the forwarding of messages, because it only requires a fixed amount of protocol data per message. In turn, our symbolic routing is less expensive regarding the required topology information (symbolic coordinates versus geographic coordinates). Both approaches have some limitations regarding scalability: For long symbolic routes, the overhead per message would become large which has to be avoided using an explicit route setup phase. For geographic routing, the maximum overhead for planarizing the graph grows with the size of the network in extreme cases.

Overall, our symbolic routing approach does not exhibit significant weaknesses in any of the areas discussed above. Clearly, there does not exist one solution solving the routing problem in its entirety without incurring any costs or disadvantages. However, our symbolic routing reaches a good compromise between the required topology information, the base costs of the routing mechanism and the performance of forwarding messages.

4.5.2 Experimental Analysis

In this section we use simulations to analyze the performance of symbolic routing between mobile client devices and wireless sensor nodes both for our basic approach and the various extensions that deal with holes and partitionings.

One important evaluation metric is the success rate of communication which is defined as the percentage of messages sent by one of the client nodes and successfully delivered at the destination area. Another important evaluation metric that allows to assess the costs for using symbolic routing is the so-called stretch, the average ratio between the real path length used and the shortest path length possible. A stretch value of 1.0 is, therefore, optimal.

For performing the analysis, we have implemented our routing approach as an extension to the ns-2 network simulator [1]. The ns-2 simulator allowed us to simulate large scenarios and also provided us with more flexibility concerning the heterogeneity of the network than TOSSIM, the TinyOS sensor network simulator. We have used TOSSIM to test our TinyOS implementation and to verify the results obtained with ns-2.

To complement our simulation environment, we have written a custom scenario generator that allows us to create scenarios with different combinations of symbolic areas, nodes and node communication properties. We have also used the scenario generator for an offline analysis of the scenarios.

Simulation Setup

For the simulations discussed in the following paragraphs, we have used a deployment area of 36x36 meters which we divide into between 15 and 100 rectangular symbolic areas with a random layout. For our sensor nodes we decided for a maximum communication distance of 7 meters, a value selected based on our experiences with sensor nodes in office scenarios, using the Two Ray Ground radio model. We have also varied the number of nodes in our experiments and show results starting from a low density with 50 static sensor nodes (corresponding to 0.039 nodes per square meter) up to very high densities with 400 sensor nodes (corresponding to 0.309 nodes per square meter). In all experiments, each simulation was repeated 100 times with randomly generated scenarios.

A purely random distribution of nodes in the simulation area is not a good representation of real-world deployments of wireless sensor nodes and can lead to extreme results in individual scenarios with symbolic areas not covered by nodes at all. However, using a completely uniform distribution of nodes is equally unrealistic and can lead to unexpected patterns in the routing structures. For our simulations, we opted for a mixture of both models using uniform distribution but adding an additional random factor to move the nodes between 0 and 20 meters away from their originally assigned position.

We used 40 mobile client nodes and let them send query messages to randomly selected destination areas every 2 seconds. We placed the client nodes randomly and moved them to different locations every 5 seconds in order to cover a large set of possible communication pairs.

Success Rate of the Basic Approach

As a first step of our investigations of the success rate of the basic approach, we considered node connectivities in the deployment area. Fig. 4.5 a) and b) show the percentage of expected connectivities between neighboring symbolic areas that are missing in the node communication graph. The larger the number of symbolic areas defined in the deployment area, the higher is the percentage of missing connectivities. Even in our scenarios with 400 nodes, as an example of a very dense topology, the percentage of missing connectivities caused by communication and coverage holes grows to over 10 percent when increasing the number of symbolic areas up to 100. Note, however, that such very large numbers of areas are not too realistic given the size of

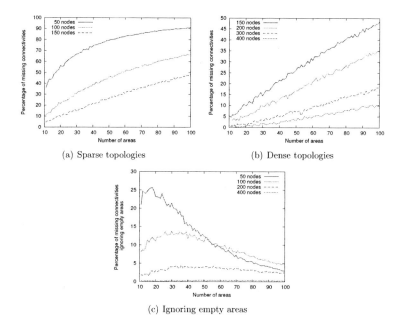

(a) Sparse topologies

(b) Dense topologies

(c) Ignoring empty areas

Figure 4.5: Percentage of missing connectivities

our deployment area. In the range between 1 and 30 areas, the results show reasonable percentages of missing connectivities even for the sparser topologies. Nevertheless, the results confirm the importance of being able to deal with communication and coverage holes.

Fig. 4.5 c) provides some interesting insight regarding the question what causes missing connectivities. It repeats the analysis from Fig. 4.5 a+b) but ignores empty areas, i.e., missing connectivities caused by a symbolic coordinate not being covered by nodes at all. Obviously, empty areas are responsible for a large portion of these missing connectivities. For dense deployments, hardly any missing connectivities between populated symbolic areas occur at all.

Based on the analysis of the percentage of missing connectivities, we then simulated message communications on the generated topologies to investigate the success rates of our basic routing approach. Fig. 4.6 shows the results of these simulations for both sparse and dense node populations when varying the number of symbolic areas and neither a message recovery nor any of the described hole prevention mechanisms is used. As the results show, only the densely populated scenarios are able to maintain acceptable success rates when increasing the number of symbolic areas. In the other

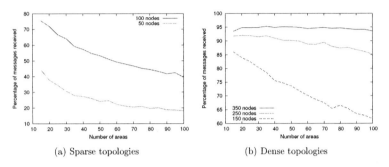

(a) Sparse topologies   (b) Dense topologies

Figure 4.6: Average success rate without recovery mechanisms

scenarios, the success rate quickly falls with the sparse topologies already starting at quite low levels.

Given our results on missing connectivities among areas, these success rate results were to be expected. Since the client devices selected the destination area randomly and also periodically moved to different areas, the symbolic paths typically consist of several hops with a large and increasing probability of missing connectivities between symbolic areas along the path. Again, this confirms the need for hole prevention and recovery mechanisms.

Preventing Holes

Adding knowledge about communication holes and coverage holes to the mobile nodes – our simplest method for preventing the occurrence of holes on the communication path between client node and destination area – directly impacts the success rate of communication: The more knowledge a node possesses about holes, the higher is the success rate it is able to achieve when sending messages to random destination nodes. An analysis of the more advanced problems related to this (e.g., costs for storing and processing this information on the mobile devices) is highly scenario specific and out of the scope of our work.

Another option for preventing holes that we have discussed is the use of node density information to estimate the success probabilities of route alternatives. We calculate a density measure d_{A_x} for a symbolic area A_x by dividing the node density of the area A_x and the node density of the complete network area A using the following equation:

$$d_{A_x} = \frac{numNodes(A_x) \cdot areaSize(A)}{numNodes(A) \cdot areaSize(A_x)} \qquad (4.2)$$

$numNodes(A_x)$ is the number of sensor nodes located in the symbolic area A_x and $numNodes(A)$ is the total number of nodes in the complete network area A. $areaSize(A_x)$ is the size of the geographic area represented by A_x and $areaSize(A)$ is the total size of the deployment area.

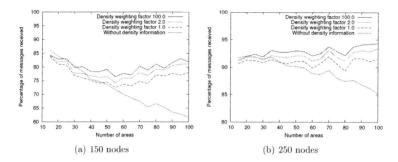

(a) 150 nodes (b) 250 nodes

Figure 4.7: Average success rates using density information

Equation 4.2 gives us a density value larger than 1 if the node density lies above average and smaller than 1 if it lies below average. We then use this density to calculate a path metric m_p for a symbolic path $p = \{A_1, A_2, \ldots, A_n\}$ (where $A_1, A_2, \ldots, A_n$ are the symbolic areas on path p) using the following function:

$$m_p = \frac{1}{(d_{A_1})^g} + \frac{1}{(d_{A_2})^g} + \ldots + \frac{1}{(d_{A_n})^g} \qquad (4.3)$$

The metric considers both the path length (by adding up the cost values of the individual areas) and the densities of the areas. The influence of these two factors can be controlled using the density weighting factor g with $g \geq 0$. In our experiments we used $g = 1.0$, $g = 2.0$ and $g = 100.0$. Using $g = 0.0$ corresponds to the routing without using density information. In this case, the client node uses the shortest symbolic path to the destination area.

Taking the path length into account in the calculation of the path metric m_p is important, because longer symbolic paths increase the window of opportunity for communication holes on the path. Even more important, the communication costs grow with the path length as the messages are routed along safer but also longer communication paths. We will see this in the discussion of the average stretch of our routing paths later in this section.

Fig. 4.7 compares the resulting success rates for different density weighting factors for our scenarios with both 150 and 250 nodes. As the results show, using density information has the desired effect of increasing the success rate of communication. Particularly interesting is that it prevents the decrease of the success rate when increasing the number of areas. This can be explained by the higher quality of the density information available when using symbolic areas of small sizes.

As expected, increasing the density weighting factor can only improve the success rate within certain limits so that the results for a density weighting factor of 100.0 are only slightly better than the results for the factor of 2.0.

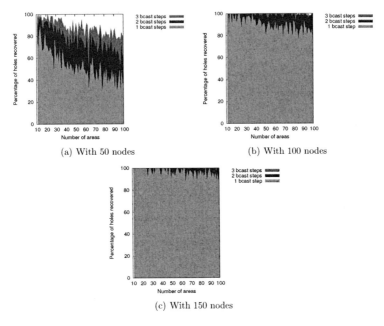

(a) With 50 nodes   (b) With 100 nodes

(c) With 150 nodes

Figure 4.8: Percentage of required broadcast steps for hole recovery

Recovering from Holes

With the help of feedback messages it is possible to reach an almost 100% success rate over time (when ignoring message loss due to collisions and the like) assuming that the network is not partitioned. How long it takes for a mobile node to arrive at this reliability level mainly depends on the rate of messages it sends to different receivers. As this is a highly application-dependent and scenario-dependent factor, we do not analyze this here but concentrate on recovery using local symbolic broadcasts.

We have analyzed the number of broadcast steps required to recover from a communication or coverage hole by randomly selecting 1000 communication paths for each scenario. For each hole appearing on these paths, we then determined the minimum number of steps required for recovering from this hole. Fig. 4.8 shows the percentage of holes recoverable with one, two and three broadcast steps for scenarios with 50, 100 and 150 nodes. For scenarios with more than 150 nodes, the proportion of holes recoverable by one broadcast step quickly approaches 100%.

The results might look discouraging for sparse topologies like for the scenarios with only 50 nodes. However, one has to consider that it is only possible to cover a very

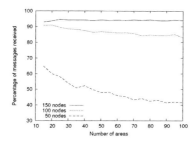

Figure 4.9: Average success rates with a maximum of one broadcast step

small number of areas with 50 nodes in the first place. If we do not consider more than 25 symbolic areas – leaving us with 2 nodes per area on average – the percentage of holes recoverable in one broadcast step lies at around 70% and around 90% of the holes are recoverable in two broadcast steps. This is a promising result considering that some symbolic areas still are without coverage due to our randomized deployment of nodes.

Fig. 4.9 now shows the average success rate when using a maximum of 1 broadcast step for recovering from communication or coverage holes. The positive effect of the recovery by local symbolic broadcasts compared to the results without recovery is considerable for all three node densities (compare the success rate results shown in Fig. 4.6). However, as expected, in the sparse scenarios with 50 nodes, it still declines sharply when increasing the number of areas. Not reaching a 100% success rate with 150 nodes despite the results shown in Fig. 4.8 can in large parts be attributed to moving client nodes that try to send queries to neighbors they have lost the connection to before receiving beacon messages from their new neighbor nodes. In parts, this is an artifact of us moving the client nodes from one random location to the next instead of using continuous node movements.

Recovering from Area Partitionings

Area partitionings can affect both the forwarding of messages along symbolic routes and the delivery of messages within symbolic areas. To assess the impact of the area partitioning problem, we first investigated how often this occurs in different scenarios. Fig. 4.10 (a) shows the average number of area partitionings that can be found depending on the overall number of areas the simulation area is split into. As the graphs show, the ability to cope with partitioned areas is obviously less important for dense topologies and for scenarios with symbolic areas that are small compared to the transmission range of the sensor nodes. A particularly interesting observation is that the curves are not monotonically decreasing with an increasing number of areas but exhibit a maximum (clearly visible for the case of 150 nodes at around 40 symbolic areas). This behavior is due to the fact that for very small numbers of areas only few

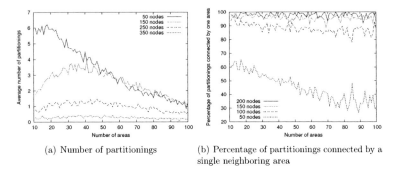

(a) Number of partitionings

(b) Percentage of partitionings connected by a single neighboring area

Figure 4.10: Analysis of partition recovery

partition candidates exist whereas for cases with a large number of areas, critical parts of the network communication graph that are susceptible to creating partitionings tend to get split up to different symbolic areas.

Our solution for the area partitioning problem presented in Section 4.4.3 that lets neighboring areas help in connecting partitions only works for cases where the partitions are connected through a single intermediate symbolic area. Fig. 4.10 (b) shows for which percentage of the partitionings this is the case. The results in the figure show that sparse topologies not only tend to have more area partitionings than dense topologies but are also only able to recover a very limited portion of them using our solution. However, already in the scenarios with 100 nodes it is possible to recover a very large percentage of partitionings. Even more dense topologies can recover partitionings in the vast majority of cases. Here, the interesting question rather is whether the overhead of a recovery solution is justified considering the small number of partitionings expected to occur in practice.

Connectivity Information Collection

Evaluating to what extent and how fast mobile client nodes can collect connectivity information by listening to beacon messages while moving in the network area is very difficult as such a collection is influenced by many external factors specific to the particular scenario. On the one hand, it heavily depends on the topology of the network and the semantics of its parts (e.g., in office scenarios client nodes move more in hallways than in offices). On the other hand, it depends on the movement model of the nodes (e.g., does the user visit the complete office building or only specific parts).

In the general case, no mobility and topology model for simulations captures this, so a solid analysis can only be done given the specific application scenario. To give at least an idea of the potential of such a collection of connectivity information, we have simulated mobile nodes on our maps that move randomly with the typical speed

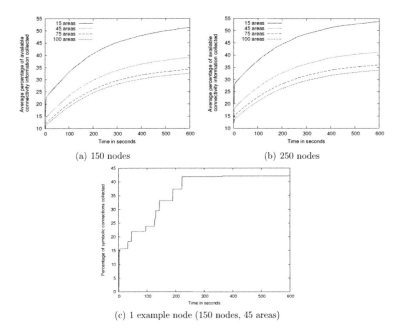

(a) 150 nodes   (b) 250 nodes

(c) 1 example node (150 nodes, 45 areas)

Figure 4.11: Average percentage of collected connectivity information over time

of a pedestrian (between 0 and 1.5 meters per second) and collect connectivity information from the beacon messages they hear. Fig. 4.11 shows the average percentage of connectivities the moving nodes have learned about over a period of 600 seconds for different numbers of areas with (a) 150 sensor nodes and (b) 250 sensor nodes. Individual mobile nodes learn connectivity information in discrete steps – adding new information whenever they enter the communication range of a node from a symbolic coordinate they have not heard of yet. This is illustrated by Fig. 4.11 (c) with the help of measurements from one example node moving in the network.

The analysis shows that a considerable part of the connectivity information is learned in a relatively short time (between 30% and 55% in 10 minutes). However, the curves also level off very quickly so that a complete knowledge of the connectivity information can only be expected – if ever – after a very long time.

Stretch

As a final step of our experimental analysis, let us now consider the stretch – the path length overhead of our node-to-node communication paths over the shortest paths possible connecting sender and receiver nodes. Fig. 4.12 shows the average stretch of

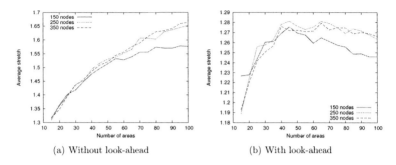

(a) Without look-ahead   (b) With look-ahead

Figure 4.12: Average stretch

our symbolic routing depending on the number of symbolic areas for scenarios with 150, 250 and 350 nodes. Fig. 4.12 (a) shows the stretch for the standard case whereas Fig. 4.12 (b) shows the results for the case when our path look-ahead optimization is used.

Without the path look-ahead optimization, the overhead of our routing paths lies between 31% and 66%. With path look-ahead, the overhead is significantly smaller and lies between 19% and 28%. For the cases with path look-ahead, the stretch is caused by the purely local path length optimization of the algorithm. This means that each node knows and uses the shortest paths to its neighboring symbolic areas but not the shortest paths to all symbolic areas in the network. The larger stretch for cases without path look-ahead is due to possible short cuts the algorithm does not take.

We have also measured the effect of using density information for the prevention of holes on the average stretch of the resulting routing paths. The results are shown in Fig. 4.13 for scenarios with 250 nodes and different weighting factors that we also used for evaluating the influence on the success rate of communications. Clearly, selecting "safer" paths using density information increases the average path length significantly. However, even for the very high density weighting factor of 100.0, the path length overhead hardly grows over 50%.

To set the results on the stretch of our symbolic routing mechanism into perspective, we simulated the communication between nodes in the same scenarios using the geographic routing algorithm GPSR [93] and measured its stretch values. Table 4.2 compares the average stretch achieved by GPSR with the average stretch of symbolic routing when communicating in the same scenarios. For GPSR the stretch does not depend on the number of areas as it does not use symbolic areas but geographic coordinates for its routing decisions. For that reason, the table only shows a single value for GPSR and a range of values for our symbolic routing. While the path length overhead for our symbolic routing is larger than for GPSR, we still consider an overhead of between 20% and 30% (or below 50% when using density information) compared to

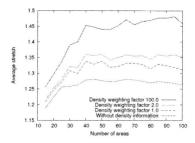

Figure 4.13: Average stretch for 250 nodes using density information

Table 4.2: Average stretch of GPSR and symbolic routing

Number of nodes	Average stretch		
	GPSR	Symbolic routing without look-ahead	Symbolic routing with look-ahead
150	1.10	1.31 - 1.58	1.23 - 1.28
250	1.14	1.31 - 1.65	1.19 - 1.28
350	1.16	1.32 - 1.66	1.19 - 1.28

the shortest path as reasonably small considering the limited amount of position and topology information we are using.

4.5.3 Discussion

While our theoretical analysis has demonstrated the positive properties of symbolic routing in general, our simulations have confirmed that symbolic routing in sensor networks is possible with relatively low overhead compared to the optimal path and a promising success rate. Dealing with inevitable holes and partitionings is possible with our recovery and prevention methods. In particular, local symbolic broadcasts turned out to be a simple and in most cases very effective method for recovering from communication problems.

The simulation results support our decision to support both local symbolic broadcasts and the sending of feedback messages in our implementation. While local broadcasts are very effective in most cases, they can become expensive for very sparse topologies without being able to circumvent all holes. Feedback messages, in turn, give the message sender all information and control about the message transfer process. This is advantageous both in sparse scenarios and when the client node expects to send multiple messages to the same destination area.

Using density information has also been shown to be worthwhile for scenarios where such data is available. Using density information is particularly attractive as it does not require any implementation on the sensor nodes and therefore does not incur any runtime overhead for processing or storing data on these nodes.

4.6 Summary

The focus of this chapter was a novel routing approach based on the concept of symbolic coordinates that we specifically developed for our heterogeneous pervasive computing scenarios consisting of mobile client devices and static wireless sensor networks. The idea of our approach is to split the routing task between the mobile client devices that specify a symbolic source route to the destination area and the static wireless sensor nodes that realize the node-to-node forwarding of messages based on this source route.

Our extensive evaluation of the approach has shown that it works in a variety of scenarios with different node densities. It generates a small overhead below 30% on the path length and is able to achieve high success rates with the help of different failure prevention and recovery mechanisms. One important advantage of the protocol is its flexibility concerning the amount of topology information known to the clients which allows using it in various types of application scenarios.

4.6.1 Future Directions in this Area

One very interesting direction that we see for future research in this area is the integration of our concepts on routing based on symbolic coordinates with topology control mechanisms for wireless sensor networks that manage duty cycles and transmission power levels of the sensor nodes. Symbolic coordinate information could provide useful input to these topology control mechanisms in two ways: On the one hand, it could be used to enforce application-level requirements like making sure that some node in each area is active at all times. On the other hand, the topology control mechanism could use the coordinate information to actively support our routing mechanism so that neighboring coordinates are able to communicate with each other while at the same time minimizing the energy consumption of the sensor network as a whole. In addition to potential energy savings, a topology control mechanism can also be interesting for our approach by limiting the amount of neighborhood state that must be managed on the individual sensor nodes.

Another important improvement for our routing approach could be the integration of routing metrics with our routing based on symbolic coordinates. On the node-to-node routing level, this could make our approach aware of factors like the link qualities and the forwarding costs of alternative paths.

To complement our work and to make it useful in a wider range of different pervasive computing scenarios, it would be interesting to investigate how limited support from an infrastructure (e.g., a limited number of sensor network base stations) can be used to improve the efficiency of our approach. The routing mechanism would then determine case by case whether to route messages through the sensor network or whether it is preferable to take the detour through the infrastructure.

A final future direction for work in this area is the investigation of how hybrid location models that combine symbolic coordinate data with geographic information can be used.

5 Coordinate Assignment

With our symbolic routing approach discussed in the previous chapter, we have introduced one exemplary application of symbolic coordinates in heterogeneous pervasive computing scenarios integrating wireless sensor networks. However, for symbolic coordinates to become a viable alternative to traditional approaches like using geographic coordinates, we also need to show that there is a simple and efficient way of assigning symbolic coordinates to wireless sensor nodes. This coordinate assignment problem is the focus of this chapter.

We start the discussion with a thorough definition of the problem and motivate the difficulty of doing such coordinate assignments efficiently. In the main part of this chapter, we introduce and describe three different methods for the coordinate assignment in indoor scenarios: The simplest but also most costly approach is the individual assignment of coordinates where the administrator needs to send symbolic coordinates to each individual node. The second approach, the assignment by broadcast, significantly reduces the assignment overhead by sending out coordinate messages once per area by broadcast. Finally, our third approach, the assignment of coordinates by assisted broadcast, improves on the assignment by broadcast by filtering out false positive assignments based on sensor events.

In the evaluation section of this chapter, we demonstrate that our three approaches are effective solutions to the coordinate assignment problem. We also show that the assignment by assisted broadcast in particular is easy to use and only generates a very low overhead while effectively preventing false coordinate assignments. It also works without any prior knowledge of the sensor network topology. This makes it a good candidate for use in real-world wireless sensor network scenarios.

5.1 Preliminaries

Providing sensor nodes with information on the spatial context they are operating in is an important part of the network configuration process at the beginning of system operation. Independent of whether geographic or symbolic coordinates are to be used by the algorithms and protocols running on the wireless sensor nodes (see Section 4.3), we need to make sure that the nodes learn about their respective coordinates during the setup of the network structure. In principle, one can do this either manually by assigning coordinates to nodes or use a localization algorithm to let the nodes determine their coordinates autonomically based on certain input data.

When working with geographic coordinates, the common approach is to determine the locations of individual nodes with the help of a localization algorithm. These algorithms usually require a limited amount of input information (e.g., coordinates of anchor nodes, distances among neighboring nodes, ...) to compute the approximate positions of the nodes in the network. Major limitations of localization algorithms in wireless sensor networks are the high computational complexity of most approaches and the lack of precision of common ranging methods which leads to significant localization errors, particularly when used over multiple hops or in indoor scenarios. We will discuss the different classes of localization algorithms and approaches and their limitations in some more detail in the related work section of this chapter.

Assigning geographic coordinates to sensor nodes manually is usually not an acceptable solution. On the one hand, it is very difficult and costly for an administrator to determine the correct geographic coordinate of a node. This is particularly true for indoor scenarios where GPS receivers do not work well. On the other hand, the assignment has to be done once per node, because each node has a different geographic coordinate. This severely limits the scalability of such a manual assignment.

So far, there do not exist any algorithms for the automatic localization of sensor nodes that support symbolic coordinates – if one ignores the possible approach of determining geographic coordinates for the nodes and then inferring the symbolic coordinates based on this geographic coordinate information. We also do not expect such algorithms to become available in the foreseeable future. The main reason for this lies in the fact that symbolic coordinates are not based on a global or local coordinate system that an algorithm could base its calculations on. Instead, the definition of symbolic coordinates is highly scenario and also application dependent. For example, the size of the symbolic areas can vary significantly and there is no real concept of distance among symbolic coordinates.

While there is no solution for the automatic localization of nodes based on symbolic coordinates, it is – unlike for geographic coordinates – often acceptable to require an administrator to perform the assignment of symbolic coordinates. There are two reasons for this: Firstly, it is usually simple to determine the symbolic coordinate of the area a node is placed in. The administrator either knows directly which coordinate to assign (e.g., knowing the room number of the current room) or can consult a map specifying the symbolic coordinates of the different areas. Secondly, in most scenarios there will be multiple nodes placed in the same area that share the same symbolic coordinate. Using an appropriate coordinate assignment mechanism, it can be possible to reduce the assignment overhead by performing the assignment once per area instead of once per node.

A central argument in this thesis is that it is possible and beneficial in many cases to use symbolic coordinates instead of geographic coordinates when integrating wireless sensor networks in pervasive computing scenarios. To support this statement, we need to show that simple and efficient mechanisms exist for the assignment of symbolic coordinates to sensor nodes. In fact, it should be significantly easier, cheaper and more reliable to assign symbolic coordinates than to do a similar assignment or localization using geographic coordinates. We focus on such coordinate assignment approaches for symbolic coordinates in the rest of this chapter.

5.1.1 Problem Definition

We now define the problem that must be solved as part of the assignment of symbolic coordinates.

As before, we have a set of sensor nodes $S_{sensors} = \{sensor_1, sensor_2, \ldots, sensor_n\}$ with node identifiers $Id_{sensors} = \{id_{sensor_1}, id_{sensor_2}, \ldots, id_{sensor_n}\}$ which have been deployed in an application area A which consists of a set of symbolic areas $A_1 \ldots A_m$ with symbolic coordinates $C_{areas} = \{c_1, c_2, \ldots, c_m\}$. The partitioning of A into the symbolic areas is given by the symbolic location model. We assume that the symbolic location model is both complete and unambiguous. **Completeness** implies that for each object x lying within the application area A there exists a symbolic area A_i to which the object belongs:

$$\forall x \in A \qquad \exists i : x \in A_i$$

Unambiguity requires that each object x lies in at most one symbolic area, meaning that symbolic areas do not overlap:

$$(x \in A_i) \wedge (x \in A_j) \implies i = j$$

Note that we do not deal with the problem of defining symbolic location models here. Instead, we assume that a symbolic location model is available for the complete area where we need to assign symbolic coordinates to nodes. Formally, such a symbolic location model defines a mapping from geographic positions to symbolic coordinates. However, this mapping does not have to be explicitly expressed by the model. For example, a floor plan provides symbolic coordinates in the form of room numbers for the individual rooms in a building. This allows to unambiguously assign a symbolic coordinate to each object in this building (i.e., the room number of the room the object is located in) without ever referring to the geographic position of nodes.

For being able to assign symbolic coordinates to the sensor nodes, we need to find a function f mapping from node identifiers to symbolic coordinates.

$$f : Id_{sensors} \longrightarrow C_{areas}$$

In reality we do not compute a solution of f on one device but rather perform a coordinate assignment procedure which implicitly determines the solution for each sensor node and assigns the correct symbolic coordinate.

Note that we do not make any assumptions concerning the deployment of nodes. Consequently, the node identifier encodes no information on the location of nodes.

5.1.2 Requirements

As usual, the primary requirement for methods dealing with the assignment of coordinates is the **correctness** of the solution. The assignment of a symbolic coordinate should neither produce false positives nor false negatives. A false positive thereby represents the case where a node gets assigned a symbolic coordinate without lying in the area represented by the coordinate. A false negative occurs if a node is ignored in the coordinate assignment procedure of the area it belongs to.

To make the use of symbolic coordinates a viable alternative to the use of geographic position information, the assignment of symbolic coordinates should only generate a **small overhead**. It must be significantly simpler and less time consuming to assign symbolic coordinates to nodes than to determine their exact geographic coordinates and assign them to the nodes.

We are particularly interested in making the coordinate assignment process **simple** enough so that it can be done by a non-technical person without receiving extensive training beforehand. This is important as we envision sensor node functionality becoming integrated in a variety of appliances and everyday items. Users should be able to setup smart environments in their homes without requiring help by a technician.

A **low overhead** of the coordinate assignment process facilitates the use in a variety of scenarios. If the number of sensor nodes of a deployment is large, then the time required per node for the coordinate assignment becomes an essential factor for the scalability of the solution.

To provide for an applicability in a wide range of scenarios, a method for the assignment of symbolic coordinates should only set **low requirements on the sensor node hardware**. In particular, the solution should not require any special hardware that needs to be added only for the purpose of coordinate assignment.

Finally, as we concentrate on applications in indoor settings in the work of this thesis, the coordinate assignment solutions must be **applicable to indoor scenarios** – ideally without setting further constraints regarding the properties of the environment.

5.1.3 Application Scenarios

Applications for the coordinate assignment methods discussed in this chapter can be found in all systems and scenarios using symbolic coordinates. One example is the routing based on symbolic coordinates that we presented in the previous chapter.

We are specifically aiming for indoor scenarios here. On the one hand, this provides us with a natural way of defining symbolic areas using the rooms of a building as the symbolic areas and the room numbers or room names as symbolic coordinates. On the other hand, we are provided with a clear separation between neighboring areas in the form of walls, doors and windows. The first of our three approaches works independent of such area boundaries whereas the other two heavily profit from such a clear separation.

While the primary application we are aiming for here is the assignment of symbolic coordinates, the approaches presented in this chapter can also be used within a more general setting, the room-level configuration of wireless sensor networks. Just like we assign a symbolic coordinate to all nodes within a room, other room-level information could be distributed the same way. One example application is to form clusters of nodes with all nodes within a room joining the same cluster. We describe more examples of applications of room-level configuration in chapter 6 of this thesis where we discuss the automatic grouping of nodes based on room boundaries.

5.1.4 Overview of Approach

Our discussion in the main part of this chapter involves three different methods for assigning symbolic coordinates to the nodes in a wireless sensor network: Individual assignment, assignment by broadcast and assignment by assisted broadcast.

The idea of individual assignment is very simple: The approach requires the administrator to visit each node individually and to directly communicate the respective symbolic coordinate to each node. This individual node-by-node assignment of symbolic coordinates provides the administrator with complete control over the assignment process. However, it is also very expensive and requires detailed knowledge of the administrator on the location of individual nodes.

The goal of the second approach, the coordinate assignment by broadcast, is to reduce the overhead for the administrator. To achieve this, a coordinate assignment message is sent out by broadcast only once per symbolic area instead of once per node. The main challenge using this approach results from nodes receiving such broadcast messages from neighboring areas, therefore assigning the wrong coordinate.

The final approach that we discuss in this chapter, the coordinate assignment by assisted broadcast, constitutes the main contribution of this chapter. Like for the second approach, the idea is to let the administrator visit the individual symbolic areas and let him send out the symbolic coordinates by broadcast. However, now the administrator also needs to confirm the coordinate assignment by triggering a sensor event in the target area. Only sensor nodes that both receive the coordinate assignment message and detect the sensor event perform the coordinate assignment step. This allows to effectively filter out false positive coordinate assignment messages received from neighboring areas.

5.2 Related Work

As mentioned before, our work on assigning symbolic coordinates to wireless sensor nodes is most closely related to the area of localization. After a short look at the widely-known Global Positioning System, we therefore discuss the solution space of localizing nodes in wireless sensor networks in some more detail. In the second part of this section, we then thoroughly discuss several existing localization techniques that are particularly related to our coordinate assignment solutions in the way they approach the node localization problem.

5.2.1 Global Positioning System

The most widely known localization system used in numerous application areas is the **Global Positioning System (GPS)** [90]. A GPS receiver determines its distance to at least three GPS satellites using the time of flight of a microwave signal and then determines its position based on this information. GPS provides position information with a relatively high accuracy nearly everywhere worldwide. The main disadvantage of GPS in the context of our scenarios is that the receiver requires a clear view of the sky for the localization to work well. This is not provided in many typical sensor network and pervasive computing scenarios (e.g., indoors). While other disadvantages like the size, the cost and the resource consumption of GPS receivers and antennas are slowly getting alleviated by new developments, these factors are still a significant obstacle to a widespread use on wireless sensor nodes. Nevertheless, for some sensor node platforms, matching GPS receiver boards are commercially available (e.g., the MTS420 from Crossbow Technology [38] for the MICA family of motes).

5.2.2 Localization in Wireless Sensor Networks

Localization is one of the fundamental research problems in the area of wireless sensor networks that has received considerable attention by many research groups in previous years. Due to the huge number of existing localization approaches for wireless sensor networks, this discussion of related work can only give a coarse overview of the area. For a deeper discussion of the fundamental localization techniques and the variety of sensor node localization approaches we refer to existing survey publications [66, 128].

Distance Measurement and Estimation

Determining the distance between nodes plays a central role in many localization mechanisms, because this distance information – together with the location of several anchor nodes – can be used to calculate the position of nodes in the network. Besides using established techniques, some localization approaches stand out from others by using special, sophisticated mechanisms for measuring or determining distances.

Basic distance measurement techniques include Time of Arrival, Time Difference of Arrival, Received Signal Strength Indication and hop distance. The idea of the Time of Arrival technique is to measure the time it takes for a signal to travel from the sender of the signal to the receiver of the signal. The distance is then inferred from the known propagation speed of the signal. Time Difference of Arrival builds upon the same idea but uses the difference in the arrival time of two signals for calculating the distance. The Received Signal Strength Indication technique aims to calculate the distance of a signal receiver from a signal sender using the strength of the signal received. This calculation is based on a model of the relationship between distance and signal attenuation. Finally, the hop distance technique refrains from measuring actual distance values but estimates the distance among arbitrary pairs of nodes using the number of hops of the shortest communication path between the nodes.

Novel, alternative distance measurement techniques include using minimal transmission power, the neighborhood similarity of nodes and radio interferometry. The idea of the minimal transmission power technique [18] is to infer the distance of two nodes from the minimal transmission power required for a successful communication between the two nodes. The neighborhood similarity technique [25] compares the sets of neighbors of two nodes and estimates the distance of the nodes based on the size of the overlap of these two sets. The radio interferometry technique [130] infers node distances based on the properties of two superimposed waves received at different nodes in the network.

Localization Techniques

As mentioned above, many localization techniques for wireless sensor networks are based on measuring distances between nodes. The basic geometric approach for doing this is called trilateration and is based on the geometric property that the position of a node can be unambiguously defined by the position of three reference points and their respective distances to the node [109]. If more than three nodes are used, then we speak of multilateration. In contrast to lateration, statistical approaches (e.g., [181]) to distance-based localization can model the locations of nodes both without and with noise in the distance measurements. The underlying idea is to express the probability of a node being located at a certain position. Each distance measurement is then used to refine the estimation.

Different distance-based localization techniques mainly differ in the way they determine distance values. There are approaches using the time of flight of radio signals [91, 111] or of acoustic signals [154], RSSI values [142, 149], radio interferometric measurements [130, 106] and external sensor events [107].

One alternative to using distances for determining the location of nodes is to use angles between nodes. This approach requires special hardware that is able to identify the direction from which a signal is received [148, 155] or to send out signals in specific directions [145]. Like trilateration for distance-based localization, the basic concept of angle-based localization is called triangulation. In the optimal case, the position information of two reference points and the angle of these points to the node in question (with respect to a given coordinate system) is sufficient to determine the position of the node.

Range-free localization approaches abstain from measuring distances or angles and solely work based on connectivity information among the nodes. Some of these approaches require a regular deployment of nodes [24] or a centralized analysis of the complete topology information [185]. The DV-hop algorithm [149] is a popular representative of range-free localization approaches. It requires the nodes to collect their hop distances to a set of anchor nodes and uses the geographic distances of these anchor nodes to determine average distance values for these hop distances.

Critique

Despite the multitude of approaches that have already been developed, localization is still considered a very difficult problem and no standard solution is foreseeable. For the classical localization approaches based on distance measurements, the limited precision of the available ranging methods remains the most critical problem. Distance measurements are influenced by many factors including multipath propagation, irregular signal fading, limited models of the environment and inaccuracies of the sender and receiver devices.

Elnahrawy, Li and Martin [46] discuss the fundamental limits of localization techniques based on signal strength when used in indoor scenarios. Their analysis indicates that the quality of the localization results is mainly determined by the (lack of) accuracy of the distance estimation and not by the localization algorithm. Whitehouse, Karlof and Culler [215] also studied the localization based on received signal strength. While they found that it RSSI-based localization can be usable in outdoor scenarios, they could not determine a useable level of correlation between RSSI values and distance in indoor scenarios. Savvides et al. [180] found that increasing the network density or increasing the number of anchor nodes can only provide strongly limited improvements to the localization result.

We expect that a significant improvement of the quality of the measurement results across different scenario types would require novel hardware technologies (e.g, optical ranging using lasers, ultra wideband radios, . . .) whose applicability to wireless sensor networks remains to be shown.

5.2.3 Techniques Related to Coordinate Assignment

The Spotlight localization system [194] is particularly related to our coordinate assignment approach in that it also uses sensor events for the localization of nodes. A helicopter (the Spotlight device) which knows its own position flies over the sensor network and generates light events at certain points of time. The sensor nodes report when they detect events back to the helicopter, which is then able to compute the geographic coordinates of the nodes. However, as the authors aim to calculate geographic coordinates, the required calculations are rather complex and a precise time synchronization of nodes is required.

Similar to our assignment of symbolic coordinates, Corke, Peterson and Rus [37] assign geographic coordinates to sensor nodes using radio communication. In their scenario, a robot helicopter equipped with a GPS receiver flies over the network area and periodically broadcasts beacon messages containing its current geographic coordinate. The sensor nodes on the ground typically receive multiple such beacons and need to estimate their position based on this information. The authors propose different methods for this calculation including taking the mean of the positions or the signal strength weighted mean of the positions. A constraint-based method performed best in their experiments.

Like our coordinate assignment by assisted broadcast, StarDust [195] and the Lighthouse location system [171] also use light signals as part of the node localization process, albeit in a completely different manner. StarDust [195] passively localizes sensor nodes with the help of reflected light. Each sensor node is equipped with a retroreflector which reflects light coming from an aerial vehicle. This vehicle records an image of the deployment area with a digital camera showing the light reflections and image processing techniques are used to identify the locations of the nodes. A mapping of nodes to the set of determined positions is found with the help of a relaxation algorithm based on information like the neighborhood relationship among nodes.

The Lighthouse location system [171] has been specifically designed for Smart Dust sensor nodes [208]. These sensor nodes are only able to communicate passively by either reflecting or not reflecting an incoming light beam. Consequently, Lighthouse also requires a passive system for the localization of these nodes. The basic idea is to have a set of lighthouse-like devices each equipped with a rotating light beam. It is then possible for a node to infer its distance to such a lighthouse based on the time it takes for the light beam to pass over the light sensor of the node. With the help of the position information from three lighthouses and distance estimates determined as described, a node is able to calculate its own position without having to perform any active communication itself.

MSP [225] uses sensor events to sort the sensor nodes in a node sequence based on the order in which they detected the event. Using this node sequence, knowledge on the propagation type of the event (e.g., linear or circular) and a set of anchor nodes, it is possible to infer an area in which a node can be located in. By repeating this process with multiple events from different sources and different directions, it is possible to shrink the candidate location area of the nodes and infer increasingly accurate location information. The lack of a precise time synchronization as well as effects like delays in the processing of events on the nodes can cause permutations in the node sequences used for calculating the positions of the nodes which in turn can severely affect the localization result. To avoid these effects (at the cost of a lower precision), MSP uses a so-called protection band compensation approach which extends the boundary of the location area a little to compensate for flippings and to avoid erasing nodes from the map.

5.3 Assignment of Symbolic Coordinates

In this section we introduce three different approaches to the problem of assigning symbolic coordinates to wireless sensor nodes. We describe the properties of the approaches and discuss their respective advantages and disadvantages. We start by describing the properties of our target scenarios in more detail.

We have already defined the general coordinate assignment problem in Section 5.1.1. Let us now take a closer look at our specific target scenario – indoor pervasive computing scenarios with pervasive computing devices and wireless sensor nodes forming a smart environment – and describe the properties of these target scenarios with respect to the assignment of symbolic coordinates.

Our target system consists of a set of wireless sensor nodes and other small, statically-deployed devices with similar resource constraints that are distributed to different rooms in a building. Each room is uniquely identified by a symbolic coordinate, which can, for example, correspond to the respective room number. As mentioned before, we do not assume any relation between the node identifiers of the nodes and their location in the network. Consequently, in the beginning the sensor nodes do not have any information about the symbolic coordinate of the room they are located in.

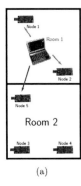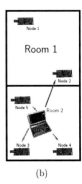

(a)   (b)

Figure 5.1: Coordinate assignment example scenario

After the deployment of the sensor nodes, there is one person (who we call administrator) responsible for assigning the correct symbolic coordinates to the nodes in the network. The administrator has a mobile client device that is able to directly communicate with the nodes of the sensor network. The client device can be used to send so-called coordinate messages to the nodes.

Fig. 5.1 illustrates the starting point of our coordinate assignment approaches with a simple example scenario with five sensor nodes distributed in two rooms. The administrator first visits room 1 (see Fig. 5.1 (a)) and then room 2 (see Fig. 5.1 (b)). In each room, the client device is able to directly communicate with the nodes deployed in this room. However, its set of neighbors in the communication graph does not have to be limited to these nodes but can also include nodes located in neighboring rooms. In the example, the client device can communicate with node 5 in room 2 while the user is in room 1 and with node 2 in room 1 while being located in room 2.

5.3.1 Individual Assignment

The most basic way of assigning symbolic coordinates to nodes is to assign the correct coordinate to each node in the network individually. There are two basic approaches for doing this. Firstly, it might possible to directly encode the symbolic coordinate and other configuration information in the program code installed on the individual sensor nodes. The second option is to assign the symbolic coordinate to the node at deployment time or during the normal node operation using one-to-one communication between the administrator's device and each individual node.

Presetting Symbolic Coordinates

The first option – encoding the symbolic coordinate in the program code of each node before it is deployed in the field – is similar to what is typically done with the node identifier of sensor nodes. TinyOS, as an example, allows to set the node identifier when uploading the program code to a sensor node. For this purpose, the installer creates an adapted version of the code image writing the node identifier to a predefined location in the code image before uploading it to the node's program memory. It would be straightforward to extend this procedure to also write symbolic coordinate information.

The main problem with including the symbolic coordinate or similar configuration information in the program code of the node is that it severely limits the flexibility for the placement of nodes. Basically, it must be known at the time of programming in which symbolic area the node will be placed. Special care must then be taken to ensure that all nodes are placed correctly to avoid confusion by wrongly assigned coordinates. This generates significant overhead during the preparation and the deployment of nodes – the very reason why we assumed that nodes initially have no information on their (symbolic) location in the network area.

When the application field of a wireless sensor network lies outside of typical research settings, we expect that future sensor nodes will be delivered with preinstalled software ready to use. If we do not want to reprogram the nodes before deployment, the symbolic coordinate would have to be preset correctly in the factory – an unrealistic assumption in most cases. Consequently, a preconfiguration of the symbolic coordinate information at programming time is not possible in this case.

Setting Symbolic Coordinates Dynamically

For using the second option – assigning the symbolic coordinates to the nodes at deployment time or during the node operation – the administrator needs to communicate with the individual nodes one by one and send the correct symbolic coordinate to each node. Typically, this is done using the node's wireless communication interface. Upon receiving such a coordinate message the node stores the new symbolic coordinate and uses it from this point on.

While assigning the symbolic coordinates at deployment time provides more flexibility than presetting coordinate information, it has the disadvantage that the administrator needs to communicate with each individual node. That is an additional work step taking the administrators time.

Advantages and Disadvantages

The individual assignment of symbolic coordinates provides the clear advantage that it avoids ambiguity in the assignment process. The administrator has complete control over which nodes receive which symbolic coordinate and he is able to ensure the correctness of the assignment process. Since every node is addressed individually, it is possible to go beyond the initialization with symbolic coordinates and to set any type of node-specific configuration information.

Unfortunately, assigning symbolic coordinates to individual nodes separately also exhibits a number of disadvantages. First of all, the assignment of coordinates requires individual communication with each sensor node in the network. Consequently, the required time and effort (and also the message complexity) grow with the number of nodes in the network. This is particularly true for the dynamic assignment of coordinates during or after deployment. For the assignment of coordinates at programming time, the main additional cost lies in the creation and the management of separate code images including the correct symbolic coordinate and the installation of the nodes at the correct place in the deployment area. For the dynamic assignment in turn, the administrator needs to be aware of the location of the individual nodes. This means that he needs to know the mapping from node identifiers to symbolic coordinates.

5.3.2 Assignment by Broadcast

With our second approach, the assignment of symbolic coordinates by broadcast, we aim to address the disadvantages of having to separately assign a symbolic coordinate to each individual node in the network. Instead, the goal is to distribute the coordinate information to all nodes in an area in a single step.

The basic working principle of the coordinate assignment by broadcast is simple. The idea is to let the network administrator visit the different rooms covered by nodes of the network (representing the symbolic areas $A_1 \ldots A_m$) and send out a message containing the current symbolic coordinate information in each room. The message is sent by broadcast so that all nodes in the one-hop neighborhood of the client device receive the information. Upon receiving such a coordinate message, a sensor node overwrites its symbolic coordinate information with the newly received data. In the example scenario in Fig. 5.1, the administrator visits the two areas room 1 and room 2 and sends out a coordinate message by broadcast in each area.

Advantages and Disadvantages

One important advantage of sending out coordinate information by broadcast is the lower overhead both for the administrator and in terms of the number of messages sent as the configuration has to be done only once per room instead of once per sensor node. Consequently, the assignment cost and the message complexity do not grow with the number of nodes in the network but only with the number of symbolic areas.

A second advantage of the assignment by broadcast is that no information is required on the position of individual sensor nodes, because the coordinate information sent out by the client device does not have to be addressed to specific nodes. This is a very important property as it allows to perform the coordinate assignment process independent of the node deployment.

The main disadvantage of the assignment by broadcast is the difficulty of ensuring that all nodes from $S_{sensors}$ assign the correct coordinate. It is typically desirable that sensor networks are connected across area boundaries like walls between rooms to provide for communication between different network parts. However, this also means that nodes can receive coordinate messages from neighboring rooms and falsely assign the symbolic coordinates from these messages. Depending on the sequence of messages sent, these nodes might overwrite the correct coordinate information with data belonging to a neighboring room. The problem is illustrated in the example in Fig. 5.1 where a broadcast sent in room 1 also reaches node 5 in room 2 and a broadcast sent in room 2 also reaches node 2 in room 1.

The basic approach to address the problem of coordinate messages affecting nodes in neighboring rooms is to control the signal strength of the messages sent by the client device. Ideally, the strength of the signal should still allow the message to reach all nodes inside the current room and should at the same time prevent the message from reaching any of the nodes in neighboring rooms. However, the propagation of radio signals in indoor scenarios is very difficult to understand or even precisely control. So it might be difficult or even impossible to find this balance especially if two nodes in adjacent rooms are located very close to each other and the attenuation of the signal by the wall between them is small.

Extensions of the Approach

We have developed two extensions for the assignment of symbolic coordinates by broadcast that address the problem of conflicting coordinate assignments from different areas. The first extension is very simple in its approach and allows sensor nodes to store and manage multiple symbolic coordinates in parallel so that different coordinate messages do not overwrite each other's information. The underlying idea is that if a node has received multiple symbolic coordinates, then it lies in the border area of the rooms represented by these coordinates. How these multiple coordinates of a node are then used is application dependent. For example, a node might participate in the operations of all areas it supposedly is a member of.

Our second extension follows a more sophisticated approach and tries to reach an informed decision on which symbolic coordinate to assign. The idea is to analyze the signal strength of the different coordinate messages received at a node, called Received Signal Strength Indication (RSSI) value, and use this information to assign a coordinate to the node. We assign the symbolic coordinate from the message received with the highest RSSI value reflecting the assumption that a coordinate message sent from the same room should be received with a higher signal strength than coordinate messages from neighboring rooms. However, this only works reliably if the signal attenuation of the walls between rooms is significant. This can be problematic, because RSSI – despite its strong limitations in indoor scenarios [46] – is more of an indicator for geographic distances among nodes than an aid for the localization of nodes to different areas. We are going to evaluate the suitability of the RSSI criterion for filtering coordinate assignment messages in Section 5.5 using measurements from a typical office scenario.

5.3.3 Assignment by Assisted Broadcast

Both approaches to the assignment of symbolic coordinates presented so far have disadvantages. Individual assignment is quite intricate and requires detailed knowledge

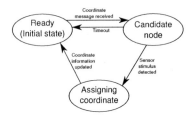

Figure 5.2: State diagram of coordinate assignment by assisted broadcast

on the nodes' positions in the network whereas the coordinate assignment by broadcast is susceptible to errors due to the propagation of coordinate messages across room boundaries. In the following, we present a third approach, the assignment by assisted broadcast, which avoids all of these problems.

Like for the assignment of coordinates by broadcast described above, the administrator uses the client device to send out coordinate messages by broadcast in the individual rooms of the deployment area. It is again his task to ensure that he sends out the correct coordinate information in each room. The novelty of our third approach lies in the handling of a received coordinate message by the sensor nodes: Instead of directly assigning a symbolic coordinate received in a coordinate message, a node first checks whether the coordinate message is followed by a sensor stimulus that confirms the new coordinate information.

Directly after the administrator has sent out a coordinate message (within a pre-defined time interval $t_{eventTriggerMaxDelay}$) he needs to trigger an event in the environment that can be detected by one of the sensors of the nodes. The goal is to distinguish nodes that are located in the same room as the administrator and that both receive the coordinate message and detect the following sensor event from nodes in neighboring areas that only receive the coordinate message but are not affected by the sensor event triggered by the administrator.

Fig. 5.2 shows the state diagram of the receiver side of our coordinate assignment by assisted broadcast. The nodes start in the "Ready" state and pass into the "Candidate node" state upon receiving a coordinate message. There they start an internal timer to check whether the expected sensor stimulus is received within $t_{eventTriggerMaxDelay}$. If this is the case, then the node proceeds to the "Assigning coordinate" state and updates its symbolic coordinate information based on the received coordinate message. Otherwise the node times out and returns to the "Ready" state.

The method described above relies on two important assumptions. Firstly, it assumes that it is possible for the administrator to change the external conditions in a way that allows all sensor nodes in the room to detect these changes as an event. Secondly, it also assumes that similar changes to the external conditions in the neighboring rooms are unlikely to happen at the same time without an explicit intervention by an external party.

Sensor Stimuli for Assisted Broadcast

Different types of sensors and different types of sensor stimuli can be used to confirm coordinate messages. The main preconditions are that the sensor stimuli can be easily triggered by the administrator and that the resulting sensor event can be detected in the whole symbolic area but not in neighboring areas. In our indoor pervasive computing scenarios, it is important that the sensor event reaches all nodes within a room but does not spread into neighboring rooms.

We work with two types of sensor events, namely light level changes and acoustic events. In indoor scenarios, the light level in rooms can easily be influenced by turning the artificial lighting on or off. The room lighting in one room typically only affects this room and does not spread to neighboring rooms. Acoustic events can be generated and detected using special devices attached to the sensor nodes as described in the implementation section below. Given an adequate volume of the acoustic signal, we expect it to be effectively absorbed by walls, windows and doors (unlike radio signals which are only attenuated to some unknown degree) which prevents the event from being detected in neighboring rooms.

Which behavior constitutes an event and how such an event is detected using sensor readings captured on the nodes depends on the type of sensor and the monitored characteristic of the environment. For light sensors we define an event as a significant change of the recorded luminance level within a limited time period. Fig. 5.3 shows the pseudo code for checking whether a light event has been detected and whether the received symbolic coordinate should be assigned. Directly after having received a new coordinate message, the node records its current sensor value and starts a timer. When the timer fires, it records its sensor value again and calculates the absolute difference of the two sensor values. If this value is above a specified event threshold, the sensor node detects an event and assigns the new symbolic coordinate.

We define events differently for acoustic signals: A sensor node detects an event when it detects a sound of a certain frequency. For the coordinate assignment by assisted broadcast this means that the node assigns the symbolic coordinate if it detects a predefined sound within a limited time period after it has received the coordinate message.

Advantages and Disadvantages

The main advantage of the assignment by assisted broadcast is that the additional sensor stimulus triggered by the administrator prevents ambiguities in the assignment of symbolic coordinates. While a coordinate message might be received by nodes in many different areas surrounding the administrator, the confirming sensor stimulus is only received by nodes in the target area. This allows to assign the coordinate to a specific set of nodes without having to address each of the nodes in this set individually.

The cost of using coordinate assignment by assisted broadcast is the additional effort required for generating the external sensor stimulus and for checking this sensor stimulus on the receiving nodes. A disadvantage of the approach is that it only works

```
int ownSymbolicCoordinate;
int candidateSymbolicCoordinate;

event receivedCoordinateMessage(int newSymbolicCoordinate) {
  candidateSymbolicCoordinate = newSymbolicCoordinate;
  initialSensorValue = getSensorValue();
  startTimer(eventDetectionTimerLength);
}

event timerFired() {
  int finalSensorValue = getSensorValue();
  if (abs(currentSensorValue - finalSensorValue) > eventThreshold) {
    ownSymbolicCoordinate = candidateSymbolicCoordinate;
  }
}
```

Figure 5.3: Checking a new symbolic coordinate for applicability

for actual sensor nodes that possess the sensor chip required for detecting the sensor event. In contrast, individual assignment and assignment by broadcast also work on other devices that are part of the pervasive computing environment, for example gateway nodes without any sensing functionality.

5.4 Implementation

We have implemented our three approaches for the assignment of symbolic coordinates based on the TinyOS 2 operating system with support for both the TelosB and the MICAz (and MICA2) sensor node platforms. For the experiments with assignment by broadcast and the assignment by broadcast using light events, we used TelosB sensor nodes and their integrated total solar radiation (TSR) light sensors.

For our experiments with acoustic events, we used MICA2 and MICAz sensor nodes in combination with MTS300 sensor boards from Crossbow. In addition to a light and a temperature sensor, the MTS300 contains a sounder element and a microphone. The sounder is able to emit sounds with a frequency of 4kHz. The microphone is connected to a hardware tone decoder that reports an event when a sound in the 4kHz frequency range is recorded by the microphone. This way, the administrator is able to trigger an acoustic event using the sounder element of an MTS300 sensor board on one sensor node while other sensor nodes use the microphone and the tone decoder on the MTS300 to detect such events.

We have implemented the client application in C++ based on the Qt software toolkit. It runs on our standard PDA platform, Linux PDAs from Sharp (Sharp Za-urus SL-3200) that communicate with the sensor network using a TelosB sensor node connected to the PDA over USB as a bridge node (see Section 2.2.2). The client ap-

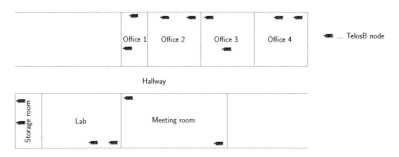

Figure 5.4: Floor plan of the experiment area

plication supports all three approaches presented in this chapter and both light and acoustic events. Thus, symbolic coordinates can be sent to individual nodes or broadcasted with or without advertising a following sensor stimulus. Note that acoustic events can be directly triggered by the client application by activating the sounder on the sensor node connected to the PDA after the coordinate message has been sent whereas triggering a light event requires explicit activity by the administrator. This is an important advantage of the solution using acoustic events.

The output power of the CC2420 radio chips used by the TelosB and the MICAz sensor nodes is programmable. The possible range of values starts with a minimum output power of -25 dBm and goes up to a maximum output power of 0 dBm. The client application allows to select any of the valid output power values.

5.5 Evaluation

In this section, we present an evaluation of our different approaches to the assignment of symbolic coordinates to wireless sensor nodes. Since the manual assignment of coordinates to individual nodes should work in all cases as long as no packets are lost due to the unreliability of the wireless channel, we do not discuss our first approach in detail here but concentrate on the evaluation of coordinate assignment by broadcast and coordinate assignment by assisted broadcast.

5.5.1 Assignment by Broadcast

For evaluating our approach, we deployed 14 TelosB sensor nodes in 7 different rooms of the computer science building at the Universität Stuttgart. Fig. 5.4 shows the floor plan and outlines the location of the nodes in the rooms. Note that we tried to create a somewhat irregular distribution of nodes with different distances among nodes in different rooms.

In a first set of experiments, we investigated how reliable the assignment of symbolic coordinates using broadcast works and to what extent the analysis of RSSI values can

Table 5.1: Average performance for different sender signal strengths

	Output power -25 dBm	Output power -14 dBm
Maximum number of nodes assigned correctly	13	13
Minimum number of nodes assigned correctly	11	10
Average percentage of nodes assigned correctly	88.57	77.14

be used to filter out false positive coordinate assignments. For this purpose, we used our prototype client device to send out coordinate messages in each room with different output power levels and collected information on which nodes received the coordinate message with which RSSI value. We repeated each experiment five times for each signal strength level of the client device.

As a first result, our experiments showed that effectively and reliably limiting the dissemination of coordinate messages to a single room is hardly possible even when using the minimum transmission power of the TelosB sensor nodes. To illustrate this, Fig. 5.5 (a) shows the average number of nodes reached from each room with the minimum output power of approximately -25 dBm and Fig. 5.5 (b) shows the same analysis for an output power of approximately -14 dBm. Even for the minimum output power, the overall average of 5.66 nodes reached from each area is much higher than the expected number of two nodes actually located in each area. On average, each node received coordinate messages from 2.83 different areas for an output power of -25 dBm and from 5.26 areas for an output power of -14 dBm. The maximum number of different coordinate messages received lay between 5 for an output power of -25 dBm and 7 for an output power of -14 dBm.

To deal with multiple coordinate messages received from different rooms, we proposed to consider the RSSI values of the received messages and assign the symbolic coordinate from the message with the highest RSSI value. Using this extension results in a promising performance of the symbolic coordinate assignment using broadcasts: Table 5.1 shows the maximum and the minimum number of nodes with correctly assigned symbolic coordinates for the experiments with signal output powers of -25 dBm and -14 dBm as well as the average percentage of nodes assigned correctly.

In our experiments, coordinate assignments with a smaller transmission power level clearly outperformed the assignment with a higher transmission power level and only assigned a wrong coordinate to between one and three nodes. An explanation for this can be found looking at the RSSI values as summarized in Table 5.2: On average, the RSSI values of messages sent in the same room were only 8% larger than the RSSI values of messages sent from different rooms when using an output power of -14 dBm and 6% larger when using an output power of -25 dBm. While the ratio between inside and outside RSSI values is a little higher for -14 dBm than for -25 dBm, this cannot compensate the much higher number of coordinate messages each node receives. Due

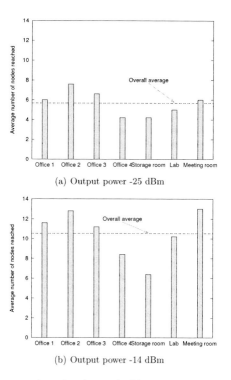

(a) Output power -25 dBm

(b) Output power -14 dBm

Figure 5.5: Average number of nodes reached by coordinate message broadcasts

to the inherent variations of the RSSI values of received messages, a larger number of coordinate messages received from neighboring rooms increases the likelihood that the RSSI value of one of these messages is larger than the RSSI value of the message received from within the room.

Overall, the coordinate assignment by broadcast together with a filtering based on the RSSI values of coordinate messages produced good results in our experiments. However, our analysis also clearly showed that RSSI is a fragile criterion that is not able to produce 100% reliable results. Due to the large variety of environmental factors influencing the radio signal (e.g., thickness and material of walls between rooms), we also expect significant differences in the performance of coordinate assignment by broadcast in different scenarios. The results of our experiments mainly show the feasibility of the approach in general but also illustrate the limitations with respect to reliability.

Table 5.2: Average RSSI values of coordinate messages sent from inside and outside a room

	Output power -25 dBm	Output power -14 dBm
Average RSSI inside	226.07	237.54
Average RSSI outside	213.64	220.1
Ratio inside / outside	1.06	1.08

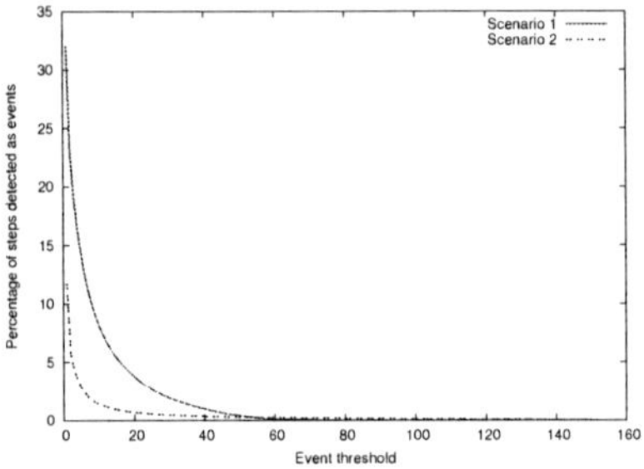

Figure 5.6: Percentage of events detected for different event thresholds

5.5.2 Assisted Broadcast Using Light Events

Based on the results of the experiments described above, we next investigated the assignment of symbolic coordinates by assisted broadcast using light events. We used the raw sensor data read from the analog-to-digital converter for our experiments without converting the data to a light measuring unit like lux.

First, we wanted to investigate how often TSR light events typically occur when they are not explicitly triggered by the user. To acquire input data for this analysis in a wide range of situations, we collected sensor data in two different indoor scenarios. We distributed 12 nodes to 4 different rooms in both scenarios and collected the value of the TSR light sensor every 10 seconds over multiple days with each sensor node. In the analysis, we evaluated how often an event is detected for two consecutive measurements when varying the event detection threshold. Fig. 5.6 shows the result of this analysis for both scenarios with the event threshold based on raw sensor data forming the x-axis and the percentage of steps detected as events forming the y-axis of the graph.

The results show that for very small event thresholds a considerable percentage of measurement pairs triggers events. This is not surprising, because the ambient light level in a room underlies constant small-scale variations. However, with an event threshold of 10 only in 8.1% of the cases in scenario 1 and in 1.4% of the cases in scenario 2 an event has been detected. With an event threshold of 20, the numbers are even smaller with 3.7% in scenario 1 and 0.7% in scenario 2. This indicates a quite small probability of unintended events occurring during the coordinate assignment

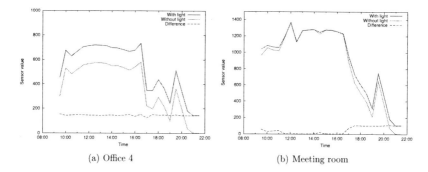

(a) Office 4   (b) Meeting room

Figure 5.7: Light sensor data with and without room light

using these thresholds especially since the event detection time period (10 seconds) was selected quite large for these measurements. Since changes to the level of illumination of the sensor nodes during the daytime are the main sources of events, the considerable differences between scenario 1 and scenario 2 can be explained by the fact that more nodes in scenario 1 were exposed to direct sunlight than in scenario 2.

Besides unintentionally detected events, a second potential issue is how to trigger light events when the room is already brightly lit by sunlight coming through the window. To investigate how big of a problem this is, we recorded TSR light sensor values in two of the rooms from our office scenario shown in Fig. 5.4 for one day. One recording was done in office 4 which has its windows to the north. To explore more extreme conditions we placed the sensor for the second recording directly behind one of the south-bound windows of the meeting room. Values were recorded every 30 minutes on a sunny day both with the room lighting turned on and with the light turned off. Fig. 5.7 shows the resulting graphs comparing the recorded light levels over time for both rooms.

The difference between the sensor values recorded with and without light is relatively stable over the day in office 4 (Fig. 5.7 (a)). With difference values in the range of 140, a reliable detection of light events is possible irrespective of the time of day the coordinate assignment is done. The situation is different for the sensor at the window of the meeting room (Fig. 5.7 (b)). Here, the influence of the artificial light is considerably lower and the difference between the sensor values shrinks down to values around 0 at noon. Obviously, the artificial light in the room cannot add to the recorded sensor value anymore once a certain light level is reached in the environment.

In theory, the effect of two light sources (i.e., the ambient light and the artificial room lighting) on the light sensor of a sensor node should be completely additive. That this can be the case is nicely illustrated by the measurements from our experiment in office 4 where the difference between the light levels with and without room lighting is approximately constant throughout the day. In our experiment in the meeting room,

Table 5.3: Average success rates for different event thresholds

Event detection threshold	Average percentage of nodes assigned correctly
5	53.57
10	100.0
20	100.0
100	78.57

however, the sensor chip partially operated in its saturation region where it cannot capture additional light radiation anymore. Only later in the day, the recorded sensor values were again in a region where the difference between recordings with and without light is approximately constant.

Based on the results of our experiments, we conclude that the time period of the coordinate assignments must be carefully selected if nodes are placed at particularly exposed locations. However, our experience also shows that for normal conditions event detection is possible all day if the event detection threshold is set to a reasonable value.

Our last step of evaluating coordinate assignments by assisted broadcast using light events was to investigate the success rate with different event detection thresholds. We performed a set of experiments choosing different event thresholds at different times of the day. In all of these experiments the client application sent the coordinate messages with the minimum possible transmission power and we used an event detection timer length of 4 seconds. Table 5.3 shows an overview of the results. Note that we deliberately ignored the RSSI values for this evaluation to emphasize the benefit of using events. However, the RSSI values of the coordinate messages received from different areas could be used as an additional criterion, for example to filter out false positive coordinate assignments after a node has detected a false positive light event.

If the event threshold is set to a too small value, then events can occur without being explicitly triggered by a user simply due to the normal variations of the sensor readings over time. The consequence of this are false positives during the assignment of symbolic coordinates – nodes that assign a coordinate in reaction to a coordinate message without lying in the room where the event has actually been triggered. In our experiments we could observe this for an event threshold of 5 (see Table 5.3). The results of experiments performed in the evening or at night with this threshold lay above the average but even then the artificial light oscillated enough to generate some false positives.

To explore the other end of the spectrum, i.e., a high event detection threshold, we performed experiments with a threshold value of 100. As expected, the high event detection threshold reliably prevented the occurrence of any false positives. However, now some of the intended recipients also did not detect an event (resulting in a false negative) and consequently did not assign the symbolic coordinate resulting in a success rate well below 100%.

The goal must be to select an event detection threshold that lies between these two extreme cases and avoids both false positives and false negatives. With an event threshold of 10 or 20, all of our experiments assigned the correct symbolic coordinates to all nodes in the network irrespective of the time of day the experiment was performed. Therefore, selecting an event threshold in this range provides for a reliable assignment of symbolic coordinates to sensor nodes.

We imagine that adequate thresholds for the detection of light events could be determined automatically as part of a calibration process. A sensing device carried by the administrator (possibly attached to the PDA) could record both the ambient light level and the effects of the user-triggered light event and could – based on the light level difference – dynamically set appropriate thresholds for other nodes to decide whether they are part of the symbolic area or not.

5.5.3 Assisted Broadcast Using Acoustic Events

In addition to our experiments with the assignment of symbolic coordinates based on the detection of light events, we also experimented on a smaller scale with the assignment by assisted broadcast using acoustic events. The main purpose of these experiments was to determine whether acoustic events are a viable and useful alternative to light events. One clear advantage of using acoustic signals is the lack of sensitivity to daylight and light level variations as experienced in our experiments with light events. However, the question to be answered is whether there exist similar (or even worse) limitations and disadvantages when using acoustic events.

The first insight of our experiments with acoustic events on the MTS300 sensor boards was that false positives – acoustic events detected by the tone detector without a signal sent by a sounder – are a much more critical problem than for light events. The simple tone detection circuit on the MTS300 sensor boards does not react exclusively to the sounds emitted by the MTS300 sounder element but can also be triggered by a variety of other sounds. For example, in many cases the simple knocking on a table, a lively conversation or the sound of typing on a keyboard was able to trigger an event at nearby sensor nodes. Besides the simplicity of the tone detection circuit, another explanation for this behavior is the fact that the particular frequency range the tone detector is tuned on appears as part of a variety of natural sounds in the environment and not only in the signal generated by the sounder on the MTS300.

To evaluate the severity of this problem, we recorded acoustic events in experiments in a set of different situations: We collected data in an office environment, in a room with a running radio and in a very quiet room without any activity. We used the measurements from the office environment as an example of typical everyday activity to be found in many indoor scenarios where sensor nodes are likely to be deployed as part of a pervasive computing environment. The measurements from the room with a running radio represent the extreme case of a particularly noisy environment whereas the quiet room represents optimal conditions to be found during the coordinate assignment. In each of these experiments, a MICA2 sensor node continuously listened for sound events for a time period of one hour and incremented its counter for each

Table 5.4: False positive analysis for acoustic events

Scenario	Number of false positive events in 1 hour
Office environment	336
Radio running	6068
Quiet room	2

occurrence of an event detected during this time.

Table 5.4 shows the results of our false positive experiments. Clearly, in noisy environments like our room with a running radio, the number of false positive events detected is unacceptably high with an event occurring every 0.59 seconds on average. While the number is significantly lower for the quieter office environment, a false positive event every 10.71 seconds still poses a high risk of errors during the assignment of symbolic coordinates using acoustic events. Note that for the experiment with the running radio, the recording sensor node was placed near the loudspeaker of the radio and the radio was operated at a relatively high volume. In another experiment where we placed the sensor node in a different part of the room, the results for the number of false positive events resembled the results of the standard office scenario. As expected, in a quiet room the number of false positives remains in the range of zero. However, it is probably difficult to guarantee such conditions during the whole assignment of symbolic coordinates in a building.

Like for the coordinate assignment based on light events, the window of opportunity for false positives is limited, because the acoustic sensor is only sampled in reaction to the reception of a coordinate message. Nevertheless, we still considered the rate of false positive events as too high for a reliable assignment of symbolic coordinates. Our solution to this problem is to extend the event detection process and to listen for a sequence of sound events instead of a single event. The underlying assumption is that the probability of the random occurrence of a sequence of sounds (or one long-lasting sound) detectable as events is smaller than for the occurrence of a single sound event.

The extended event detection procedure is shown in pseudo code in Fig. 5.8. It works as follows: After receiving a coordinate assignment message, a sensor node starts a timer that fires after x milliseconds. It checks whether an acoustic event occurred during this time interval. The timer is restarted a maximum number of y times. If more than z acoustic events are detected during these y time intervals, then the sequence is marked as detected and the symbolic coordinate is assigned. As an example, a node waits for 4 time periods with a length of 500 milliseconds each and is required to detect an acoustic event in 3 of these time periods to actually assign the symbolic coordinate it received. Only requiring the detection of z out of y possible sensor events reflects our experiences during preliminary experiments where none of the sensor nodes was able to detect all sensor events triggered by a nearby sounder.

We repeated our false positive analysis now requiring the detection of multiple events in a row. Table 5.5 shows the number of false positive events recorded in

```
int intervalsCounter = 0;
int intervalsWithEventCounter = 0;

event receivedCoordinateMessage(int newSymbolicCoordinate) {
  intervalsCounter++;
  startTimer(x);
}

event timerFired() {
  boolean toneDetected = checkMicrophone();
  if (toneDetected) {
    intervalsWithEventCounter++;
  }
  if (intervalsWithEventCounter == z) {
    assignCoordinate();
  } else if (intervalsCounter < y) {
    intervalsCounter++;
    startTimer(x);
  }
}
```

Figure 5.8: Event detection for acoustic signals

Table 5.5: Extended false positive analysis

	Office environment	Radio running
Single event	336	6068
5x1000ms, detect 3	46	926
6x500ms, detect 2	116	2469
12x250ms, detect 8	0	391

the office environment and in the scenario with a running radio for three exemplary combinations of x, y and z. As expected, the higher the number of events to be detected in a sequence of time intervals, the lower is the number of false positives recorded by the nodes. In the office scenario, this allowed us to effectively limit the number of false positives and to even reduce the number to zero for the case with 8 events detected within 12 time periods of 250 milliseconds each. For the extremely noisy environment with a radio running, the extended event detection mechanism was also able to reduce the number of false positive events. However, the remaining number of false positives remained significant. This implies that – like for the assignment of coordinates using light events – a certain control over the environmental conditions during the assignment of symbolic coordinates using acoustic events is essential.

After considering false positive events, our next step was to evaluate the success rate of assigning symbolic coordinates with the help of acoustic events. For this purpose,

Table 5.6: Average success rates for acoustic events

Values for x, y, and z	Average percentage of nodes assigned correctly
5x1000ms, detect 3	100%
5x1000ms, detect 4	98.33%
6x500ms, detect 2	100%
6x500ms, detect 4	96.88%
6x500ms, detect 5	3.13%
12x250ms, detect 8	100%
8x250ms, detect 4	93.33%

we distributed four MICAz sensor nodes in a room and performed a set of experiments assigning symbolic coordinates to these nodes. The distance between the sounder and the receiving sensor nodes varied between one and four meters. We experimented with different combinations of x, y, and z. Table 5.6 gives an overview of the success rate results that we obtained across 15 runs for each setting.

The results shown in Table 5.6 illustrate that the coordinate assignment by assisted broadcast works well using acoustic events and that it is possible to achieve success rates in the range of 100% using appropriate combinations of x, y and z. The event detection process works equally well for different lengths x of the event detection time periods. However, the experiments also confirmed our expectation that the tone detection mechanism is not able to detect events in all of the y time periods as shown by the measurement using six event detection time periods with a length of of 500 ms each: While four events could be detected with an average success rate of 96.88%, the success rate dropped to only 3.13% when requiring the detection of an event in five out of the six time periods. We mainly attribute this behavior to the specific tone detection hardware used in our experiments and its interaction with the implementation of the timers on the sensor nodes.

We also placed nodes in neighboring rooms to test whether the acoustic signals are able to propagate across room boundaries and trigger events at these nodes thereby causing false positive coordinate assignments. However, even though the sound was sometimes still hearable for humans in neighboring rooms, none of the nodes detected any events during the coordinate assignment experiments so that no false positives occurred. The attenuation of the sound signal by walls and doors is obviously strong enough for limiting the propagation of the sound signal to the current room.

For light events it was reasonable to assume that the effect of an event can be detected irrespective of the location of a sensor node, because the light sources at the ceiling usually cover the complete area of a room. Our acoustic signals, however, are generated by the PDA of the administrator at a specific point in the room and spread from this location. The strength of the acoustic signal decreases with the distance from the signal source. Consequently, the detection of acoustic events can only work reliably within a certain radius around the administrator. This does not constitute a serious limitation, because the administrator can safely send the signal multiple times from different locations when assigning coordinates in particularly large rooms. Nevertheless, it is important to consider this factor in assessing the usability of coordinate assignment using acoustic events.

We evaluated the influence of the distance on the coordinate assignment based on acoustic events with a set of controlled experiments measuring the success rate for different distances between a sender node and a receiver node of acoustic events. We placed MICAz sensor nodes on the floor without any obstacles between the sounder node and the receiver nodes and used two events detected in six 500 ms timer intervals as the condition for the coordinate assignment (see the first line in Table 5.6). Up to a distance to five meters, the experiments showed a success rate of 100%. At six meters distance, the success rate fell to 76.7% across 30 runs. At a distance of seven meters, the success rate was slightly lower at 70.0%. Note that these results strongly depend on the environment and the placement of nodes in real scenarios. This can be illustrated by an additional experiment where we placed sounder and receiver node eight meters apart but at a height of one meter above the floor. Now we achieved a success rate of 96.7% in the coordinate assignment.

The results confirm that the distance between the sender of acoustic events and the sensor nodes receiving the events is indeed a limiting factor that can occur in practice if the rooms of the target scenario exceed a certain size. In most office-sized rooms or normal-sized rooms in residential buildings, the maximum distances determined in our experiments should suffice to perform the coordinate assignment for the complete room in a single step. In larger rooms it is easy to walk around the room and trigger the event multiple times.

For many of the problems and limitations described here, we expect that sounder and sensor hardware specifically developed for the problem at hand could improve the results significantly. However, assuming such special hardware would also imply increased requirements in terms of the sensor node equipment deployed in the pervasive computing scenario.

5.5.4 Comparison of Approaches

Summarizing the results of our evaluation, assigning symbolic coordinates by broadcast has shown a good performance when used together with RSSI filtering. It allowed us to assign symbolic coordinates to nodes in a simple and efficient fashion while achieving a high success rate. If, however, an even higher degree of reliability is required, then assigning symbolic coordinates by assisted broadcast is able to provide a reliable solution achieving success rates in the range of 100% as we have shown in our experiments.

The assignment by assisted broadcast using light events clearly outperformed the assignment using acoustic events in terms of reliability. Dealing with the light sensors also proved to be much easier than with the sounders and microphones of the MTS300 board whose behavior was difficult to understand in some cases. We also expect that more future wireless sensor nodes will feature a simple light sensor than a microphone.

The coordinate assignment solution based on the detection of acoustic events might be more interesting in connection with other small-scale pervasive computing devices which are more likely to be equipped with microphones.

One important reason why considering acoustic events is attractive is that it allows to directly trigger the events from the client device without explicit action (i.e., manually turning on the light) by the administrator.

5.6 Summary

In this chapter we have introduced two canonical approaches for the assignment of symbolic coordinates to wireless sensor nodes – the individual assignment and the assignment by broadcast – and have discussed their advantages and disadvantages. With coordinate assignment by assisted broadcast, we have then presented a third solution that combines the advantages of both approaches with only minor additional effort for an externally triggered sensor event.

In the evaluation of our approaches we have shown that the assignment by broadcast and particularly the assignment by assisted broadcast allow for a simple yet reliable assignment of symbolic coordinates to sensor nodes in indoor scenarios. Due to its ease of use and its good performance, the manual configuration of symbolic coordinates after the deployment of a sensor network is a viable alternative to more sophisticated node localization approaches.

A reliable indoor localization system for wireless sensor networks that is able to determine the position of nodes (expressed either on the geographic or the symbolic level) without requiring user interaction or expensive hardware while only generating a low message and computational overhead is definitely desirable. However, while such a perfect localization solution is not foreseeable, our coordinate assignment solution provides a reliable assignment of symbolic coordinate information to sensor nodes that only generates a low overhead and only requires a reasonable amount of support by the user. Moreover, such static wireless sensor nodes preconfigured with coordinate information based on our approach could also provide symbolic location information to mobile devices during the normal system operation as part of a localization solution.

5.6.1 Future Directions in this Area

One interesting direction for future work lies in a combination of wireless sensor networks and building automation systems that automate the control of different mechanical and electrical systems in buildings. Such a combination would make it possible to turn on and turn off the lights in the rooms of a building automatically. This way, we could completely automate the assignment of symbolic coordinates using a control algorithm that first sends out symbolic coordinate messages and then activates the light in the corresponding rooms of the building to trigger the light sensors of the affected nodes. We have already done the first steps in this direction by developing our prototype light control system integrating sensor networks with a home automation platform that was introduced in Section 3.4.1 of this thesis.

We are also going to take on ideas from our coordinate assignment approaches in two of the following chapters of this thesis: In the next chapter, we are going to discuss the grouping of nodes based on sensor data. Instead of relying on sensor stimuli deliberately triggered by the user, there we are interested in analyzing the sensor data collected by sensor nodes as part of their normal operation and group the nodes based on a similarity analysis of this data. In chapter 7 we are going to discuss various approaches for initiating interactions with wireless sensor nodes. One idea for selecting nodes for such an interaction is to trigger sensor events on these nodes – just like we triggered sensor events on all nodes in a room in the methods described in this chapter.

5 Coordinate Assignment

6 Node Grouping

Information on the context of users and devices is an essential building block of most pervasive computing applications. If sensor nodes and sensor networks are used as part of pervasive computing scenarios, they can provide such context information. However, to make this possible, a precondition is for the sensor nodes to have information on the spatial context they are operating in.

In the previous chapter, we have described how an administrator can assign spatial context information to sensor nodes in the form of symbolic coordinates. In this chapter, we investigate how sensor nodes can learn about certain aspects of their spatial context autonomously as part of a self-organization process. Specifically, we aim for an intelligent clustering of nodes that considers real-world criteria in the formation of node groups: Nodes that are located in the same area (the same room in our scenarios) should also be assigned to the same group.

The idea of our approach is to collect time series of sensor values on the individual nodes and use correlations among these values as input for making clustering decisions. This proceeding is based on the assumption that nodes located within the same area experience similar external conditions whereas nodes placed in different areas detect clear differences of their sensor recordings over time.

We investigate different criteria and methods in a centralized analysis and, based on that, design a sensor-based node clustering method that performs large parts of the operation distributed in the network. In the evaluation, we show that our approach allows to automatically create clusters (groups of nodes) that adhere to room boundaries using inexpensive and broadly available sensors.

6.1 Preliminaries

The self-organization of nodes plays a very important role in wireless sensor networks. It lets nodes cooperate with their peers to form structures in the network without being explicitly guided by external entities thereby keeping the human out of the loop. As part of a self-organization procedure, nodes learn about their neighbors, the structure of the network or, in general, their context and can use this information to optimize their operation and to fulfill the overall task of the sensor network.

Self-organization capabilities are essential for two reasons. Firstly, with growing network sizes it becomes more and more difficult and costly for human administrators to manually organize all aspects of the network operation. Secondly, the complexity and variability of sensor network structures hardly allow to keep an up-to-date view of the sensor network properties that would be required to completely organize the operation of the sensor network from the outside. Note that this argument does not contradict our efforts of supporting administrators in configuring a sensor network (as discussed, for example, in the previous chapter). The provided configuration information constitutes important input and a starting point to self-organization mechanisms that then deal with many details of the network operation.

There are examples of self-organization mechanisms to be found in many parts of the operation of wireless sensor networks. One is the formation of routing structures where nodes cooperate with each other to calculate optimal routing paths to a destination based on reliability requirements, link quality information or energy considerations (see for example [177]). Another example is node clustering: Sensor nodes organize themselves in clusters based on certain optimization criteria and cooperate within the clusters and coordinate among neighboring clusters [223]. Other popular examples of self-organization in wireless sensor networks include boundary recognition (e.g., [178]) or the assignment of roles to sensor nodes [51].

Many existing self-organization solutions for wireless sensor networks work in a purely network-centric fashion. They consider factors like communication links between nodes, the quality of communication links or similar properties of the node communication graph. If available, some methods also use information on the distance between nodes or the geographic positions of nodes. However, most self-organization mechanisms ignore the properties and the semantics of the real world relevant to the applications and the users when forming structures in the network.

While existing solutions to the problem of self-organization in wireless sensor networks play an essential role in the operations of wireless sensor networks, we argue that there also exists a need for self-organization capabilities that are oriented on real-world criteria and that support the formation of structures that reflect the properties of the real-world scenario the sensor network is operating in.

Our motivation to consider the self-organization of nodes based on real-world criteria as part of this thesis results from the insight that such real-world structures are of particular importance in the context of pervasive computing scenarios. In these scenarios, sensor nodes are not only required to provide sensor data reflecting the current state of their respective surroundings but they should also be able to provide more complex context information of the area they are operating in. This is simplified considerably if the sensor nodes are aware of the properties of their environment and organize themselves in a way that reflects this knowledge.

In this chapter, we are looking into a specific type of self-organization, namely clustering of nodes in the network. Our goal is to form clusters in such a way that they reflect real-world semantics that are meaningful to the application. For the indoor scenarios we are mainly targeting, the notion of rooms provides a natural unit of clustering and our goal is to create groups of nodes located in the same room. To emphasize the difference between conventional clustering approaches and our clustering that is oriented on real-world semantics, we speak of a node grouping rather than clustering in the rest of this chapter. Fig. 6.1 illustrates our idea using an example of such a grouping with nodes organizing themselves in four groups that reflect the four rooms of the indoor scenario they are deployed in.

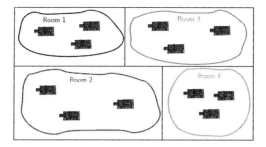

Figure 6.1: Example of a node grouping in indoor scenarios

In the previous chapter, we have introduced an efficient method for the room-level assignment of symbolic coordinates to nodes. By assigning the same coordinate to all nodes in a room, we can also solve the problem of grouping the nodes with regard to the room they are located in. While such an assignment of grouping information is possible, here we aim for a more automatic and autonomic solution with the nodes organizing themselves into groups. Actually, we will describe below how our node grouping approach can be used as a part of a coordinate assignment solution.

One possible way of grouping sensor nodes would be to use the geographic coordinates of the individual nodes, map them to the different areas and then use this mapping to group together nodes located in the same area. However, as we have discussed in the previous chapter, for our indoor scenarios such position information is difficult or too costly to acquire with the required precision. Moreover, once the geographic coordinates of the nodes are known, this approach would also require a mapping to areas to determine whether neighboring nodes really lie in the same area.

The connectivity between nodes can provide proximity information with some limited accuracy [184] – nodes that are able to directly communicate with each other also lie in each others vicinity. However, connectivity information does not allow to distinguish neighboring nodes located in adjacent areas. The same is true for distance measuring techniques like Received Signal Strength Indication (RSSI) or Time Difference of Arrival (TDOA): If the network is connected across area boundaries, then the distance between nodes is an insufficient criterion for deciding whether two nodes lie within the same area. The very assumption that RSSI and TDOA can be used for estimating distances between nodes despite area boundaries (e.g., walls and floors) contradicts the use of these criteria for detecting area boundaries between nodes.

As position information is too expensive or even impossible to acquire and connectivity or distance information are unsuitable for the grouping of nodes, we need to come up with other means of obtaining meaningful groups in sensor networks automatically. The idea of the approach discussed in the rest of this chapter is to collect time series of sensor data on the individual nodes (or reuse sensor data collected for other purposes) and do a statistical analysis of the data looking for correlations among the sensor readings of different sensor nodes. The sensor data of nodes located in the same room is expected to exhibit a stronger correlation than the data of nodes placed in different rooms as colocated nodes experience similar external conditions.

6.1.1 Problem Definition

The formal definition of the problem to solve for a grouping of nodes based on the area they are located in is very similar to the problem definition of symbolic coordinate assignment shown in the previous chapter. Both deal with partitioning the set of nodes based on their area membership with coordinate assignment additionally requiring to assign the correct symbolic coordinate to each node. In this regard, our node grouping solves a subproblem of the coordinate assignment problem. However, in this chapter we aim for a solution that determines the group membership of nodes automatically whereas we presumed explicit interactions with an administrator in the coordinate assignment approaches discussed in the previous chapter.

Again, we have a set of sensor nodes $S_{sensors} = \{sensor_1, sensor_2, \ldots, sensor_n\}$ with node identifiers $Id_{sensors} = \{id_{sensor_1}, id_{sensor_2}, \ldots, id_{sensor_n}\}$. The nodes have been deployed in an application area A which can be divided into a set of areas $A_1 \ldots A_m$ based on some well-known real-world criteria. In our scenarios, the partitioning of the application area is given by the partitioning of the building into rooms. Each sensor node is located within one of the areas which we express using the "element of" relation (e.g., $sensor_i \in A_j$).

The goal of our node grouping is to divide the n nodes among l different node groups $G_1, G_2, \ldots, G_l$. The membership of nodes to groups has to fulfill the following four conditions:

$$\forall s \in S_{sensors} \qquad \exists i : s \in G_i$$

$$\forall s \in S_{sensors} : ((s \in G_i) \wedge (s \in G_j)) \implies (i = j)$$

$$\forall s_x, s_y \in S_{sensors} : ((s_x \in A_i) \wedge (s_y \in A_i) \wedge (s_y \in G_j)) \implies (s_y \in G_j)$$

$$\forall s_x, s_y \in S_{sensors} : ((s_x \in G_i) \wedge (s_y \in G_i) \wedge (s_x \in A_j)) \implies (s_y \in A_j)$$

The first two conditions express that each sensor node belongs to exactly one node group. The third condition requires that two nodes located in the same area are also member of the same group. Finally, the fourth condition provides the equivalent requirement for the opposite direction: Two nodes that have been assigned to the same group must also be located in the same area.

Note that we again do not make any assumptions on the relationship between the location of nodes and their node identifier which could be used to assign nodes to the correct groups. Also note that there is no direct relationship between the set of areas and the set of node groups. We know that the number of node groups l must be smaller or equal the number of areas m, because not all areas have to be populated with nodes. However, without using additional domain knowledge, we cannot infer which node group belongs to which area.

6.1.2 Requirements

The solution to a grouping of nodes based on real-world criteria has to fulfill several requirements. As usual, an important goal is the **correctness of the node grouping**. In this case, correctness is defined according to the four conditions given above: All sensor nodes are assigned to exactly one group and nodes in the same area belong to the same group and vice versa.

The node grouping should generate a **low overhead** on the individual nodes. This overhead refers both to the required amount of processing and the amount of communication required. A certain amount of message exchange is inevitable as part of the process to provide nodes with information on the characteristics of the sensor recordings of other nodes. However, the approach should limit itself to **mainly local communication and coordination** to support the scalability of the approach.

Finally, to follow the idea of self-organization, the node grouping should require only **few input by external entities**, like the network administrator.

6.1.3 Application Scenarios

As in most parts of this thesis, we are mainly aiming for applications in indoor scenarios. Indoor scenarios not only help with a natural definition of areas in the form of the rooms in a building, they also provide for a clear separation between neighboring areas in the form of walls, doors and windows. This property has already been used for the assignment of symbolic coordinates discussed in the previous chapter. Here, the separation of area helps in distinguishing nodes from different areas using their sensor value recordings.

Our primary motivation for sensor-based clustering is to allow sensor nodes to **learn about an important aspect of their spatial context** in the pervasive computing scenario, namely which nodes are located together in the same area. This node grouping information can then form the basis for various types of applications and is part of our effort on supporting the network configuration of wireless sensor networks in pervasive computing scenarios.

A successful grouping of nodes based on the rooms they are located in can be a first, fully automated step in the **assignment of symbolic coordinates** to a wireless sensor network: Since the nodes in a group know that they are located in the same area, it suffices if one of them is aware of its symbolic coordinate for all of them to learn their coordinate information. One can equip one node per area with symbolic coordinate information either by placing one symbolic beacon node per area or by assigning the coordinate information to one node using one of our node interaction mechanisms that we later describe in Chapter 7. Moreover, we also expect the coordinate assignment by broadcast to work more reliably if the nodes have determined their group memberships before starting the assignment as now individual nodes are less susceptible to wrongly switch their coordinate to a coordinate of a neighboring area. We thereby get an alternative to the coordinate assignment mechanism presented in the previous chapter that requires less involvement of the administrator at the cost of the grouping effort required among the nodes.

One very important application of grouping or clustering is the **management of redundancy** in the sensor network or the pervasive computing environment. Sensor nodes are commonly deployed with a high level of redundancy to deal with the unreliability and the strong resource constraints of the individual nodes. During the normal operation of the sensor network, nodes are then intermittently deactivated to prolong the lifetime of the overall network. Various clustering approaches have been developed for the purpose of such a duty cycling of nodes [76, 222]. They ensure that at least one node per cluster is awake at all times providing for the coverage of the application area. Our sensor-based clustering can improve upon these approaches as it allows to ensure that at least one node in each area monitored by the sensor network is kept awake. This integrates important real-world criteria into the decision made by the redundancy management.

Another typical application that clusters in wireless sensor networks are used for is the **aggregation of data**. Again, our room-level grouping of nodes can be of advantage here: Data aggregation among nodes covering the same area can be done with less information loss than aggregation across area boundaries. By aggregating data within a node group, the nodes basically generate a summary of the sensor data of the area they cover. Related to that is the **cooperation of nodes** for complex sensing tasks involving multiple nodes where the room-level grouping can help in bringing the right nodes together for a cooperative sensing task.

Our clustering based on real-world criteria can also help in the **detection of anomalies** of sensor recordings which is an important aspect of the autonomous operation of wireless sensor networks. After the nodes of an area have been grouped together, we can expect the sensor readings of these nodes to remain correlated to a certain extent. If a single node of this group then starts to significantly deviate from the behavior of the rest of the group, then we can suspect an erroneous behavior of this node rather than an unexpected change in the external conditions of the area monitored by the nodes. Note that such inferences would not be that easy if we just compared the behavior of neighboring nodes as those nodes might monitor different areas of interest with different characteristics of their sensor recordings.

Finally, we also see applications of our node grouping in the **assignment of roles** to sensor nodes as discussed by Frank and Römer [51]. This goes back to our original goal of the nodes learning about their spatial context which can be an important part of the input of a role assignment algorithm but also relates to the other application fields discussed in this section like redundancy management or aggregation. For example, a grouping of nodes might determine how to assign the role "data aggregator node".

6.1.4 Overview of Approach

The idea of our approach is to group sensor nodes based on the similarity of the sensor values they record. This idea is based on the assumption that sensor nodes operating in the same room experience similar external conditions that – given adequate sensor criteria – result in a similar behavior of the sensor values the nodes record over time. In contrast, nodes located in different rooms are subject to different external influences and are likely to record time series of sensor values with different characteristics.

We perform a statistical analysis of the correlations of time series of sensor values among different pairs of nodes and use these correlation values to group nodes together. To do this, we apply methods from the area of statistical data clustering which is a common technique for statistical data analysis used in a variety of application fields. We also investigate how these data clustering methods must be adjusted to fit the special properties of wireless sensor networks.

We start the investigation with a centralized analysis of the applicability of different sensor criteria, relevant data filtering and statistical data clustering methods for the task of grouping nodes based on sensor measurements. Based on the results of this analysis, we then discuss how large parts of the node grouping algorithm can be distributed in the network to allow for a computation of node groupings in real wireless sensor network deployments and in large pervasive computing environments.

6.2 Related Work

Our work on grouping wireless sensor nodes based on sensor data to reflect the distribution of nodes to different areas is strongly related to node clustering in wireless networks. In fact, our grouping approach can be considered a special type of clustering that takes real-world criteria into account instead of, for example, network-centric criteria like connectivity.

A second important area of research our work builds on is statistical data clustering. Data clustering methods assign data objects to groups in a way so that objects belonging to the same cluster are more similar than objects from different clusters. We take a short look at statistical data clustering and its various applications at the end of this section.

6.2.1 Node Clustering in Wireless Networks

The clustering of nodes is an important concept in wireless sensor networks (but also in general wireless networks) that has been used for a long time to hierarchically structure the network into groups of nodes [223]. For example, node clusterings are used for routing, data aggregation or duty cycle management. Each cluster typically consists of a cluster head node and one or multiple cluster member nodes. There exist several types of approaches that mainly differ in the type of information they use and the method used to select cluster heads based on this information.

Simple Cluster Head Selection

The clustering of nodes has already been discussed in early work on wireless networks (e.g., [9, 123]), mostly in the context of allocating resources to the nodes like the radio channel. These clustering mechanisms use relatively simple criteria for the selection of cluster heads and the assignment of nodes to clusters.

Both Lin and Gerla [123] and Baker and Ephremides [9] describe clustering approaches for wireless networks that are based on the node identifiers of the nodes. In the selection of cluster heads, Baker and Ephremides favor nodes with lower identifiers. This approach only works reasonably well if the assignment of these identifiers is done uniformly throughout the application area. Lin and Gerla [123] describe an approach aimed at calculating clusters for the distribution of spread-spectrum codes in wireless networks. Despite using the simple node identifier criterion, the worst-case runtime of the algorithm grows with the number of nodes in the network.

Another mostly static and therefore simple criterion for selecting cluster heads is the neighborhood degree [102], i.e., the number of neighbors a node possesses. By favoring nodes with a high degree, it is possible to create dense clusters and cover the network with relatively few cluster heads.

Selecting Optimal Cluster Heads

The ultimate goal of cluster head selection is achieving a clustering structure that optimally supports the network operation and minimizes the costs in order to maximize the network lifetime. A variety of approaches aim for such an optimal selection of cluster heads starting from different premises.

Calculating a set of cluster head nodes in a way so that all non-cluster head nodes lie in the direct neighborhood of a cluster head node corresponds to the dominating set problem known from graph theory. Unfortunately, it has been shown that determining whether there exists a dominating set consisting of a maximum of k nodes is an NP-complete problem. Consequently, the problem of calculating a minimal dominating set is also NP-complete. An even more challenging requirement to clusters of nodes is when the cluster head nodes are required to form a connected communication backbone so that data can be exchanged among cluster heads without requiring the cooperation of non-cluster head nodes. This corresponds to the connected dominating set problem which is also an NP-complete problem.

The NP-completeness and the required centralized calculation prohibit calculating the optimal dominating set or connected dominating set for wireless sensor networks. Instead, several heuristic approaches have been developed that approximate the optimal connected dominating set in linear time. The approaches differ in their degree of localization with some approaches working on purely local neighborhood information (e.g., [218, 219, 193, 211]) while others require the exchange of information over larger parts of the network (e.g., [120, 12]). Basagni, Mastrogiovanni, Panconesi and Petrioli [133] compared the performance of several of these approaches and conclude that protocols working on purely local information perform well both in terms of clustering quality and in terms of clustering overhead. In the following, we only provide a short overview of a few approaches to give an idea of the range of existing solutions.

Wu [218] and Wu and Li [219] describe a method for the computation of a connected dominating set that works completely distributed only using information from the local neighborhood of the nodes. The execution of the algorithm is split int two phases. In the first phase, candidates for the connected dominating set are determined using a simple rule that guarantees to generate a connected dominating set: A node belongs to the candidate set if it connects two nodes that are not directly connected with each other. In the second phase, two pruning rules are used to eliminate a large fraction of the candidate nodes while conserving the connected dominating set property. The intuition of these rules is that a node can be removed from the candidate set if another node or a pair of nodes cover its neighborhood. In later work, Dai and Wu [40] have generalized the pruning rules thereby achieving a smaller connected dominating set in many cases.

The main intuition underlying the Clustering algorithm via waiting timer (CAWT) [211] is that nodes with many neighbors are better candidates for being cluster heads than nodes with fewer neighbors. Based on this insight, CAWT probabilistically determines cluster heads using a waiting timer at each node. At the beginning of the system operation, each node in the network starts a waiting timer setting a random wait time. When the waiting timer expires, a node declares itself cluster head and sends a cluster head notification message to its neighbors. The nodes inform each other about their existence using hello messages. For each hello message a node receives, it reduces its remaining wait time by a specified amount. This way, the more neighbors a node has the shorter it needs to wait for the expiry of its timer. When a node receives a cluster head notification message, it cancels its own waiting timer and joins the cluster. This prevents two neighboring nodes from both becoming cluster heads.

The Distributed Clustering Algorithm (DCA) [12] generalizes from the different criteria that indicate the level of qualification of a node to serve as cluster head. It uses a weight factor for each node which can incorporate different criteria like, for example, the degree of the node, the stability of the node's links or the remaining energy of the node. This makes the algorithm independent of the specific requirements of the application and the resulting preferences on the clustering criteria.

Clustering with Cluster Head Rotation

One important goal of node clustering in wireless sensor networks is to prolong the lifetime of the overall network. For example, this is achieved by aggregating data at the cluster heads before transmitting it to the base station. However, while this reduces the burden on the overall network, it requires considerable effort from the cluster heads. The premature death of cluster head nodes due to their higher load can in turn shorten the lifetime of the overall network. To prevent this, some clustering approaches periodically recompute the partitioning into clusters and the assignment of the cluster head role.

LEACH [76] repeats the assignment of the cluster head role in regular time intervals to achieve an equal distribution of the additional load of cluster heads to all nodes in the network. The system operation time is divided into rounds where each round starts with a short cluster head selection phase and then continues with a long steady operation phase. LEACH assumes that the optimal number of cluster heads is known in advance and uses this information to calculate how often each node should act as a cluster head (i.e., every p rounds). At the beginning of each round, a node decides whether to become cluster head for this round only if it has not already acted as cluster head in the current set of p rounds. The probability of becoming cluster head increases with each round so that each node is guaranteed to play the role of a cluster head exactly once in each set of p rounds.

The main goal of the HEED clustering algorithm [222] is to optimize the lifetime of the sensor network by distributing the additional workload of the cluster heads over all nodes in the network while maintaining a relatively uniform distribution of cluster heads over the network area. The main criterion for the cluster head selection is the remaining energy of the node so that nodes with more remaining energy become cluster heads with a higher probability than nodes with less remaining energy. As for LEACH, the cluster head selection is executed in rounds. At the beginning, each node calculates a probability of becoming cluster head based on its remaining energy. In each round, a node decides whether to become a cluster head based on this probability value. If it decides against becoming a cluster head it checks whether there is a cluster head available in its direct neighborhood. If not, the node doubles its probability value and goes into the next round.

HEED operates in a completely distributed fashion and only requires that all nodes start the clustering process at approximately the same time. Doubling the probability of becoming a cluster head in each round guarantees that HEED terminates after a finite (small) number of steps.

Clustering Considering Sensor Data

There also exist a few approaches that – like our node grouping – use sensor data as part of computing a clustering of nodes in wireless sensor networks.

The work by Nagata, Oguma and Yamazaki [144] is strongly related to the approach presented in this chapter in that they also aim to group nodes based on sensor data. They describe a middleware that creates clusters of nodes as part of a two step process. In the first step, the tentative clustering algorithm is used to compute a first, tentative grouping of nodes. Nodes that detect the same event at approximately the same time form a so-called tentative cluster and elect the most powerful node as their cluster head. In the second step, the nodes of the tentative cluster record their sensor data for a certain time interval and compare this data with the data recorded by the cluster head. The comparison of the sensor data from different nodes is done using domain knowledge that is not provided by the middleware. So how the sensor nodes actually determine their level of similarity to other nodes – a central question in the work presented here – remains an open question.

Yoon and Shahabi present a technique called Clustered AGgregation (CAG) [221] that dynamically creates clusters of sensor nodes based on the similarity of sensor values when a base station sends a query to the sensor network. The goal is to save on the number of messages as only the cluster heads report their sensor values back to the base station. The other nodes in a cluster can remain quiet as their sensor values are similar to the value reported by the respective cluster head.

CAG supports both an interactive mode where the clustering is done for a one-shot query and a streaming mode where the cluster head nodes periodically report back to the base station. The basic principle is the same for both modes of operation: A forwarding tree is generated for each query like it is done in other sensor network query systems. The root node of this tree records records its own sensor value, declares itself cluster head and sends out the query together with the recorded sensor value to its child nodes. A node receiving a query records its own sensor value and compares it with the sensor value received from the cluster head. If the difference is below a threshold specified by the user issuing the query, then the node joins the cluster, forwards the query unmodified and does not participate in answering the query. If, however, the difference lies above the threshold, then the node declares itself cluster head and includes its own sensor value in the query message before forwarding it to its child nodes. This way, all sensor nodes either become cluster head or associate themselves with a cluster head node that generates similar sensor data. For the streaming mode of CAG it is additionally necessary to check in regular intervals whether a cluster is still valid based on the current sensor data. If a node detects that it does not fit its current cluster anymore, then it first tries to join another, neighboring cluster. If this is not possible, it creates a new cluster, declares itself cluster head of this cluster and starts delivering data to the base station.

Meka and Singh [137] also describe a system that creates clusters based on the similarity of sensor data. Their approach is based on the concept of δ-clusterings. A δ-clustering is defined as a clustering of nodes where the dissimilarity – or the distance – between any two nodes inside of a cluster does not exceed δ. An optimal δ-clustering consists of the minimal number of clusters possible. However, even deciding whether a δ-clustering of a certain size exists is already a NP-complete problem.

Meka and Singh approximate an optimal δ-clustering using a distributed method. They first organize the network in a quadtree structure so that each node has one parent node (with the exception of the root node) and up to four child nodes. The root node then begins the clustering process and adds all nodes to its cluster that fulfill the condition that their distance to the root node is smaller or equal $\frac{\delta}{2}$. This ensures that any two nodes within the cluster have a distance smaller or equal δ. If not all nodes of the network can be added to the cluster in the first round, the four child nodes in the quadtree initiate the clustering process in the same way their parent node did and add all nodes to their cluster fulfilling the respective distance criterion. This process is repeated with more and more nodes in the quadtree initiating the clustering until finally all nodes are part of one of the created clusters.

While we concentrate on the grouping of sensor nodes attached at fixed locations, Lester, Hannaford and Borriello [116] are interested in a similar grouping of mobile sensor devices. They aim to determine which mobile devices are carried by the same person using accelerations the devices experience while the person carrying the devices walks. The computation of the grouping is based on high-frequency measurements with 3-axis acceleration sensors attached to each device. The collected data from different sensors is then preprocessed using a fast Fourier transform and the correlation of the data is calculated using a coherence function. Their experiments showed that the method allows a matching of devices with high accuracy as long as the devices are carried on the same part of the body. The correlations among devices attached to different parts of the body were shown to be considerably lower. Consequently, the applicability of such an approach to the grouping of devices attached to arbitrary parts of the human body remains to be shown.

The characteristics of the sensor data in the approach described by Lester, Hannaford and Borriello differ significantly from the properties of the data in our approach. In particular, they investigate high-frequency recordings of a criterion with a high variability. Since this is usually not given in our scenarios, detecting correlations of static sensor devices – the goal of our work – has to be approached differently.

Summary

As the discussion above has illustrated, there exists a variety of clustering solutions for wireless networks that take different clustering criteria into account. These solutions range from very simple approaches based on node identifiers or static topology information over approaches aiming for optimal cluster structures and approaches that distribute the load using cluster head rotation to special node clustering solutions optimizing application-specific criteria, for example based on sensor data.

Unlike our sensor-based node grouping, none of the "conventional" clustering solutions directly takes real-world semantics relevant to the user into account. The reason for that lies in the different objectives of these node clustering approaches: They aim to optimize the overall network operation which mainly involves minimizing the node costs and the networking costs while maintaining connectivity. For the most part, this is possible without considering user-centric criteria. In contrast, it is the central idea of our approach to group nodes based on real-world criteria to make such groupings useful in context-based, user-centric pervasive computing applications.

6.2.2 Data Clustering

As part of this work we use different approaches from the area of statistical data clustering. The general goal of data clustering is to classify objects so that objects of the same class (or cluster) have a high degree of similarity while objects in different classes have a low degree of similarity. An overview of data clustering methods and their application areas can be found in [85].

While we apply the methods to time series of sensor data collected by wireless sensor nodes, statistical data clustering is actually used in a large variety of different application areas. Examples include data mining [15], health psychology [34] and gene analysis.

We are going to introduce selected data clustering methods in detail later in this chapter when we discuss their application to our node grouping approach.

6.3 Basic Concept

In this section we introduce the basic concept of our node grouping based on sensor data. As a first step, we consider the problem from a centralized perspective assuming that the complete data set is available for analysis at a central location. The goals are to show the correctness of our assumptions concerning the correlation of sensor data, prove the general feasibility of our node grouping and to explore different possible approaches for their suitability.

6.3.1 Motivation of Approach

The motivation to use the similarity of sensor values for grouping nodes stems from observations that sensor recordings of nodes placed in the same area often behave similarly and exhibit the same types of changes and events. To illustrate this with an example, Fig. 6.2 shows recordings from the humidity sensors of six sensor nodes deployed in two different rooms. Fig. 6.2 (a) shows the time series of recordings from nodes 1, 2 and 3 which are deployed together in one room. Fig. 6.2 (b) does the same for nodes 4, 5 and 6 which are placed together in the other room. Fig. 6.2 (c) then shows all six recordings in a single graph to visualize the overall similarities as well as the differences.

Looking at the example recordings, one can detect clear similarities of the recordings among the nodes placed in the same room and clear differences between recordings originating from different rooms. Most importantly, nodes belonging to the same group not only record similar sensor values but also often show the same trend in changing their sensor values. While the similarities are clearly visible for the human eye in this example, there are also noticeable differences. On the one hand, there exist significant differences of the absolute values recorded by different nodes at the same time. On the other hand, the nodes primarily correspond in the general trend of their behavior – small, short time variations tend to be node specific. Our assumption is that the differences of the node behavior among nodes of the same group are less significant than the similarities among these nodes and the dissimilarities to other nodes so that it is still possible to extract information useful for a grouping.

As part of our node grouping approach, we need to extract the similarities and differences from usable sensor criteria and process them in a way that allows identifying the correct groups of nodes.

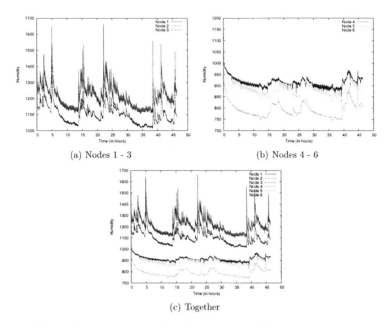

(a) Nodes 1 - 3   (b) Nodes 4 - 6

(c) Together

Figure 6.2: Example of similarities among humidity sensor readings

6.3.2 Overview of Steps

Our basic node grouping approach can be structured into four steps that are shown in
Fig. 6.3: data collection, data preprocessing, similarity calculation and node clustering.
The idea is to collect sensor data on the individual sensor nodes, preprocess and filter
the collected data and then use this as input for a calculation of similarities among
the different pairs of nodes. In the last step, the similarity values are used to calculate
a clustering of the nodes.

For both the centralized analysis and the distributed node grouping approach, domain knowledge can significantly contribute to a successful clustering [85]. As hinted
on in Fig. 6.3, we incorporate such domain knowledge mainly during the preprocessing of data and the similarity calculation and use this knowledge to emphasize certain
aspects of the data or filter out irrelevant data parts.

In our centralized analysis, the four steps of our approach are executed consecutively
as shown in Fig. 6.3. As we will later see, the first three steps are executed in parallel
when distributing the node grouping approach. In the following we explain the four
steps in more detail.

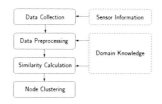

Figure 6.3: Node grouping processing steps

6.3.3 Data Collection

The process of collecting the sensor data heavily depends on whether data is collected for a later offline analysis or whether data is to be analyzed on the fly. In both cases, it is important that the data collected on different nodes is comparable. One aspect of this comparability is that data samples are collected at the same time.

When collecting data for an offline data analysis, we let each sensor node collect data samples in regular time intervals for each type of sensor it operates. This way, at the end of the collection phase it is able to provide a vector of n data samples for each sensor type. To provide for the comparability of these data vectors, all nodes should perform the data collection phase in parallel and the nodes need to synchronize their clocks so that measurements from different nodes can be associated with each other. For the expected volatility of the sensor criteria, the precision of prevalent time synchronization approaches in sensor networks is sufficient.

6.3.4 Data Preprocessing

Data preprocessing or data filtering takes the acquired sensor data and modifies or transforms it in a way that supports the following steps. One goal of such a preprocessing is to cover some of the effects of a lack of calibration of the sensor nodes as well as the differences in conditions sensors experience even when operating in the same area. Most importantly, data preprocessing is one way of including domain knowledge into the analysis by working out or emphasizing specific features hidden in the sensor data.

From the vast selection of possible preprocessing steps, we had to select a small number for evaluation in the context of our approach. We have opted for some basic methods that are particularly adequate for filtering sensor data. Each of the filters presented below is oriented towards some specific characteristic or problem of the sensor data. However, our approach is not limited to the use of these methods and can be easily extended at a later time.

The deviation between the output of uncalibrated sensor chips can increase linearly with the values. The **normalization filter** deals with this problem by bringing the sensor data from all data sources to one common scale. The filter inspects the complete data vector to identify its maximum and minimum. It then sets these values to a predefined range and adjusts all other values of the data vector accordingly.

The **data smoothing filter** is a very simple approach to remove small amplitude jittering from the sensor output. It smoothes the incoming data signal by calculating the average of the previous x values and uses this average as the output value of the filter.

The idea of the **curve tendency filter** is to abstract not only from the absolute sensor values but also from the shape of the sensor data curve and to only capture the general trend. For this purpose, the filter compares the current sensor value with the previous sensor value and records whether the curve is ascending or descending, thereby producing a binary output signal.

Strong outliers in the sensor data vector can be a handicap for detecting similarities or dissimilarities among nodes. In statistical data clustering, rank filtered data is known to be less susceptible to the effects of such outliers. The **value rank filter** takes the input data vector and calculates a ranking of its values as output. This means that if the x-th element of the input vector has the y-th largest value among all values of the input vector then the x-th element of the output vector will have the value y.

The motivation for the **event detection filter** originates from our expectations on the properties of the sensor data recorded by individual nodes. We expected that some types of sensors occasionally experience significant changes of their sensor values in between two samples. We call such a sudden change of values an event and use the event detection filter to record them. In our particular scenario, we expected the correlated detection of events by light sensors placed in the same room in situations where a person entering (or leaving) a room turns on (or turns off) the light. This way, the event detection filter is a specific form of domain knowledge incorporated in the clustering process.

6.3.5 Similarity Calculation

For the calculation of similarities among data vectors there are distance metrics and correlation coefficients. Distance metrics express how far apart two variables are according to a certain criterion. In the context of data clustering, a distance measure expresses how different two variables behave: The larger the distance, the bigger is the difference between two variables. For our application it is important not to confuse these distance values with geographic distances between nodes. In the following, distance always refers to such (dis)similarity measures and not to a geographic distance.

In contrast to distance metrics, a correlation coefficient measures the strength of a relationship between two variables. The value of a correlation coefficient lies between -1 and 1 where -1 denotes the strongest possible negative correlation, 1 the strongest possible positive correlation and 0 represents no detectable correlation. For the node grouping methods described in Section 6.3.6, both distance and correlation measures can be used.

It is possible to limit the costs generated by calculating the similarity among nodes by restricting the set of node pairs this calculation must be done for. We can use domain knowledge on the hop distance between nodes for this purpose: As nodes lying in the same area should not be more than a few hops apart it is possible to filter out correlations among nodes whose hop distance lies above a specified threshold. We use this domain knowledge in the distributed implementation where we assume that nodes in the same area are able to directly communicate with each other.

A large set of different distance and correlation measures have been developed in the field of statistical data clustering with some of them tuned to very specific problem types. In our work we use a set of elementary metrics that cover the different available classes. Specifically, we consider two very basic distance measures, the Euclidean distance and the Manhattan distance, as well as a very popular representative of the correlation measures, the Pearson coefficient. In addition, we also consider two correlation coefficients for specific types of input data: the Spearman coefficient for value rank data and the Phi coefficient for data with only two magnitudes.

The **Euclidean distance** and the **Manhattan distance** are distance metrics that are most popular for their use in the field of geometry but that are also used in a variety of other fields. The formulas for calculating the Euclidean Distance and the Manhattan Distance are shown in Equation 6.1.

$$d_{Eucl}(x,y)=\sqrt{\sum_{i=1}^{n}(x_i-y_i)^2}, \quad d_{Man}(x,y)=\sum_{i=1}^{n}|x_i-y_i| \tag{6.1}$$

A commonly used correlation coefficient is **Pearson's product-moment correlation coefficient**. Its main idea is to measure the tendency of two variables to increase and decrease together. The Pearson coefficient thereby assumes that the relationship among correlated variables is linear.

Equation 6.2 shows how Pearson's product-moment correlation coefficient r_{xy} is calculated for two variables x and y when a series of n samples has been taken. $\bar{x}$ and $\bar{y}$ are the mean values and σ_x and σ_y the standard deviations calculated over the n samples of the variables x and y respectively.

$$r_{xy} = \frac{\sum_{i=1}^{n}((x_i-\bar{x})(y_i-\bar{y}))}{n\sigma_x\sigma_y} \tag{6.2}$$

Spearman's rank correlation coefficient is a special case of Pearson's product-moment correlation coefficient that works on a ranking of data values. It uses the formula for calculating the Pearson coefficient and applies it to data preprocessed by the value rank filter. One advantage of the Spearman coefficient compared to the Pearson coefficient is that it does not assume a linear relationship among correlated variables.

The **Phi coefficient** is a popular representative of the group of correlation coefficients for dichotomous data, that is data with only two magnitudes. For our work this is relevant when looking at data generated by the event filter or the curve tendency filter. The Phi coefficient measures the degree of correlation between two binary variables x and y. It compares the product of the number of cases where x and y are both 0 or both 1 with the product of the number of cases where x and y are 1 or 0 or 0 and 1 respectively. Its calculation is shown in the equation in Fig. 6.4 (a). It

$$\phi = \frac{ad-bc}{\sqrt{efgh}}$$

(a) Formula

	x^-	x^+	Total
y^-	a	b	e
y^+	c	d	f
Total	g	h	n

(b) Counter values

Figure 6.4: Calculation of the Phi coefficient

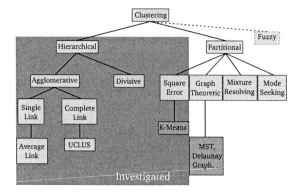

Figure 6.5: A taxonomy of clustering approaches (adapted from [85])

is based on the table shown in Fig. 6.4 (b) that collects information about how often the binary values of x and y match and how often they conflict.

6.3.6 Node Clustering

The last step of our node grouping is to use a data clustering algorithm to calculate a clustering of nodes based on the acquired similarity information. Fig. 6.5 (adapted from [85]) shows a classification of data clustering techniques with the three main classes **hierarchical clustering**, **partitional clustering** and **fuzzy clustering**. Hierarchical clustering approaches arrange the elements in a clustering tree that expresses the similarity among elements. In contrast, partitional clustering algorithms directly calculate a partitioning of elements. As the name suggests, the idea of fuzzy clustering is to calculate for each element membership probabilities to individual clusters. As we are more interested in well-defined clusters than in membership probabilities, we do not consider fuzzy clustering any further in this work but concentrate on hierarchical and partitional clustering which we discuss in a little more detail in the following subsections.

Hierarchical Clustering

The basic idea of hierarchical clustering is to arrange the individual elements of a set in a tree so that short branch distances between elements in the tree express a high level of similarity and long branch distances express a low level of similarity. The clustering process can either be done agglomerative or divisive. Agglomerative methods start with each element being its own cluster and then form larger clusters step by step. Divisive clustering starts with one single cluster containing all elements and splits a cluster in each processing step. We experimented with both types of methods and found that the agglomerative approach outperforms the divisive approach for our scenarios. For that reason, we only discuss agglomerative methods in more detail here.

In each step of the agglomerative clustering process, the two elements with the highest degree of similarity are joined together to form a new aggregated element. This is repeated until all elements are part of one large aggregated element. This creates a tree data structure with the individual elements forming the leafs of the tree and the union of all elements forming the root of the tree. Different methods are available to compare the similarity among aggregated elements: One can select the minimum similarity (**single linkage**) or the maximum similarity (**complete linkage**) among all individual elements of two aggregated elements. As an alternative, the average similarity (**average linkage**) among the individual elements can be computed and used as the similarity value of the aggregated elements. A different approach is to calculate the centroid vector of all elements of the aggregated element by calculating the average of all vectors of the individual elements and use these centroids to compute similarities (**centroid linkage**).

A clustering tree contains more information than a mere partitioning of elements and is more flexible in its use. For example, it allows a more general expression of the similarity of two nodes in the context of a group of nodes. In addition, it can still be used to acquire node relationship information even if the number of clusters to be found is not known.

If the number of clusters is known, then it is possible to deduce the desired set of clusters during the calculation of the tree. As the number of disjunct elements is reduced by one in each step of agglomerative clustering, we simply stop when the desired number of clusters is reached and use each of the calculated partial trees as one partition. If the number of clusters is not known in advance, one can stop merging tree elements once a specified minimum similarity among joined elements is not reached anymore.

Partitional Clustering

The class of **partitional clustering** approaches represents all algorithms that directly partition a data set into a set of clusters based on a given knowledge of the number of clusters to be found in the system. In our analysis, we concentrate on square error clustering methods. More specifically, we picked the k-means clustering algorithm which is the most popular representative of the square error clustering methods. Another important subgroup of partitional clustering are the graph theoretic methods with the minimum spanning tree and the Delaunay graph as popular examples.

The k-means clustering algorithm works as follows: Initially, the individual elements of the data set are randomly assigned to one of the k clusters. Next, for each cluster the mean vector of the cluster elements (the "centroid") is calculated. Each element is then reassigned to the cluster whose centroid has the highest similarity to the data vector of the respective element. The computation of the cluster centroids and the reassignments of the elements is repeated until some convergence criterion is met (e.g., assignment does not change anymore). Note that due to the random assignment of nodes to the clusters in the beginning, each run of the k-means algorithm can yield different results.

6.3.7 Combining Clustering Trees

Having more than one information source available (e.g., multiple sensors in our scenarios), it is desirable to be able to combine the similarity information acquired from these different sources. This can help distinguishing areas that appear very similar according to one criterion but that differ significantly based on another. It can also balance weaknesses and strengths different criteria have in different time periods (e.g., light sensors at night). Finally, it potentially allows the node grouping algorithm to work in a more diverse set of scenarios without requiring scenario-specific customizations.

Combining distance or correlation information from different sources is non-trivial and cannot be done by simply calculating the average of distance or correlation matrices as the range of values strongly depends on the properties of the sensor, the preprocessing methods and the similarity measure. This is most obvious for the Euclidean distance and the Manhattan distance where the distance values of sensors varying with a large amplitude can easily dominate distance values from sensors that only generate a small range of values.

We found a suitable solution to this problem coming from the field of biology where the average consensus supertree (ACS) [112] method has been developed to find a consensus based on multiple clustering trees. The main idea of ACS is not to combine distance or correlation matrices from different criteria but rather to combine the clustering results (in the form of clustering trees) obtained by applying one of the hierarchical clustering algorithms to these matrices. ACS calculates path length matrices for each of the input trees, then takes the average matrix of these path length matrices and uses it as input for a second round of clustering. The path length matrix of a tree contains for each pair of nodes the number of branches between the nodes in the input tree. While the original version of ACS used a least-squares algorithm for the second cluster calculation, we simply apply the same clustering algorithm that was used to calculate the input clustering trees.

6.4 Centralized Analysis

In the previous section, we have introduced the basic concept of our node grouping approach based on sensor data and have described the relevant data filtering and statistical data clustering methods to be used as part of the grouping. Before we describe our distributed approach to the grouping of nodes that is applicable to real wireless sensor network deployments, let us first provide an analysis of the applicability of these methods to determining the groups of sensor nodes that reside within the same room. The results of this analysis are important for two reasons. Firstly, they are used to identify appropriate methods for the node grouping approach and, secondly, they are used as the best-case scenario for evaluating the quality of the approach.

To perform the analysis, we use a centralized experimental setup to collect real sensor data in a building. Each participating sensor node first performs a series of n measurements that are stored in its local flash memory. To globally synchronize the measurements of different sensor nodes, we use the Flooding Time Synchronization Protocol (FTSP) [129] for TinyOS. After the measurement series has been completed, each sensor node forwards its stored data to a central base station where the offline analysis is performed. Clearly, this setting is not suitable for real world wireless sensor networks. However, it eliminates a number of complications that we discuss later and ensures that multiple grouping methods can be analyzed on the same set of input data.

6.4.1 Experimental Setup

For the analysis of the described methods, we collected data in two different home scenarios using temperature, humidity and light sensors in the form of photosynthetically active radiation (PAR) as well as total solar radiation (TSR). To do this, we used off-the-shelf Tmote Sky sensor nodes without performing any calibration. In each scenario, we distributed twelve nodes to four different rooms with three nodes being placed in each room. The sensor nodes were attached to the wall or to furniture in different parts of the monitored rooms at different heights (ranging from the floor to the ceiling) and with different orientations. We paid attention to the fact that none of the sensor chips was directly covered by other artifacts of the room. However, effects like some nodes lying in the shadow of an artifact or lying in the airflow of a window were deliberately not avoided.

6.4.2 Validating assumptions

Our first step was to check the validity of our basic assumption that there exists a correlation among the sensor readings of nodes located in the same area and that this correlation is significantly higher than the correlation among nodes located in different areas. For this analysis we used the complete data set collected in our two exemplary scenarios and computed the Pearson coefficient for all pairs of nodes and all types of sensors. We separately calculated the average correlation for all node pairs lying

Table 6.1: Average correlation inside areas / between areas

	Home scenario 1		Home scenario 2	
	Inside	Between	Inside	Between
Humidity	0.87	0.22	0.86	-0.02
Light PAR	0.96	0.50	0.93	0.20
Light TSR	0.98	0.39	0.95	0.34
Temperature	0.83	0.35	0.77	0.18

in the same area (Inside) and all node pairs lying in different areas (Between). The results are shown in Table 6.1.

The values shown in Table 6.1 confirm our assumption that the correlation among nodes in the same area is significantly higher than the correlation among nodes in different areas for all four types of sensors. They also illustrate differences between sensors in the levels of similarity inside of an area and among areas: The two types of light sensors show the highest level of similarity inside of an area in both of our scenarios whereas the humidity sensors show the lowest level of similarity among sensors in different areas. The results also indicate that the behavior of individual sensor types and the properties of the resulting data sets strongly depend on the respective scenario and that this dependency mainly constitutes itself in how different the conditions in the areas of the scenarios are.

Note that this analysis does not necessarily express the actual usefulness of the criteria for a node grouping yet as it only uses the Pearson coefficient, ignores any possible data preprocessing and does not consider the required size of the input data set.

As a second step, Table 6.2 analyzes correlations among different types of sensors again using the average value of the Pearson coefficient. This time it is calculated for all pairs of different sensors on the same sensor node. High correlations among different sensor types are interesting because of their potential use for node similarity calculations if two nodes do not overlap in the types of sensors they provide. Moreover, if two types of sensor output are highly correlated then operating both sensors on the same node cannot provide much additional information for the grouping of nodes. The results demonstrate that such a correlation among sensor types only exists between the TSR light sensor and the PAR light sensor which could be expected given the strong relation of the two sensors. But even in this case, the correlation tends to be smaller than the correlation among different nodes in the same area when considering a single sensor type.

6.4.3 Evaluation criteria

The basic evaluation criterion for the grouping of nodes is the correctness of the clustering result. We can express this clustering quality with the percentage of node groups that have been calculated correctly. A correctly calculated group G_i of nodes consists of at least one node $sensor_x$ and also contains all nodes that lie in the same

Table 6.2: Average correlation among different sensors

	Home scenario 1	Home scenario 2
Temp. – Light TSR	0.52	0.17
Temp. – Light PAR	0.44	0.15
Temp. – Humidity	0.17	0.28
Light TSR – Li. PAR	0.88	0.94
Light TSR – Humidity	0.08	0.07
Light PAR – Humidity	0.03	0.04

area as $sensor_x$ (in our case: all nodes lying in the same room). Furthermore, all nodes belonging to G_i must lie in the same area as $sensor_x$.

This definition of correctness is clear when applying partitional clustering. For hierarchical clustering, however, there is a difference between node groups that form a correct part of the clustering tree and node groups that additionally can be correctly deduced during the calculation of the clustering tree as described in Section 6.3.6.

Depending on the application of the clustering result it might also be useful to define a more sophisticated metric for evaluating the result of hierarchical clustering algorithms that takes the position of elements with respect to their respective peers into account. For example, one could consider the hop distance in the tree between elements of the same area to better account for the quality of a clustering when not all nodes of a group are clustered together.

Besides the correctness of the clustering result, another important metric is the size of the data vector required for the algorithm to stabilize on a solution. As the size of the data vector corresponds to the number of samples each sensor node has to collect, this directly influences the overhead and the energy consumption of the sensor nodes. Finally, it is important to consider the complexity of calculating the clustering result based on the provided data.

6.4.4 Analysis Results

Among the four sensor types we experimented with, the TSR light sensor proved to be the most reliable one that provided useful results over a large number of cases in both scenarios. While the PAR light sensor and the humidity sensor were also useful in many cases, the temperature showed to be a surprisingly weak criterion.

Among the set of preprocessing steps, the event filter is the only one that consistently proved to be useful in a large set of cases. Applying the other filters only showed improvements in a small number of cases and often not consistently across different experiments. The curve tendency filter and the value rank filter provided good grouping results. However, they required a large number of samples for stabilizing on a correct solution or tended not to stabilize at all which disqualifies them for use in real applications.

The Pearson correlation coefficient is the most reliable similarity metric. It worked well for all sensor types albeit requiring different numbers of data samples to stabilize

Table 6.3: Exemplary results of the centralized analysis

	Home scenario 1		Home scenario 2	
	Success	Steps	Success	Steps
Humidity Pearson	100%	50	75-100%	-
PAR Pearson	100%	70	100%	70
TSR Pearson	100%	70	100%	70
Temperature Pearson	100%	500	75%	900*
TSR Euclidean	75-100%	-	100%	10*
TSR Manhattan	75-100%	-	100%	10*
TSR Event10.0 Phi	100%	90*	100%	80*
TSR Event20.0 Phi	100%	40*	100%	10*
TSR Event30.0 Phi	100%	60	100%	70
PAR Spearman	100%	700*	100%	1300*
TSR Spearman	100%	800	75%	300*

(See data in Table 6.3). The Euclidean and the Manhattan metrics worked well in a smaller set of scenarios with only some types of data. No clear advantage of one of the two over the other could be detected. The Phi coefficient worked well in combination with the event filter whereas the Spearman coefficient provided good results in combination with the value rank filter but at a high cost in terms of the number of required data samples.

Both the hierarchical clustering algorithms and the k-means clustering algorithm worked well with a similar quality. For that reason the following discussion of exemplary results will only consider complete linkage hierarchical clustering and only show its results. We also defer the analysis of combining multiple criteria using ACS to the evaluation in Section 6.6.

To illustrate the overall results described above, Table 6.3 shows exemplary node grouping results with different combinations of filters and similarity measures recorded for our two home scenarios. Both experiments were started in the evening and the analysis is based on data samples taken every 200 seconds. For each combination the table shows the percentage of clusters correctly identified and the number of steps (= the number of data samples used for the calculation) required for the algorithm to stabilize on this clustering. If no entry for the number of steps is given then the algorithm failed to find a stable solution[1].

Table 6.4 summarizes the results of our centralized analysis considering the usefulness of the data preprocessing steps, the similarity calculation methods and the node clustering algorithms as well as their respective time complexities ($T(n)$) and space complexities ($S(n)$). The complexity values will be discussed in more detail later.

As Table 6.3 shows, a correct grouping grouping of nodes can be found with the help of different criteria using only a small number of data samples. However, the table does not show the dependency of such results on the start time of the analysis. Our

---

[1]If the number of steps is supplemented by a star (*) then the result shown is for the number of correct clusters being part of the tree and not for the number of clusters correctly deduced during the calculation of the clustering tree as described above.

Table 6.4: Result overview of the centralized analysis

	Time compl.	Space compl.	Useful
Normalization	$O(m)$	$O(m)$	Limited
Data smoothing	$O(m)$	$O(1)$	Limited
Curve tendency	$O(m)$	$O(1)$	Limited
Value rank	$O(m\log(m)))$	$O(m)$	Limited
Event detection	$O(m)$	$O(1)$	High
Euclidean	$O(m)$	$O(1)$	High
Manhattan	$O(m)$	$O(1)$	High
Pearson	$O(m)$	$O(1)$	High
Spearman	$O(m)$	$O(1)$	Limited
Phi	$O(m)$	$O(1)$	High
Hier. single link.	$O(n^2\log n)$	$O(n^2)$	High
Hier. compl. link.	$O(n^2\log n)$	$O(n^2)$	High
Hier. avg. link.	$O(n^2\log n)$	$O(n^2)$	High
k-means	$O(klmn)$	$O(km)$	High

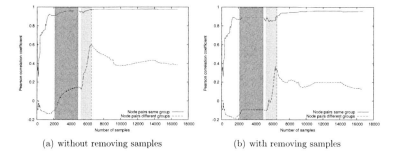

(a) without removing samples   (b) with removing samples

Figure 6.6: Average progress of the Pearson coefficient for the TSR light sensor

experiments showed that node grouping works best when the data collection is started in the evening with human activity present in the covered areas. To illustrate this, Fig. 6.6 (a) shows the progress over time of the Pearson coefficient for TSR light sensor data collected in home scenario 1 during a time period of approximately two days. Like for the results shown in Table 6.2, the graph also distinguishes between node pairs belonging to the same group and node pairs belonging to different groups. While the average correlation coefficient quickly approaches 1 for node pairs belonging to the same group one can also see two time periods (colored in the figure) that significantly increase the average correlation among nodes belonging to different groups which in turn makes distinguishing nodes from different groups more difficult.

The first colored time period corresponds to the first night during which all rooms were completely dark and all light sensors recorded values in the range of 0. Such a long period of time during which all sensors basically experience the exact same conditions make the sensor nodes appear more similar irrespective of their group affiliation. This

163

in turn expresses itself in a larger correlation coefficient as can be seen in the figure.

It is possible to use this knowledge about the existence of time periods without sensor activity to remove the data samples from the calculation of the Pearson coefficient for a pair of nodes using a simple rule: When both values of a data sample pair are below a specified threshold th then the data sample pair is not used in the calculations of the correlation. However, this rule must be slightly enhanced to account for the cases where sample pairs below the threshold provide useful information (For example when one room is dark while another room is illuminated). Since we are only interested in filtering out long time periods of inactivity, we changed the rule so that we only start removing data sample pairs from the calculation after a specified number of value pairs l below the threshold have been read. Fig. 6.6 (b) shows the result of applying this heuristic (using $th = 3$ and $l = 5$) to the collected data. As can be seen, the average correlation among nodes belonging to the same group still grows quickly while the average correlation among nodes belonging to different groups does not grow anymore during the night time. This way the average value of the Pearson coefficient only reaches a maximum value of 0.37 instead of 0.59 for the case without removing data samples.

The second colored time interval represents the time period from forenoon to noon of the second day when many of the nodes experienced bright sunlight. The problem now is that the high values collected by the light sensors during this period quickly dominate the much smaller values collected during the evening or the night in the calculation of the Pearson coefficient. A small number of these samples then suffices to loose much of the useful similarity information acquired previously. This information loss is only compensated after some time by useful similarity information provided by these high sensor values and the average correlation among nodes located in different rooms starts to get smaller again.

It is much more difficult to avoid the negative effects of the second time interval compared to the first interval. One can avoid transitions from periods with small sensor values to periods with much larger sensor values by timing the node grouping accordingly. As an alternative, it is possible to collect the data from the different value ranges separately. Finally, if enough data samples are available such effects get balanced out in the long run as shown in Fig. 6.6. In our implementation we rely on an intelligent timing of the node grouping data collection as well as on balancing out weaknesses of individual sensors by combining their node grouping data with data from other criteria using ACS (see Section 6.3.7).

While the dependency of the light sensors on the time of the day is most obvious, our experiments showed that the performance of the humidity and the temperature sensors also depend on the respective time of the day as well as on the presence of human activity in the rooms.

Another important result of our analysis of the two scenarios is the insight that it is difficult to achieve a correct grouping of nodes quickly. However, it is possible to save on the number of required data values and consequently on the number of required messages by increasing the data sampling interval. This is illustrated in Fig. 6.7 that shows the number of steps required for a stabilization of the node grouping

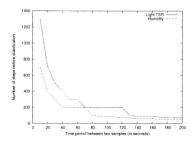

Figure 6.7: Clustering stabilization depending on the sampling interval

for the TSR light and the humidity sensors depending on the time interval between individual samples taken in home scenario 1. With small time intervals between the data samples, the number of required samples is extraordinarily high for both types of sensors shown. The higher sampling rate does not even seem to provide much additional information which becomes obvious when looking at the amount of time it takes to stabilize when sampling every 10 seconds compared to sampling every 200 seconds: 217 minutes compared to 233 minutes for the light sensor and 116 minutes compared to 167 minutes for the humidity sensors. Note that the situation can be different for other types of sensors that collect data on more volatile characteristics of their environment.

6.4.5 Node Grouping Complexity

The complexity values shown in Table 6.4 are based on the number of clusters k, the number of iterations l, the number of nodes n and the number of data samples m. The complexities given for the data preprocessing methods are per node and the complexities for the similarity calculation methods are per node pair.

It is important to note that the factors considered critical when evaluating the complexity of the various grouping approaches are different for our case compared to other applications of statistical data clustering. Normally, the size of the data vector representing each individual element to be clustered is small and fixed. The number of data samples m is therefore not considered in such complexity calculations. However, the number of elements to be clustered can be extremely large (e.g., the number of pixels of an image when using data clustering in image analysis) and strongly influence the costs of the different approaches. Consequently, the literature identifies k-means clustering as more efficient to calculate than hierarchical clustering as the number of elements only has linear influence there compared to quadratic influence for hierarchical clustering.

In our node grouping scenarios, the number of elements (nodes) stays comparatively small - even for larger scenarios. However, the size of the data vectors the calculations are based on can be significant so that their influence on the cost of calculating a node grouping cannot be ignored. The consequence is that for our grouping of nodes, hierarchical clustering is typically less costly than k-means clustering as the number of samples m only influences the similarity calculation and not the node grouping itself.

6.5 Distributed Node Grouping Approach

Up to this point, our analysis has been based on the assumption that all sensor data is collected by a central base station that is then able to process the data from the different nodes and decide on their grouping based on this global information. However, forwarding the complete sequence of collected sensor data from all nodes in the network with a reasonably high sampling rate creates a constant high traffic load despite potential optimizations like aggregation. For that reason, this section deals with the distributed implementation of significant parts of the algorithm on the individual nodes of the network and discusses how the required amount of traffic to a central base station can be minimized.

One major goal of a distributed implementation of the node grouping algorithm is to avoid interfering with the needs of the actual application running in the sensor network. For this purpose, the node grouping component running on the nodes needs to limit its resource requirements in terms of memory, processing time and energy consumption (see also the requirements specified in Section 6.1.2). Only a low message overhead should be generated both for the communication among sensor nodes and for transporting data to the central base station. As the flash memory is often needed by the applications, no logging of data should be required.

Time synchronization is a complex and expensive service in wireless sensor networks. To avoid the message overhead associated with this, the distributed approach should not require synchronized clocks and should also not be based on a concept of rounds.

Depending on the application running in the sensor network, it should be possible to take advantage of existing message traffic. This can either be done by directly utilizing sensor data that is sent out by the application or by piggybacking sensor data to other types of messages that the application sends out in regular intervals. For example, the popular routing protocol MintRoute [216] which is available as part of TinyOS uses periodic beacon messages for neighborhood management. These beacon messages could be extended to also distribute sensor data to neighboring nodes.

Note that there is an important difference between the goals of distributing data clustering methods in general and our goals in distributing the node grouping algorithm in a sensor network. In other application fields, the primary goal of such a distribution is a higher performance by spreading the workload of the data clustering calculations over multiple computers. The data for these calculations is usually completely available to all involved parties. However, ensuring the performance and the scalability of the data clustering calculation itself is not the main problem for the grouping of nodes in a sensor network. It is rather the costs incurred on the individual devices during the collection of the data required for performing a clustering of nodes.

6.5.1 Method Overview

The basic idea of our approach is that each sensor node periodically reads its own sensor data every p seconds (beacon send interval). However, instead of recording this data together with a time stamp value in its local flash memory, the node broadcasts the collected data in a beacon message to its neighbors.

When a node receives a beacon message from one of its neighboring nodes, it reads its own sensor data and compares the two data samples to extract information required for the similarity calculation. This way, comparable pairs of sensor data are generated without time synchronization. Although still following the four process steps shown in Fig. 6.3, data preprocessing and similarity calculation are now directly done on the individual sensor nodes.

Based on the results of our analysis of the centralized approach, the only data preprocessing step still supported in the distributed implementation is the detection of events. If needed, most other filters can easily be added at a later time. Exceptions are the normalization filter and the value rank filter whose space and time complexities impede a distributed implementation.

After collecting similarity values on the individual nodes in the network, only the last step of the clustering process – the actual computation of the node clustering – is still done at a central base station. This is because the calculation requires a global view on similarity information among all nodes. However, collecting such similarity information at a central point of the network is much less expensive than collecting complete vectors of sensor data.

6.5.2 Similarity Measures and Clustering Techniques Revisited

The most important requirement for the similarity measures used in our distributed implementation is that their calculation can be done online requiring only a single pass. This basically means that it should be possible to process and analyze each sample of the data vector directly at the time it is captured without having to first store all samples in the memory of the nodes and later repeatedly going through the samples to calculate the similarity.

Both the Euclidean distance and the Manhattan distance can easily be collected in a distributed way on the sensor nodes. They only require to store one sum value and the counter of the number of samples collected.

The data required for the calculation of the Pearson correlation coefficient can also be collected distributed on the sensor nodes. For this purpose, Equation 6.2 must be reformulated into Equation 6.3. Together with a reformulation of the formula for the standard deviation as shown in Equation 6.4, this results in the following list of six values that must be collected by a sensor node:

$$\sum_{i=1}^{n} x_i \quad \sum_{i=1}^{n} x_i^2 \quad \sum_{i=1}^{n} x_i y_i \quad \sum_{i=1}^{n} y_i \quad \sum_{i=1}^{n} y_i^2 \quad n$$

$$r_{xy} = \frac{\sum_{i=1}^{n} x_i y_i - \bar{y} \sum_{i=1}^{n} x_i - \bar{x} \sum_{i=1}^{n} y_i + n\bar{x}\bar{y}}{n\sigma_x \sigma_y} \tag{6.3}$$

$$\sigma_x = \sqrt{\frac{1}{n} \sum_{i=1}^{n} x_i^2 - \frac{1}{n} 2\bar{x} \sum_{i=1}^{n} x_i + \bar{x}^2} \tag{6.4}$$

Since the calculation of the Spearman rank correlation coefficient is equivalent to the calculation of the Pearson coefficient it can be distributed the same way. However, calculating the required value ranks of a data vector is equivalent to sorting the values of this vector. Besides a time complexity of at least $O(n \log(n))$ this also entails storing the complete data vector on the sensor node. This is what the distributed implementation tries to avoid. For that reason and due to the suboptimal results in the centralized implementation, we do not use the Spearman coefficient in the distributed implementation.

To compute the Phi coefficient, the sensor nodes only need to collect the four counter values shown in the table in Fig. 6.4 (b). Compared to other collected values, the advantage of the Phi counter values is that their range of values is very small as the value of all four counters is smaller than or equal to the number of samples taken.

In summary, most of the distance metrics we experimented with in the centralized analysis are also well suited for a distributed implementation. The only exception, the Spearman rank correlation coefficient, has been shown to be too expensive in terms of memory consumption as it does not allow a single pass implementation.

The different types of hierarchical clustering discussed in section 6.3.6 base their calculation on the distance or correlation matrix containing similarity information among all nodes. If the similarity values collected by the individual nodes are collected at a central base station, then the hierarchical clustering can be calculated in exactly the same way as in the centralized approach.

The situation is different for the k-means clustering algorithm. As described in section 6.3.6, the algorithm requires to recalculate the mean vector of the data vectors of all objects in a cluster in each iteration. This is not possible if the sensor nodes only store and provide similarity values calculated out of the data vectors.

Summarizing the insights on clustering, we can conclude that only clustering algorithms qualify for our distributed approach that directly work on a distance matrix and do not require the data samples themselves for their calculation. Consequently, in the following we concentrate on hierarchical clustering.

6.5.3 Inaccuracies

The distributed approach described above introduces a new set of inaccuracies that can affect the clustering results. The first inaccuracy is introduced by the delay between the measurements on a pair of nodes which is caused by the time required for the message transfer. The problem is that the sensor values of two nodes used for computing correlation values are not actually recorded at the same time. How critical this is depends on the volatility of the respective sensor data. For example, it is usually not a problem for the temperature and humidity sensors as these criteria seldom change abruptly. It might happen that the light level suddenly changes between the two sensor readings. However, the probability for this is very small as both the number of such light events and the time interval between the two recordings is small.

The second inaccuracy is caused by lost beacon messages, for example due to collisions. Without precautions, this can result in differing numbers of samples recorded at different node pairs. Given a sufficient number of samples, this is can be neglected for the Phi and the Pearson coefficient as their values are by definition normalized between -1 and 1. However, the values of the Euclidean or Manhattan distance increase monotonically with the number of samples so that only distance values based on the same number of samples are comparable. The straightforward solution is to collect a predefined number of samples for each node pair to achieve comparable Euclidean distance values. However, this does not prevent different node pairs from collecting data from different time periods which again limits the comparability of the resulting distance values.

A more fundamental potential source of inaccuracies results from the fact that it is not feasible to compute the similarities between arbitrary node pairs in a distributed manner. Doing so would require the global distribution of measurements, for example by flooding beacons. However, in many application scenarios, this problem can be mitigated by limiting the beaconing scope (i.e., its hop count) using domain knowledge. In our particular indoor scenario for instance, it is possible to limit the scope to 1 since it is reasonable to assume that sensor nodes residing within the same room are direct neighbors and nodes that are not direct neighbors are not within the same room. In these cases we use this domain knowledge to assign an infinite distance (or a correlation value of 0) to the remaining node pairs.

Since the detection of events relies on comparing the current sensor reading with previously sampled sensor data, special care is required for the distributed implementation. Data is sampled whenever a beacon message from a neighbor arrives and so the time interval between the current and the previous data sample can be arbitrarily small. This causes unbalanced conditions for the detection of events. Ideally, one would always compare a data sample with the sample recorded the last time a beacon message was received from the same neighboring node. However, this would cause a rapid increase in memory consumption.

Our solution to this problem is to let the node store the previous two sensor values it collected in reaction to its own time trigger (and not in reaction to receiving a beacon message) as reference values. It also stores the time stamp of the younger reference value. When sensor data is sampled following a received beacon message the node selects one of the two reference values for the comparison according to the following rule: If the difference between the current time and the time stamp of the younger reference value is smaller than half of the beacon send interval then use the old reference value. Use the younger reference value otherwise.

6.5.4 Optimizations

In the distributed approach described above, the number of times a sensor node needs to sample its local sensors during the time period p depends on the number of neigh-

Table 6.5: Memory consumption for storing distance metric information

Metric	Memory consumption (in bytes)
Euclidean distance	7
Pearson coefficient	25
Phi coefficient	8

boring nodes it receives beacon messages from. It is possible to reduce the overhead for this sampling with two optimizations: Firstly, it is not necessary to sample a sensor a second time if the last sample is still very fresh (less than q time units old). Second, sensor data originally sampled for calculations can be directly sent out in a beacon message if the next scheduled send time is less than r time units away.

Another optimization aims at reducing the amount of state each sensor node needs to store and maintain for the calculation of similarity information to neighboring nodes. In the basic approach, two neighboring nodes x and y both collect information about their similarity with respect to each other. While in most cases the two similarity values will not be identical (as they are based on different data sample pairs) their basic information should be the same. So we can practically cut in half the number of neighboring nodes a node has to manage state for by letting neighboring nodes negotiate which one records similarity information.

The nodes can negotiate responsibilities explicitly by exchanging messages that contain the number of node pairs each of them already manages. Alternatively, this negotiation can be done implicitly with the nodes deciding based on a static rule. A simple example of such a rule that ensures that exactly one of the nodes takes over the responsibility is the following: If the sum of the two IDs is even then the node with the smaller ID manages the node pair. If the sum of the two IDs is uneven then the node with the larger ID manages the node pair.

6.5.5 Implementation

As for the experimental analysis of the centralized implementation, we used Tmote Sky sensor nodes for our distributed implementation. The implementation was done in nesC for the TinyOS 2 operating system.

The implementation supports the Euclidean distance, the Pearson correlation coefficient and the Phi correlation coefficient. We did not implement the Manhattan distance as it did not show any advantages compared to the Euclidean distance. The three similarity measures differ in the amount of memory consumed by the data required for their calculation. The Euclidean distance requires 7 bytes per sensor and node pair, the Pearson coefficient 25 bytes and the Phi coefficient 8 bytes (see Table 6.5). This takes into account the possible range of values which requires reserving between 2 and 5 bytes per value in main memory to avoid overflows. The considerably higher memory consumption of the Pearson coefficient data motivates why considering the other criteria is still worthwhile despite the superior performance the Pearson coefficient showed in the analysis of the centralized approach.

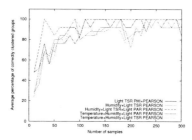

Figure 6.8: Percentage of groups clustered correctly for various criteria

In order to be able to investigate the evolution of distance and correlation values over time in the evaluation of the approach, we added a log module that writes this information in regular intervals to the node's flash memory. Such a logging to flash is not necessary when later adding the node grouping to a real sensor network application and can be removed to save on resources.

6.6 Evaluation

This section evaluates the performance of the distributed node clustering approach in different situations using real-world measurements. For this purpose, nodes were distributed in two home scenarios with 15 nodes in 5 different rooms with 3 nodes per room in each scenario.

6.6.1 Result Overview

We prepared five experiments in the two scenarios (200 seconds beacon send interval) started at different times in the evening reflecting our knowledge that this time period provides the best data for the clustering of nodes.

One important result of the experiments is that basing the clustering decision on a single criterion allows us to reach good node clustering results with acceptable effort only in a limited share of the experiments. For example, while considering the TSR light sensor alone led to correct and stable clustering after around 100 data samples in some experiments, it failed to detect more than 80% of the groups correctly or failed to stabilize at all in other experiments. This highlights the need for combining node clustering information from different criteria with the help of ACS. While such combinations also show weaknesses in a subset of experiments, their results vary less across experiments and are in general more stable over time. Consequently, the best performing node clusterings all combine two or more different criteria. An analysis of the average percentage of correctly clustered groups calculated over all experiments is shown for five particularly well performing combinations in Fig. 6.8.

In our scenarios, the light sensors are again indispensable information sources. However, both temperature and humidity sensors can play an important role as stabilizing elements that can compensate periods of weaknesses of the light sensors. Relying on temperature or humidity alone is difficult in the settings we tested and would increase the required number of samples considerably.

Fig. 6.8 shows a representative part of the result space based on well-performing combinations of criteria. Note, however, that a lot of different criteria and combinations of criteria were able to correctly cluster 80% and more of the groups correctly using a relatively small number of samples. In general, the experiments confirmed our expectations that a successful node clustering is more difficult to achieve due to the challenges of the distributed approach but still possible with only a limited amount of effort.

6.6.2 Detailed Analysis

We have identified different numbers of samples recorded by different node pairs as a source of inaccuracies and as a challenge to the successful clustering of nodes. The table in Fig. 6.9 (a) analyzes the severity of this problem for four different data collections showing the range of the number of samples recorded by different node pairs. Fig. 6.9 (b) exemplifies this for one data collection from the first scenario and shows the number of samples recorded for each node pair. The analysis shows that such irregularities in the number of samples recorded are the normal case rather than an exception and that the standard deviation is significant in some cases. Interestingly, there are even considerable differences among experiments conducted in the same scenario.

Another interesting result of our measurements related to the analysis of the number of samples is the performance of the Euclidean distance metric in the distributed implementation. In many experiments it failed to confirm the promising results the metric showed in the analysis of the centralized approach. We mainly attribute this to the radio irregularities that cause a variance in the number of samples recorded by different node pairs. As the value of the Euclidean distance strongly depends on the points in time the data samples are recorded, the absence of some samples can heavily distort the result even when the distance calculation of all node pairs is later based on the same number of samples. This reasoning is confirmed when comparing the results of experiments with a high variance in the number of samples with experiments with a lower variance. Consequently, the Euclidean distance metric should only be used if the scenario provides relatively stable communication links between all node pairs.

The analysis of the centralized approach has shown that node grouping works best when started during time periods with artificial light and considerable human activity. The other extreme of the spectrum – starting node grouping at night without any human activity – can be avoided. However, normal daylight scenarios are common and have to be supported. To explore how node grouping works in these scenarios we started two experiments (home scenario 2, data collected every 200 seconds) in the morning and made sure that there was no human activity in the covered rooms for at least the first eight hours.

	Max	Min	Avg	Std dev
Scenario 1 - Experiment 1	1040	0	829	335
Scenario 1 - Experiment 2	1130	0	924	332
Scenario 2 - Experiment 1	660	0	582	152
Scenario 2 - Experiment 2	670	410	630	31

(a) Analysis

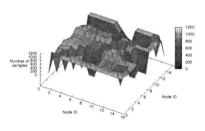

(b) First home scenario

Figure 6.9: Number of samples

The most interesting result of these experiments is that all types of sensors are negatively affected by the lack of human activity and consequently the list of criteria stabilizing on a successful grouping in an acceptable amount of time is smaller. Fig. 6.10 (a) shows the number of groups correctly detected over the number of samples considered for a set of criteria performing reasonably well in this setting.

To explore the other extreme – how explicit human activity can positively influence a grouping of nodes – we set up an experiment in the second home scenario with the nodes recording their sensor values every 10 seconds for a time period of 20 minutes. As an explicit trigger, we alternately turned on or turned off the light in one of the five areas every 20 seconds. As expected, the data from the temperature and the humidity sensor could not generate useful results during this short experiment. Based on the TSR light sensor, however, the grouping stabilized on a correct result after only little more than three minutes. The PAR light sensor and the combination of both light sensors took a little longer to stabilize as shown in Fig. 6.10 (b) and the PAR light sensor alone was not able to identify all groups correctly. This shows that deliberately influencing the external conditions recorded by the sensor nodes can help in achieving good node grouping results quickly.

Above we have proposed an optimization that allows to reduce the number of node pairs each node has to manage by only requiring one of the two nodes of a pair to record similarity information based on exchanged sensor data. This optimization assumes that for a node pair $(sensor_x, sensor_y)$ the similarity information collected by node $sensor_x$ is basically equivalent to the similarity information collected by node $sensor_y$. We verified the correctness of this assumption with the help of correlation

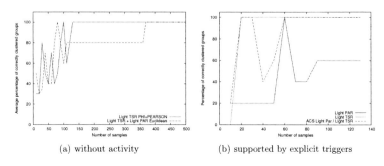

(a) without activity   (b) supported by explicit triggers

Figure 6.10: Node clustering results

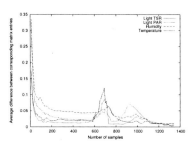

Figure 6.11: Correlation matrix symmetry analysis

matrix data collected in the second home scenario for the Pearson coefficient. For each correlation matrix, we calculated the average deviation between corresponding entries in the matrix:

$$\frac{\sum_{x,y=1}^{n} |corr(sensor_x, sensor_y) - corr(sensor_y, sensor_x)|}{n(n-1)} \qquad (6.5)$$

Fig. 6.11 shows this average deviation plotted over the number of samples the correlation matrices are based on. It shows that this deviation quickly falls below 0.1 for all sensor types and seems to converge to 0 in the long run. It also shows that certain events (e.g., sunrise in the morning) can temporarily cause a higher deviation. In general, however, we see our assumption confirmed.

6.7 Summary

Clustering is a powerful technique. For many sensor network applications, however, it is beneficial and sometimes even mandatory to form clusters on the basis of real-world semantics. Pervasive computing scenarios are a prime example of an application domain that could benefit from such a real-world reference of the clusters.

With the work presented in this chapter, we have shown that it is feasible to automatically create clusters or groups of nodes that reflect rooms and the boundaries between rooms by analyzing the measurements of inexpensive and broadly available sensors. To this end, we have performed an extensive analysis of the suitability of relevant data filtering and statistical data clustering methods. Based on the results of this analysis, we have devised a largely distributed approach to automatically determine clusters that adhere to room boundaries in real deployments.

As the variety of possible external conditions and influencing factors is very large, it is difficult to provide the ultimate set of criteria that will work flawlessly in all kinds of scenarios. However, we have been able to show that a grouping of nodes is possible with good results at acceptable costs despite quite diffuse conditions.

Our results indicate that adding domain knowledge significantly improves the results. When deploying our node grouping method as part of a real sensor network application, domain knowledge about this specific application and its scenario can help in making node grouping work there.

6.7.1 Future Directions in this Area

One possible future direction for research in the area of node grouping based on sensor data is to extend the presented approach to other scenarios that do not exhibit the comparatively clear correlations as present in and between individual rooms. In this context it might be useful to perform a thorough analysis of fuzzy data clustering approaches.

To push the level of distribution of our approach one step further, an interesting approach is to investigate to what extent sensor nodes are able to autonomously detect stabilization of the similarity values to their neighboring nodes or even to determine when the required amount of information for the clustering of nodes has been collected. Based on this information the nodes could adapt their beacon interval p and avoid spending energy on further beacon messages that do not provide any additional information for the grouping of sensor nodes. Ultimately, the goal would be for nodes to determine a clustering in a completely distributed fashion without the need for a coordinated collection of similarity values at a central base station.

We are sure that the idea of clustering devices based on sensor data does not have to be limited to sensor nodes but could also be useful in other application domains or on other types of pervasive computing devices. With the availability of cheap, high-quality sensor chips it might even be reasonable to add sensor chips to devices for the sole purpose of grouping devices together. Potential applications that come to mind include self-configuring home entertainment systems, home automation systems or alarm systems.

7 Interacting with Sensor Nodes

In this chapter, we discuss the problem of supporting users in interacting with wireless sensor nodes in their vicinity. We start with a motivation of why such individual node interactions or interactions with specific groups of nodes are important in pervasive computing scenarios. We then discuss the difficulty of providing such interaction capabilities on wireless sensor nodes.

In the main part of this chapter, we introduce three different interaction approaches that we have developed as part of this thesis work. The idea of gesture-based interaction is to select a sensor node for an interaction by performing a simple gesture in front of the node that can be detected with the help of the nodes' light sensors. The Sensor Node Lamp interaction approach uses a special hardware device to send light signals to sensor nodes in order to select them for interaction. Sensor nodes report back to the client device when they detect such a light signal to inform the client about them being selected. The idea of *NextOnePlease* interaction is to let the user quickly browse through the set of nodes in its vicinity using feedback from the LEDs available on the wireless sensor nodes.

In the evaluation we show with the help of practical experiments and a user study that our three approaches are effective and easy-to-use solutions to the node interaction problem.

7.1 Preliminaries

The traditional view of a sensor network as a black box with individual nodes being of little importance is not always helpful when mobile devices are able to communicate with individual sensor nodes while moving through the deployment area of a wireless sensor network. Instead, mobile devices should be able to exchange information directly with individual nodes, for example to send queries or tasks to specific sensor nodes and to receive back replies from them. We expect that a significant part of such communication will be among the mobile devices and sensor nodes in their direct vicinity. This is particularly true in pervasive computing scenarios where applications rely on information about the current context of the user which can often be provided by sensor nodes operating in the neighborhood of the user.

While providing for basic communication with neighboring nodes is straightforward, we have identified another challenge in this context that is the focus of this chapter: Supporting explicit interactions between the user and sensor nodes in his vicinity. More specifically, the difficulty lies in initiating interactions with one specific sensor node or with a specific set of sensor nodes. The user might select nodes based on various real-world criteria (e.g., "I would like to read the history of temperature values recorded by the sensor node mounted above the door") and the system needs a way of communicating (and thereby interacting) with exactly the specified set of nodes.

There are various types of interactions possible for a mobile device operating in the area of a wireless sensor network. Besides interacting with all neighboring nodes (broadcast interaction) or with a single, randomly selected node (random interaction), we are particularly interested in interactions with a specific node (individual interaction) or a group of nodes (group interaction) that the user selects based on real-world criteria. Selecting all nodes or a single random node for interaction is trivial to implement, the first using a simple broadcast, the second by selecting any node in the neighborhood. For that reason, we concentrate on individual and group interaction in the following discussion.

Establishing an interaction between a mobile device and a sensor node is particularly difficult due to the properties of the wireless sensor nodes. They do not possess any of the conventional user interface components for inputting and outputting information like a keyboard or a display. Instead, sensor nodes usually interact with neighboring devices solely by exchanging messages using the wireless communication interface.

Traditionally, there are two ways of selecting a sensor node for an interaction, either using its node identifier or with the help of geographic position information. If the client device knows the node identifier of the target node, then initiating an interaction with this node is trivial: The client device can directly start sending unicast messages to this node. However, mobile users usually do not have access to this mapping between nodes and node identifiers even though it might be known at deployment time. Moreover, having to deal with node identifiers on the user level is not always intuitive and might be error prone.

If the sensor nodes are aware of their respective geographic positions and the client device knows the coordinate of the target node, then it can use this information to initiate the interaction. This can either be done by comparing the coordinate information of the candidate nodes with the specified geographic coordinate of the target node and determining its node identifier this way or by directly communicating with the target node using geographic routing. However, in addition to the problems of node localization in sensor networks, it is also very complex for the user to determine the exact geographic position of the target node he wants to interact with. Symbolic location information can be used when the goal of an interaction request is to reach all nodes or any node within a symbolic area (compare area anycast and area broadcast discussed in Chapter 4) but not when individual nodes within that area have to be selected.

To facilitate the interaction between mobile users and wireless sensor nodes, we need to find an easy-to-use solution for selecting nodes based on real-world criteria. It should not require preexisting knowledge on the properties of the nodes (e.g., the node identifiers) or the structure of the network (e.g., the node positions). Moreover, it should not require additional hardware or special preparations on the wireless sensor nodes deployed in the environment.

7.1.1 Problem Definition

Let us now define the problem of providing interaction capabilities with wireless sensor nodes in a more formal way. In doing this, we are also going to introduce some terminology used throughout the rest of this chapter.

Assume that there exist a set of mobile client devices $S_{clients}$ and a set of sensor nodes $S_{sensors}$ that these devices can interact with. Both types of nodes have a common wireless communication interface that allows them to exchange messages with each other. Each client node and each sensor node possesses a unique node identifier i that can be used to address the nodes.

An interaction is initiated by a client node $n_{client} \in S_{clients}$ on behalf of its user. The user wants to interact with a subset of the nodes $S_{target} \subseteq S_{sensors}$. $|S_{target}| = 1$ holds for an individual interaction, $|S_{target}| > 1$ for a group interaction. Interactions initiated by different client nodes do not overlap and can be considered separately.

While the user is typically able to informally describe which node or which set of nodes he targets (e.g., by describing its position: "I want to query the node mounted on the wall to my left"), it is often difficult or impossible to specify the identifiers of the target nodes which would be required to establish a one-to-one communication between the client node and the target node. At the same time, interaction messages sent by broadcast might reach a whole set of candidate nodes S_{neigh} with $S_{neigh} \subseteq S_{sensors}$. When users interact with nodes in their vicinity, it is usually realistic to assume that $S_{target} \subseteq S_{neigh}$ holds. The problem of performing a targeted, purposeful interaction is to select the set of target nodes from the set of candidate nodes while avoiding to also select any undesired node.

The final goal of the procedure is for the client node to receive a set of node identifiers Id_{target} that represent the nodes of S_{target}. Id_{target} is then used to communicate and actually interact with the nodes.

7.1.2 Requirements

The primary goal for our interaction mechanisms must be a **high accuracy** in the selection of nodes. The occurrence of both false positives (i.e., selecting nodes that the user did not intend to interact with) and false negatives (i.e., ignoring nodes chosen by the user) should be avoided. Closely related to that is our second goal, a **good usability of the system**. It must be simple and intuitive to use – despite the limitations of the sensor nodes involved in the interaction. Finally, we also need to take the resource limitations of the wireless sensor nodes into account. For that reason, we need to **limit the complexity** of the operations performed on the individual nodes. Moreover, we cannot require additional hardware like a display on the sensor nodes just for facilitating the interaction.

As for all solutions discussed in this thesis, the main target scenario for our interaction approaches are indoor deployments of wireless sensor networks as part of pervasive computing scenarios like in homes, office buildings or factories. Consequently, we need to make sure that the solutions are **applicable to typical indoor deployments,**

However, some of the presented solutions can also be used in outdoor settings.

7.1.3 Application Scenarios

So far, we have provided a general motivation for the need of node interaction capabilities in wireless sensor networks. Let us now discuss a few specific examples of application scenarios.

The canonical application field for node interactions is to **query sensor data from specific nodes** that the user selects based on real-world criteria. Even if multiple nodes cooperate in providing a consistent overall view of the application area, users might still want to investigate the data from individual sensor nodes more closely during an analysis of the system behavior.

A very important application field is the **configuration of sensor networks** during or after the deployment and the **reconfiguration of nodes** during the normal network operation. While – as noted before – the optimum would be a completely autonomous self-configuration of the network, real-world deployments still require some human intervention to setup the desired structures. Such manual configuration steps are simplified considerably if nodes can be contacted individually and if the selection of nodes can be performed based on the administrator's own criteria.

In chapter 5 we have discussed the room-level configuration of sensor networks that we used to assign symbolic coordinates to sensor nodes. The node interaction approaches discussed in this chapter can be considered as the logical continuation of this idea that allows the configuration of individual nodes or arbitrary groups of nodes instead of configuring based on room boundaries. Naturally, the node interaction approaches can also be used for **assigning symbolic coordinates** which might be useful in border cases or to check the success of the room-level assignment process.

The proposed interaction mechanisms can also be useful for **debugging wireless sensor networks**. Selecting individual nodes, reading out their state information and interpreting the behavior based on this data are essential steps in gaining insight on the network behavior. Our interaction mechanisms allow to do this on the fly for any node in the network which is important when debugging large-scale, real-world deployments outside of controlled lab settings. Such a debugging does not always have to be a sophisticated error searching process but can be as simple as an administrator **checking the correct functionality of individual nodes** to determine whether hardware needs to be exchanged.

Finally, all application scenarios discussed so far build on a largely traditional view of sensor nodes and wireless sensor networks. We imagine that many different types of applications are possible if we consider **pervasive computing scenarios** with a variety of small-scale devices distributed in the environment or integrated into appliances that the users might want to interact with.

7.1.4 Overview of Approach

We introduce three different approaches to the problem of initiating interactions with wireless sensor nodes in this chapter. They build on different assumptions concerning the capabilities of the wireless sensor nodes and the type of involvement of the user in the selection of nodes.

The idea of **gesture-based interaction** is to let the user perform a simple gesture by moving his hand in front of the sensor node he wants to interact with. Candidate nodes are informed of the upcoming interaction in advance and a sensor node is then selected for interaction if it detects such a gesture following the announcement. The main difference between our gesture-based interaction and related approaches from the areas of mobile and pervasive computing lies in the very low hardware requirements of our approach: It can be implemented on standard sensor node hardware using only a light sensor for detecting the gesture and requiring only very simple processing on the node.

For the **Sensor Node Lamp interaction** approach, we provide the user with a special hardware device, the Sensor Node Lamp. It combines the functionality of a sensor node with a controllable light source that can be used to generate different light signals. The idea is to let the user illuminate the target node with the Sensor Node Lamp like he would do with a flashlight. A sensor node is then selected for interaction if it detects the predefined light signal generated by the Sensor Node Lamp based on light level variations recorded by its light sensor.

Note that both gesture-based interaction and Sensor Node Lamp interaction take advantage of sensors integrated on the nodes (in this case the light sensors) to perform tasks originally not related to sensing the node's environment. This utilization of sensors for other tasks is a recurring theme in this thesis found in several of the discussed approaches.

Our third approach, **NextOnePlease interaction**, in some sense inverts the idea of gesture-based interaction and Sensor Node Lamp interaction. While in the two aforementioned approaches the user provides input to the sensor nodes, now the sensor nodes provide information using their LEDs that allows the user to select the correct target node for an interaction. The idea is to let the user quickly browse through the list of sensor nodes in his vicinity until he reaches the target node. *NextOnePlease* highlights one node at a time by activating its LEDs. The user repeatedly requests the next node by pressing a button on his client device until the target node is highlighted. He can then select this node for interaction using a second button on the device.

7.2 Related Work

Techniques for mobile interactions between users and embedded devices are an important research topic in mobile and pervasive computing. To set our solutions for wireless sensor nodes into perspective, we discuss the fundamental interaction techniques touching, pointing and scanning that are established in mobile and pervasive computing. We also consider existing interaction solutions developed specifically for wireless sensor networks and discuss related approaches from the area of gestures. Finally, we take a short look at one specific application area and flavor of selective interactions: Security and authentication. This already motivates the next step of our work, the secure assignment of keys, presented in chapter 8.

7.2.1 Touching, Pointing and Scanning

There are three fundamental techniques for the mobile interaction with objects and devices in the environment: Touching the object, pointing at the object or scanning through a collected list of objects. Each of these techniques sets different requirements on the contribution of the user and the capabilities of the objects or the supporting infrastructure.

Touching

The idea of the touching interaction technique is to require direct physical contact between the user and the object he wants to interact with. The user needs to walk up to the object and select it by touching the object or performing a similar action that represents a direct contact. Touching is usually considered a very simple and intuitive interaction technique that, due to the direct physical contact, allows to select objects in an unambiguous manner.

Typical methods for implementing the touching interaction technique in mobile and pervasive computing include RFID tags and readers, proximity sensors or user buttons on the target device (e.g., [207, 173, 127]). If the target devices possess integrated RFID chips, then the selection of a device for interaction can be done using a short range RFID reader that is moved over the target device. Similarly, proximity sensors can be used to measure the distance between a mobile client device and potential target devices and select devices that are within a threshold distance when an interaction is initiated. Requiring the user to press a button on the device is a very simple way of implementing touching interaction. However, it is not necessarily intuitive in all scenarios and many types of devices do not allow adding a user button for initiating interactions.

Our gesture-based interaction technique can be considered a member of the group of touching interaction techniques in that it also requires the user to walk up to a sensor node to select it for interaction. Instead of asking the user to touch the sensor node (which might not be desirable for small devices including sensitive sensor chips), he performs a gesture in front of the sensor node. We will discuss related work from the area of gestures later in this section.

Pointing

The pointing interaction technique requires the user to point a device in the direction of the object he wants to interact with. The selection of the object is then done by transmitting a directed signal from the client device to the target object or by using the client device to receive or read in data from the target object. Compared to touching, pointing provides the advantage that it allows selecting objects from a certain distance if a line of sight between the user and the object is given. However, it is generally more susceptible to errors, for example when the user is pointing in a slightly wrong direction.

In previous work, one way of implementing the pointing interaction technique was to use cameras on the mobile client devices that read visual codes attached to objects to identify which object a user is pointing at [168, 169]. An even more sophisticated solution also using cameras is to perform object recognition on the mobile device to identify the target object of the interaction [49].

Merrill and Maes [138] use another approach where the mobile device detects signals actively sent out by physical objects. For this purpose, the physical objects need to be equipped with a transponder that sends out a directed infrared signal identifying the object. With the help of two client devices – an extended Bluetooth headset and a finger-worn ring these signals are received and interpreted. This allows, for example, to point to an object with the ring finger and explicitly interact with the object this way.

A third group of pointing interaction techniques uses light signals sent out by the client device for the pointing action. Ma and Paradiso [125] describe a system using a modified laser pointer that transmits a high-frequency optical signal to custom-built tags that are able to filter out interferences and use the data signal to detect whether they are target of the interaction. Rukzio et al. [173] use a similar approach receiving light from a laser pointer with a special array of light sensors attached to the objects of interest. The approach by Ghali et al. [67] is a little different. They use a camera to track the light cone of a flashlight the user points at the application area. This way, they are able to identify target objects without having to attach any hardware to the objects of interest.

Our Sensor Node Lamp interaction mechanism belongs to the group of pointing techniques that use light signals sent out by the client device for the pointing action. While related approaches rely on custom-built hardware on the receiver side [125, 173], a special challenge in the context of our work is to detect interaction attempts with standard wireless sensor node hardware.

Scanning

While touching and pointing rely on a direct exchange of information between the client device and the target object of an interaction, the scanning interaction technique works in a more indirect fashion. The idea is to collect information about smart objects in the vicinity of the user on the user's client device. This information is then presented to the user in appropriate form to allow him to select objects for an interaction. The collection of information is usually done using radio communication [173].

For the scanning technique to work, the individual objects must be able to describe themselves in sufficient detail in order to provide the user with enough information to perform a selection. Examples of such information include the location of the node, the node functionality or the context of the node.

Our third interaction approach *NextOnePlease* also lets the user select the target node for an interaction from the set of neighboring nodes. However, it differs from existing scanning interaction techniques in that it cannot rely on the sensor nodes describing themselves sufficiently and therefore works with additional visual feedback. This way, *NextOnePlease* again uses a direct exchange of information between the target object and the user instead of an indirect selection as for the scanning interaction techniques.

Rukzio et al. [173, 172] investigated the mobile interaction techniques touching, pointing and scanning concentrating on the preferences of users. They found that people generally prefer touching for nearby objects and pointing for objects farther away. Scanning is only preferred for objects outside of the user's line of sight.

7.2.2 Interacting with Sensor Nodes

Since sensor nodes and sensor networks are not traditionally used in interactive applications, there have only been few approaches on interacting with wireless sensor nodes so far. Peterson and Rus [161] describe a device they call Sensory Flashlight that allows to interact with sensor nodes lying in a specific direction of the user. They assume that both sensor nodes and the Sensory Flashlight know their exact positions. Using this location information together with directional information from an analog compass, they are able to determine which devices the Sensory Flashlight is pointing at. Although the names suggest a similarity of the Sensory Flashlight approach with our Sensor Node Lamp approach, the applied concepts are actually completely different: The Sensory Flashlight works based on location information and directional information whereas the Sensor Node Lamp uses directed light signals to initiate interactions with nodes in the environment.

The Tricorder [122] realizes the selective interaction with sensor nodes in an indoor environment also using location and direction information. The Tricorder determines its orientation using an integrated compass and its approximate location using a simple RSSI-based localization mechanism with the static sensor nodes acting as location beacons. The display of the Tricorder then shows a map of the building centered at the position of the device with the positions of the sensor nodes overlayed. Sensor nodes can be selected on the map and their data can be browsed. Unlike both the Sensory Flashlight and the Tricorder, our approaches work without relying on location information.

MoteFinder [179] uses a special directed antenna (a so-called cantenna) to strengthen the reception of radio messages from a certain direction while attenuating messages from other directions. The RSSI values of received beacon messages can then help to identify a specific node by pointing the cantenna in its direction. However, signal propagation effects limit the applicability of MoteFinder, particularly in indoor scenarios.

The follow-me application presented by Wang, Silva and Heidemann [206] is a guidance system for indoor scenarios that is based on wireless sensor networks. It is an example of an application that uses the LEDs provided by sensor nodes to interact with the user of the system: After the user has specified its destination, the system searches the shortest walkable path from the current position to the destination and marks this path for the user by having the sensor nodes on this path blink their LEDs in a synchronized fashion.

7.2.3 Gestures

There is a large body of work on the detection of gestures in the areas of mobile and wearable computing. The focus lies on allowing the user to provide input to a computing device in a simple and unobtrusive manner. Instead of only detecting that a gesture has been performed, these systems have to be able to differentiate between various gestures with each gesture triggering a certain command or providing some data input.

The Gesture Pendant [190] is a small camera device that is worn like a necklace and records and analyzes gestures performed in front of the body. It can either recognize a set of predefined gestures or user-defined, trained gestures for which hidden Markov models are used. The Gesture Pendant works independently of the external lighting conditions as it provides its own light source in the form of a large number of small infrared LEDs placed in a ring around the camera. The camera filters out non-infrared light which minimizes interferences by external light sources.

The Pendle [203] is worn like the Gesture Pendant and detects gestures in the form of explicit movements of the device with the help of a touch sensor and an acceleration sensor. The main goal is to allow explicit interactions with the environment of the device.

FreeDigiter [139] detects gestures by counting the number of fingers passed over a proximity sensor. It works with the help of infrared light that is emitted by the FreeDigiter device and reflected by the fingers moved over the device. The reflected light induces a current in the sensor which allows to detect each finger as a peak in the sensor signal. The use of infrared light allows FreeDigiter to work relatively independent of the external conditions. To filter out false positive gestures, the user must explicitly trigger the gesture recognition by shaking his head which is detected using an acceleration sensor.

Rekimoto describes the GestureWrist and the GesturePad [167], two devices for the unobtrusive detection of gestures. The GestureWrist is integrated with a wristwatch and uses capacitance and accelerations sensors. The GesturePad integrates capacitance sensors in clothing and provides for touch interaction on the body of the user.

Some projects aim to generalize the use of gestures beyond specific applications. The Georgia Tech Gesture Toolkit [213] provides a generic toolkit for gesture recognition based on hidden Markov models. Different gestures can be implemented by designing a model, specifying a grammar and training the gestures model. Ferscha and Resmerita [47] propose a generic library of gestures that can be used by different applications.

They use a 3D orientation sensor attached to an object for gesture detection. The approach of the Ubi-Finger [201] combines the selection of devices with an interaction using gestures. The device is attached to the forefinger of one hand and consists of an infrared transmitter for object selection and an acceleration sensor and a bending sensor for gesture detection. Physical objects must provide an infrared receiver to interact with the Ubi-Finger.

Compared to the gesture recognition approaches described here, the hardware requirements of our gesture-based interaction are much lower (only a light sensor). While this does not allow the recognition of more sophisticated gestures as would be required for data input using gestures, the limitation allows an efficient implementation on wireless sensor nodes.

7.2.4 Selective Interaction for Security and Authentication

The selective interaction with devices also plays an important role in the context of security, namely for authentication. Smart-Its Friends [81] connects ("peers") two devices when a user holds them together and shakes them together. This way, the explicit intention of the user to peer these devices is easily checked. Patel, Pierce and Abowd [153] describe a system that verifies that a user wants to release data from his mobile device to a public terminal by displaying a gesture challenge on the public terminal. Only if the user confirms his intention to release the data by performing the requested gesture with the mobile device, then the data is transmitted to the untrusted infrastructure device. The gesture challenge consists of a sequence of shakes and pauses and is captured using an accelerometer sensor in the mobile device.

We will pick up the idea of using selective interaction for security related goals in the next chapter again where we discuss how to securely assign keys to wireless sensor nodes.

7.3 Gesture-Based Interaction

In our first sensor node interaction approach, we aim to implement a simple gesture recognition mechanism that can be used to initiate an interaction between the user and a wireless sensor node. The main challenge lies in realizing such a gesture recognition with the very limited resources of wireless sensor nodes.

7.3.1 Approach

The idea of gesture-based interaction is to define a simple gesture that the user is able to perform in front of a sensor node using one of his hands. A node is selected for interaction if it detects such a gesture performed by the user. Since our goal is that no special hardware needs to be added to the sensor nodes (in particular no dedicated light sources [190, 139], no cameras [190] or special proximity sensors [139]), we limit ourselves to using the light sensor available on many sensor node platforms and detect gestures by analyzing variations in the recorded light level over time that result from temporarily covering the light sensor with an object or a hand.

As the light sensor only provides a generic output that is not focused on the recognition of the gesture but can be influenced by many other environmental factors (e.g., natural light level variations in the vicinity of the sensor), the recorded sensor values must be carefully interpreted to extract actual gesture information. Moreover, the complexity of gestures recognizable with a light sensor is inherently limited. However, this is acceptable in our scenario as the gesture is solely used to perform a pairing between the client device and the sensor node and not to convey complex data.

We do not let sensor nodes sample and look for gestures all the time but only after they have been explicitly activated by a trigger message coming from a client node. This provides us with two advantages: Firstly, it significantly reduces the load on the sensor node: Continuously sampling the light sensor and analyzing the readings for gestures would be expensive in terms of energy and processor cycle consumption. It might also interfere with the rest of the application running on the sensor node by consuming resources required for the execution of the application. Secondly, only sampling for gestures on demand greatly reduces the potential for false positives in the gesture detection: A random sequence of light level changes that qualifies as a gesture based on the recognition mechanism only affects the gesture-based interaction if it occurs right after a client node has sent a gesture trigger message.

There are multiple reasons why we chose the detection of simple gestures over more traditional implementations of the touching interaction paradigm. Firstly, a user button or similar equipment for receiving direct input from the user is not available on most sensor node platforms. Even when available, like on the TelosB sensor node platform, such buttons are usually very small and inconvenient to use. Secondly, asking the user to touch the light sensor (thereby completely covering it and providing a clear sensor stimulus) would require the user to know where on the node the light sensor is located. This makes the approach more difficult to use than just moving the hand over the node. Thirdly, in many cases we do not want the user to touch the sensor node as the node might provide sensors or other hardware sensitive to such contacts and touching the node might interfere with the normal operations. Finally, blocking nearly all ambient light also happens during the normal node operation (e.g., people moving in front of a node in dimly lit scenarios). To avoid false positives, we need the ability to check for multiple "uncovered" – "covered" – "uncovered" sequences which are easily provided by moving the hand back and forth in front of the node.

7.3.2 Gesture Types and Gesture Recognition

We detect gestures performed by the user moving his hand over the sensor node. Such a gesture results in a uncovered-covered-uncovered sequence of states that can be detected using the light sensor values recorded during this time. We expect the sensor node to record significantly lower light sensor values while it is covered by the hand of the user compared to the uncovered state.

As an illustrating example, Fig. 7.1 shows the light levels recorded by a TelosB sensor

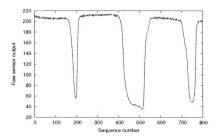

Figure 7.1: Example light levels recorded with gestures

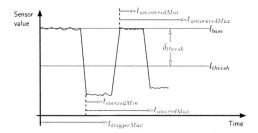

Figure 7.2: Illustrated gesture recognition process

node over a time period of approximately seven seconds while the user performed a gesture. In this case, the gesture consisted of the user moving his hand over the node three times in a row. All three movements are clearly identifiable as short time periods exhibiting considerably lower sensor values. However, the example also illustrates that we have to expect differences in the length of both the "sensor covered" time periods and the "sensor uncovered" time periods in between. Consequently, the gesture detection mechanism cannot set tight bounds on the event timings here but must be able to deal with varying gesture speeds. The maximum speed of the hand movement that can still be recognized as a gesture depends on the sampling frequency of the light sensor.

We detect a gesture starting with the base sensor value l_{base} and require to go below a threshold sensor value l_{thresh} to detect a transition to the "sensor covered" state. Our gesture detection mechanism also defines minimum and maximum lengths of the "sensor covered" ($t_{coveredMin}$ and $t_{coveredMax}$) and "sensor uncovered" ($t_{uncoveredMin}$ and $t_{uncoveredMax}$) time periods. Defining not only maximum but also minimum times helps in filtering out false positive state changes. Fig. 7.2 illustrates the threshold and timeout values used as part of the gesture recognition process.

Larger values for δ_{thresh}, the difference between the base sensor value l_{base} and the threshold value l_{thresh}, decrease the likelihood of false positive events caused by normal light level variations. However, too large values impede the detection of gestures, particularly in dimly lit scenarios. Moreover, initial experiments showed that the absolute ambient light levels recorded by nodes can vary significantly even within the same room requiring different values for δ_{thresh} on each node. To provide the required flexibility in that regard, the nodes perform a self-calibration process each time the gesture recognition procedure is started and determine the threshold value l_{thresh} dynamically. We found that – while the absolute light levels change – the ratio between the base sensor value and the sensor values recorded in the "sensor covered" state $\frac{l_{base}}{l_{covered}}$ remains relatively constant. We therefore calculate the threshold value using the following equation:

$$l_{thresh} = a \times l_{base} \qquad (7.1)$$

a is a constant value with $0 < a < 1$ predefined at compile time or configured by the client device when announcing the gesture interaction attempt. Smaller values of a reduce the probability of false positives but also complicate the detection of legitimate gestures.

An additional method for avoiding false positive gesture events is to define gestures that require the user to move his hand over the sensor node multiple times (like shown in the example in Fig. 7.1). Requiring a longer sequence of changes between the "sensor uncovered" and the "sensor covered" states reduces the likelihood of such light variations occurring randomly. However, it is important to consider that the burden on the user grows with the number of times he needs to move his hand over the sensor node. Our implementation supports specifying the required number of state changes dynamically at runtime.

7.3.3 Interaction Protocol

Fig. 7.3 shows the time diagram of a successful interaction between a client node and a sensor node (called target node in the figure). The following explanation of the individual protocol steps refers to events numbered in the time diagram in Fig. 7.3.

The client node initiates the process by sending out a *gesture announcement message* by broadcast (1). It contains information on the type of gesture (i.e., the number of times the sensor is required to be covered to qualify as a gesture). The *gesture announcement message* is received by all sensor nodes S_{neigh} lying within the communication range of the client node (2). They form the candidate set for the subsequent gesture recognition process. In the example these are the target node and node 2. In reaction to this message reception, the nodes sample their light sensors in order to record their respective base sensor values l_{base} before the actual gesture starts[1]. They then continue to sample their light sensors every $t_{sampleInterval}$ time units.

As part of the gesture, the user temporarily covers the target node with his hand. This is detected when the sampled value l_{sample} lies below the threshold value l_{thresh}

---

[1]We will discuss some peculiarities of this sampling process in Section 7.4.3 when we discuss a similar sampling as part of the Sensor Node Lamp interaction protocol.

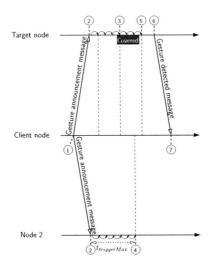

Figure 7.3: Time diagram of a gesture-based interaction

for the first time (3). The target node then continues to check for light events until the specified gesture is completed. In the example in Fig. 7.3 we use a simple uncovered-covered-uncovered gesture which means that the user needs to move his hand over the node only once. When the complete gesture has been detected (5), then the target node reports back to the client node with a *gesture detected message* (6). Node 2, together with all other nodes from S_{neigh} that did not detect a gesture performed by the user, times out after $t_{triggerMax}$ time units (4), stops sampling its light sensor and does not send any feedback to the client node.

Upon receiving the *gesture detected message* (7), the client node is informed about the node identifier id_{target} of the node its user wants to interact with. Using this node identifier, the client device is able to initiate a one-to-one communication with the target node or simply report it to the user for later use.

If the sensor node has the capability to provide (visual) feedback (e.g., the LEDs on TelosB nodes), then we use this to directly inform the user on the success of the gesture recognition. If the node does not provide the expected feedback, then the user knows that his gesture has not been correctly detected and is able to repeat the process.

Fig. 7.4 shows the state diagram of wireless sensor nodes that are candidates for interaction attempts using gesture-based interaction. Starting from the "Ready" state, a node passes to the "Sampling base value" state upon receiving a *gesture announcement message*. Once the node has determined its base sensor value, it proceeds to the "Uncovered" state and then switches back and forth between this state and the

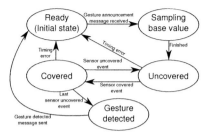

Figure 7.4: Gesture-based interaction state diagram

"Covered" state with each sensor event until either the expected gesture has been detected (going to the "Gesture detected" state) or until a sensor event did not occur within the specified time bounds (going back to the "Ready" state).

7.4 Sensor Node Lamp Interaction

While our gesture-based interaction provides a very simple and effective way of pairing a client device with the target sensor node for interaction, it requires that the user has direct physical access to the sensor node in order to perform the gesture. In this section we present an alternative mechanism that overcomes this limitation with the help of a special hardware device, the Sensor Node Lamp (SNL).

7.4.1 Approach

Like gesture-based interaction, the Sensor Node Lamp interaction mechanism also uses the light sensor of a node to detect whether it is the target of an interaction. The idea is to have the user point the Sensor Node Lamp in the direction of the node he wants to interact with (the target node). A light source integrated into the Sensor Node Lamp is then used to illuminate the target node which is able to infer that it is the target of the interaction request based on the significant difference between its original light level and the light level recorded while the Sensor Node Lamp is active and pointing at the node. The light levels of all other nodes not lying within the light beam of the Sensor Node Lamp remain unaffected.

Using a predefined sequence of time intervals with the Sensor Node Lamp in the "light on" or "light off" state (instead of just turning on the Sensor Node Lamp) helps the receiver nodes filtering out false positive interaction events as they only participate in the interaction if they were able to decode the expected signal correctly.

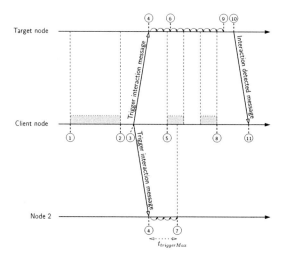

Figure 7.5: Time diagram of an interaction using the Sensor Node Lamp

7.4.2 Interaction Protocol

Fig. 7.5 shows the time diagram of a typical sequence of events for the interaction between client and sensor nodes using the Sensor Node Lamp. As in the time diagram illustrating gesture-based interaction, it shows the client node, the target node and a third node (node 2) located in the neighborhood of the client node and therefore part of S_{neigh} but not participating in the interaction. The user starts the interaction process by pressing the user button on the Sensor Node Lamp. This does not trigger any communication yet but only activates the LED (1) to help the user in pointing the light beam in the direction of the target node. We call this the aiming phase. When the user releases the button, the light is turned off (2) and the actual interaction protocol is started.

As a first step, the client node broadcasts a *trigger interaction message* (3) to alert the neighboring nodes in S_{neigh} of the upcoming interaction. Upon receiving this message (4), a sensor node starts sampling its base sensor value l_{base} which is then – together with a threshold distance δ_{thresh} – used to differentiate between "light on" and "light off" sensor readings.

After having recorded l_{base}, the node continues to periodically sample its light sensor every $t_{sampleInterval}$ time units. The client node meanwhile waits for $t_{triggerDelay}$ time units. It then activates the LED of the Sensor Node Lamp (5) for a time period of $t_{lampActive}$ time units, waits for $t_{lampInactive}$ time units with the lamp deactivated and then activates the Sensor Node Lamp for another $t_{lampActive}$ time units. This way, it sends a simple on-off-on-off light pattern that can be detected by any sensor node lying

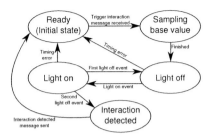

Figure 7.6: Sensor Node Lamp interaction state diagram

within the light beam of the Sensor Node Lamp. Unlike for gesture-based interaction, we are able to precisely control the timings of this pattern (using 200 ms for each time interval in our experiments) and can use them on the receiver side to filter out false positive light level changes.

The target node detects the first "light on" event triggered by the Sensor Node Lamp after a few sampling cycles (6). This triggers the light pattern recognition mechanism which continues to sample the light sensor and checks whether the sequence of light events is detected within the expected time intervals. Since only the intended receiver node lies within the light beam of the Sensor Node Lamp, only this node is able to detect the advertised on-off-on-off light pattern. Node 2 and all other nodes from $S_{neigh} \setminus \{n_{target}\}$ time out after $t_{triggerMax}$, stop sampling their light sensors and do not participate in the rest of the protocol (7).

Once the receiver node has successfully finished the light pattern detection with the end of the second "light on" period (9), it knows that it belongs to the set of target nodes S_{target}. It reacts by sending an *interaction detected message* back to the client (10).

After having finished sending the light pattern (8), the client node has started waiting for *interaction detected messages* coming back from neighboring nodes (11). It waits for $t_{replyDelayMax}$ time units for such messages and adds the node identifiers of all responding nodes to the set Id_{target}. More than one node can reply with an *interaction detected message* if multiple nodes lie within the light cone of the Sensor Node Lamp. All further communication as part of the interaction can now be directly addressed to the target node (or the set of target nodes).

Fig. 7.6 shows the state diagram of the Sensor Node Lamp interaction receiver nodes. Comparing it with the state diagram of gesture-based interaction in Fig. 7.4 again shows the high level of similarity of the two approaches. All states and state transitions of gesture-based interaction have a direct counterpart in the Sensor Node Lamp interaction approach. Major differences like the expected light value patterns or the checking of the event timings do not affect the state diagram significantly.

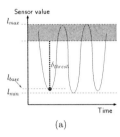 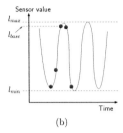

(a)   (b)

Figure 7.7: Effects of light oscillations on base value sampling

7.4.3 Dealing with Light Level Variations

Preliminary experiments with the Sensor Node Lamp have revealed an additional challenge not covered by the original protocol. While the described approach worked reliably in daylight scenarios, it often failed when using artificial light. We found the reason for this behavior in the properties of fluorescent tubes used for the illumination of rooms and hallways in many public buildings. Instead of providing a constant light level, their intensity oscillates with a frequency of 100 Hz (or 120 Hz in countries where the frequency of the electrical system is 60 Hz). While this flickering is usually not detectable for the human eye, it strongly influences the values recorded by the light sensors which – under seemingly stable conditions – oscillate within a certain range of values $[l_{min}, l_{max}]$.

For small values of the threshold distance δ_{thresh} (which are important for the Sensor Node Lamp approach to work over larger distances and under conditions with a high ambient light level), the outcome of the light signal detection can depend on the times the base sensor value and the subsequent light signal sensor values are sampled: If the base sensor value l_{base} lies near l_{min}, then already the oscillation of values caused by the fluorescent tubes can trigger "light on" events. The problem is that such untimely light events can disrupt the light signal detection and the interaction setup with the Sensor Node Lamp fails.

The problem is illustrated in Fig. 7.7 (a) where the base value l_{base} lies near the minimum value of the current light oscillation l_{min}. Samples taken in the shaded area are now detected as belonging to the "light on" state without the Sensor Node Lamp actually being activated.

To deal with this problem, we have extended the procedure for recording l_{base} that is illustrated in Fig. 7.7 (b): Instead of sampling only once, we sample five times in a row with 2 ms wait time in between and use the maximum of the five values as l_{base}. With a high probability, this gives us a base value which lies near l_{max} and – as the evaluation shows – effectively eliminates the problem of false positive "light on" events during the signal detection.

As mentioned before, a similar problem also exists for gesture-based interaction.

Figure 7.8: The Sensor Node Lamp prototype

There we use the same basic solution but take the minimum instead of the maximum of the five samples as the base value.

7.4.4 Sensor Node Lamp Hardware

We have built a prototype of the Sensor Node Lamp that can be mounted on top of a TelosB sensor node. Fig. 7.8 shows a side view of this prototype labeling its main components. The central element of the Sensor Node Lamp is a powerful 1 watt LED fixed behind a lens that focuses the light in a beam with a cone angle of 8.7 degrees. We use a LED that emits red light at a dominant wavelength of 625 nanometers which lies within the optimal reception range of the light sensors on the TelosB sensor nodes. Moreover, compared to LEDs emitting light in other colors (e.g., green or white), the user is still able to see and differentiate the red light of this LED well even in scenarios with a high ambient light level. The circuit board of the Sensor Node Lamp is connected to the board of the TelosB sensor node and the state of the LED (on or off) can be controlled from the TelosB node using one of its digital output pins.

The Sensor Node Lamp also provides a button that allows the user to provide input to the application running on the sensor node. For the Sensor Node Lamp interaction, we use the button to let the user initiate the protocol. Other notable features of the Sensor Node Lamp hardware are a separate power supply in the form of two AA batteries and a constant current transformer used to provide a constant light level over the lifetime of the batteries. The pure hardware cost of the Sensor Node Lamp prototype (not including the cost for design and assembly) is approximately 35€.

We decided against using a laser as the light source of the Sensor Node Lamp mainly for two reasons: Firstly, the spreading of the light in the Sensor Node Lamp helps the user in that he does not need to point directly to the light sensor and shaky hands do not prevent a successful interaction. Secondly, since we expect a device like the Sensor Node Lamp to be used in smart environments like smart homes, we were worried about the possible negative impact of lasers or laser pointers on the eyes of people in these environments.

7.4.5 Flashlight Analogy

With its LED light source, the lens focusing the light into a light beam and the button used to control the lamp, the Sensor Node Lamp not only looks a little bit like a flashlight, it is also used in a very similar manner: Pressing the user button turns on the light. The light beam can then be directed at the object of interest by orienting the Sensor Node Lamp accordingly. This flashlight analogy is an important aspect for the usability of the Sensor Node Lamp as a flashlight is a well-known device most users are familiar with. Being able to explain the functionality of the Sensor Node Lamp starting from the flashlight analogy greatly simplifies the explanation of the device and its working principle to new users.

The task that the user has to perform is kept intentionally simple. He only needs to point the device in the direction of the target node and illuminate it with the Sensor Node Lamp for a short time period. Everything else happens automatically in the background without requiring the user's attention.

Another important advantage of the flashlight analogy is the immediate visual feedback that the Sensor Node Lamp provides to the user. The user is able to see where he is pointing and which node he is targeting with the Sensor Node Lamp. By moving nearer to the target, the user is able to easily reduce the size of the target area which can be necessary depending on the deployment density.

7.5 NextOnePlease Interaction

Gesture-based interaction and Sensor Node Lamp interaction both rely on using light sensors to facilitate interactions. However, in some scenarios such light sensors might not be available or using them might interfere with the normal tasks of the sensor nodes. In this section, we introduce *NextOnePlease* (NOP), an interaction solution that works without using any sensor information. While in the first two approaches the user provides input to the sensor nodes, *NextOnePlease* inverts this procedure and lets the sensor nodes provide information to the user which he can use to select the correct target node.

7.5.1 Approach

Sensor nodes are usually very limited in the types of visual feedback that they are able to provide. However, most current sensor node platforms provide a few small, controllable LEDs (see Table 2.1 in Chapter 2). Given their relatively low cost, we expect that most future sensor node devices – whether targeted at the research community or the consumer market – will feature similar equipment. We also expect that other small pervasive computing devices that do not possess any sensors might be equipped with such LEDs that could be used as part of node interactions. *NextOnePlease* uses these LEDs to combine wireless communication with visual hints provided by the nodes that allow the user to select the correct node he wants to interact with.

We first experimented with the nodes showing and reporting random sequences of its individual LEDs turned on or off. By comparing the LED sequence shown by a node with reported sequences displayed in the user interface of the client device, the user was able to identify which node he wanted to interact with. However, we found that comparing LED states on the node and on the display in real-time is an exhausting task, particularly when the number of candidate nodes is large. Moreover, due to the small size of the LEDs and their small spacing, differentiating between different LED states is only possible from a small distance. For that reason, *NextOnePlease* only uses two LED states on the individual nodes, "LEDs turned on" or "LEDs turned off", and does not require the user to consult information on the display of his client device.

As for the other two approaches, we assume that the client node is able to communicate with a whole set of nodes in its neighborhood which form the candidate set S_{neigh} for the interaction setup. *NextOnePlease* allows the user to browse through a list of the nodes from S_{neigh} (sorted based on the context of the client) until he finds the target node. For this purpose, *NextOnePlease* highlights one node at a time by turning its LEDs on. The user can then either select the highlighted node or ask for the next one – both by simply pressing a button on the client device.

NextOnePlease keeps the task of the user intentionally simple. Selecting a node only requires to repeatedly press a button (for requesting the next node) until the LEDs on the target node are activated. Then this node can be selected using the second button. This browsing through the list can be done very quickly and without interpreting sophisticated information which allows a fast selection of the target node.

Note the important difference between the *NextOnePlease* approach and the basic concept of scanning interaction approaches. Scanning interaction techniques require the candidate nodes to describe themselves in order to allow the user to select one or multiple nodes offline based on this description. With *NextOnePlease*, in contrast, nodes are selected based on visual information directly provided from the target node to the user.

7.5.2 Interaction Protocol

Fig. 7.9 illustrates the interaction procedure in a time diagram with the help of an example interaction between a client node and a target node with two other nodes lying within the communication range of the client ($|S_{target}| = 1$, $|S_{neigh}| = 3$).

The client node initiates the procedure by sending out an *activate message* by broadcast (1). Similar to the previous two approaches, this informs the neighboring nodes about the interaction request of the user. It also triggers the nodes to turn off their LEDs and to start sending periodic *report messages* back to the client node (2-4). Based on these report messages, the client node is able to infer the set of candidate nodes S_{neigh} for the interaction and sorts them in a list.

We require the explicit initiation of the interaction procedure using the activate message in order to save on resources of the nodes (i.e., for sending report messages and for operating the LEDs) while no interaction is underway. Moreover, we use a

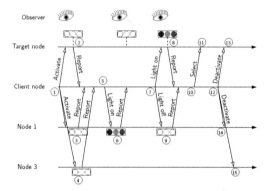

Figure 7.9: Time diagram of an example *NextOnePlease* interaction

soft state approach and let the nodes stop participating in the procedure if they have not received a message from the client node within a certain time.

The next step of the protocol is triggered by the user pressing the "Next node" button. The client device reacts by sending a *light on message* (5) to the first entry in its internal node list (node 1 in the example). Upon receiving this message, node 1 activates its LEDs and announces its new LED state with a *report message* (6). Each time the "Next node" button is pressed, a *light off message* is sent to the current node and the next node in the list is activated with a *light on message* (7-9). If the end of the internal node list is reached, then the client node starts again with the first node. This way, the user can easily browse through the node list multiple times, for example when he missed the target node during the previous iteration. This process continues until the user detects that the LEDs of the target node are turned on and presses the "Select current node" button. Since the client device knows the identifier of the highlighted node, it can add the identifier to Id_{target}. On the protocol level, this triggers a *select message* being sent to the target node (10). When the target node receives this message (11), we provide a special visual feedback to the user in the form of a short blinking sequence that confirms the successful selection.

If desired, the user is able to continue the process and to select additional nodes. In the example, however, the user ends the selection and the client node sends out a *deactivate message* by broadcast (12). Upon receiving this message (13-15), the sensor nodes stop sending periodic report messages.

Fig. 7.10 shows the state diagram of the receiver side of the *NextOnePlease* inter-action protocol. The node starts and remains in the "Inactive" state until it receives an *activate message* coming from a client device. In the "Ready" state it periodically sends *report messages* back to the client device to inform about its presence and its LED state. Upon receiving a *light on message*, the node proceeds to the "LEDs on" state where it remains until it either receives a *light off message* or a *select message*.

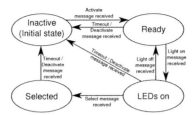

Figure 7.10: *NextOnePlease* interaction state diagram

In the first case, the node returns to the "Ready" state. In the latter case, it switches to the "Selected" state and starts the visual feedback sequence mentioned above. The node returns from the "Ready" state, the "LEDs on" state and the "Selected" state back to the "Inactive" state if it receives a *deactivate message* or if it times out in case the *activate message* has not been refreshed for a specified timeout interval.

7.5.3 Implementation

Like for the other two interaction approaches, we used TelosB sensor nodes for the prototype implementation. The TelosB nodes provide a red, a green and a blue LED which can be activated and deactivated by software. In order to get the maximum achievable visual difference between the two LED states, we always activate or deactivate all three LEDs at the same time.

The *NextOnePlease* client application runs on Sharp Zaurus PDAs. It provides a graphical user interface with a "Next node" and a "Select current node" button used for node selection. However, for an easier and faster node selection, two hardware buttons on the side of the PDA can be used for the same task.

Fig. 7.11 shows a screen shot of the application. The main elements are the "Next node" button and the "Select current node" button. The UI also shows a sorted list of all nodes lying within the communication range of the client node together with their LED states and one button per node that allows to directly select nodes from the list. This representation of all candidate nodes in a list that the user can browse reminds of the scanning interaction paradigm. Note, however, that only the "Next node" button and the "Select current node" are necessary for the interaction and that no user interface is required at all if the two hardware buttons of the PDA are used. Going beyond our prototype implementation, we imagine that in many cases the interaction with nodes using *NextOnePlease* could be done using a much simpler and smaller device than a PDA that basically only consists of two buttons.

The client application internally maintains a list of nodes it has been receiving report messages from. This list represents the set of candidate nodes S_{neigh}. To deal with very large numbers of nodes in the neighborhood of a client device, we use the received signal strength (RSSI) values of the report messages as a criterion for sorting the node list. This is based on the assumption that report messages from nodes in

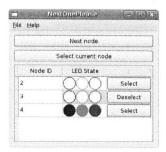

Figure 7.11: *NextOnePlease* interaction UI

the direct vicinity of the client (which the user most likely wants to interact with) are received with a higher RSSI value than from nodes farther away. Consequently, nodes with higher RSSI values should be offered for interaction first.

In chapter 5 we have discussed that many different environmental factors influence the RSSI values of messages and distort the distance/signal-strength relationship. For that reason, we do not directly sort the list by the RSSI values of the nodes. Instead, we use the RSSI values to partition the nodes into three groups: "Nearby", "medium distance", "far away". Nodes in the first group are browsed before nodes in the second group which in turn come before the nodes in the last group. It could also be useful to present the nodes from the first group a second time before the user browses through the list of nodes from the third group. To avoid frequent group changes due to the instability of the RSSI criterion, we use a weighted moving average based on the messages received over time.

7.6 Evaluation

In this section, we show and discuss results from evaluating our three sensor node interaction approaches. We start by taking a look at their memory consumption on the individual sensor nodes and continue with an evaluation of the interaction distances. We then discuss the results of a user study and end the evaluation with guidelines on selecting one of the approaches for a specific application scenario.

7.6.1 Memory Overhead

The memory consumption of our interaction mechanisms is a relevant factor, because both program memory and main memory are very limited resources on typical sensor node platforms.

The actual overhead of our three interaction mechanisms depends on the application the mechanisms are integrated with as they can share code with other application

Table 7.1: Size overhead analysis

		Blink	Oscilloscope Temperature	Oscilloscope Light	MViz
Original	ROM	2656 bytes	13442 bytes	16608 bytes	28150 bytes
	RAM	55 bytes	394 bytes	438 bytes	1912 bytes
Gesture	ROM	17498 bytes	19662 bytes	18674 bytes	29914 bytes
	RAM	528 bytes	634 bytes	602 bytes	2074 bytes
SNL	ROM	17298 bytes	19416 bytes	18442 bytes	29652 bytes
	RAM	510 bytes	616 bytes	584 bytes	2060 bytes
NOP	ROM	12084 bytes	14222 bytes	17370 bytes	28734 bytes
	RAM	354 bytes	462 bytes	506 bytes	1980 bytes

parts running on the sensor node (e.g., radio communication or sensor access modules). To evaluate this, we have integrated gesture-based interaction, Sensor Node Lamp interaction and *NextOnePlease* interaction with three well-known applications from the TinyOS source tree: Blink, Oscilloscope and MViz. For the Oscilloscope application, we used two different configurations – one using the temperature sensor (Oscilloscope Temperature) and one using the light sensor (Oscilloscope Light) on the TelosB nodes. This difference is significant, because gesture-based interaction and Sensor Node Lamp interaction both use the light sensor but not the temperature sensor for their operation. We configured MViz to also use the light sensor. Table 8.1 summarizes the resulting size values for both program memory (ROM) and the main memory (RAM) of the nodes.

Overall, the memory overhead of all three approaches is reasonably small and should allow integrating the mechanisms with a variety of applications on different sensor node platforms. As expected, the overhead is largest for the Blink application, because its original version neither uses any sensor nor the wireless communication interface. These modules then have to be added by the respective interaction mechanism (adding up to 14842 bytes in program memory and 473 bytes in main memory). Much of this overhead already disappears in more realistic applications that already include the communication components (e.g., Oscilloscope Temperature). The lowest overhead is generated for Oscilloscope Light and MViz which already contain the code for both wireless communication and for accessing the light sensor (e.g., only between 584 bytes and 1764 bytes of program memory and between 68 bytes and 162 bytes of main memory when integrated with MViz).

As expected, *NextOnePlease* has the lowest memory requirements among the three interaction mechanisms. On the one hand, this is due to not requiring access to any sensor information. On the other hand, the implementation of the interaction mechanism is particularly simple, because the application logic for the sensor node selection is implemented on the client device whereas the task of the sensor node is comparatively simple.

7.6.2 Interaction distance

The maximum distance between the user and the node he wants to interact with is an essential property as it determines in which situations the interaction mechanism

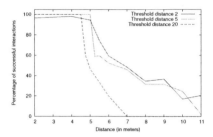

Figure 7.12: Sensor Node Lamp success rate over distance

can be used.

Gesture-based Interaction

Gesture-based interaction has the strongest limitations with respect to the interaction distance as the user needs to directly approach the node for performing the gesture. Our experiments showed that a distance of 5 centimeters between the hand and the sensor node is reasonable. While larger distances could be supported by decreasing the threshold distance δ_{thresh}, this would greatly increase the potential of false positive gestures being detected.

Sensor Node Lamp Interaction

For the Sensor Node Lamp, we evaluated the maximum interaction distance and the success rate of interactions at different distances in a controlled experiment. We placed the Sensor Node Lamp and a receiver node at specific distances of each other in the normally lit hallway of a building. We then measured the success rate of Sensor Node Lamp interactions based on 200 trials per distance. Fig. 7.12 shows the results for distances between 2 and 11 meters for three different values of δ_{thresh}. Note that we are using raw sensor and threshold values here instead of meaningful light units to avoid any conversion overhead on the nodes.

When the distance between the Sensor Node Lamp and receiver node increases, the impact of the Sensor Node Lamp on the light sensor decreases thereby decreasing the difference between the two light states. For $\delta_{thresh} = 5$ and $\delta_{thresh} = 20$, we were able to achieve a 100% success rate for distances up to 5 meters and 4.5 meters respectively. Above these threshold distances, our experiments showed a sharp decline of the success rate. However, we were still able to initiate some interactions up to a distance of 6 meters at a threshold of $\delta_{thresh} = 20$ and up to 11 meters using the smaller threshold $\delta_{thresh} = 5$. The explanation for this behavior lies in the light level variations caused by the fluorescent lamps installed in the hallway: Above a certain distance, the difference δ_{impact} between the light levels in the "light on" and the "light off" states becomes too small to compensate the continuous oscillations of the light levels in all cases. Whether a "light on" event can be detected now depends on the timing of the background oscillations while the light values are sampled. The smaller δ_{impact} becomes with an increasing distance, the more situations exist where the measured light level does not suffice for a "light on" event.

Fig. 7.12 also shows an example for the threshold distance δ_{thresh} being selected too small ($\delta_{thresh} = 2$) which allows normal light level variations to trigger light events. As we are checking the timings of the Sensor Node Lamp light signal on the receiver side, false positives are still effectively prevented and we could not detect any during extensive experiments. However, untimely light events can disturb the detection of an actual Sensor Node Lamp light signal and impede a successful interaction setup. This is illustrated in Fig. 7.12 for a threshold of 2: Even for small distances, a 100% success rate cannot be achieved as external light events interfere with some of the signal detections. For larger distances, however, the smaller threshold is able to produce a slightly higher success rate than for a threshold of 5. The explanation for this is again that a smaller threshold allows tolerating a smaller light level difference δ_{impact} between the "light on" and "light off" states.

Overall, with a maximum interaction distance of 5 meters, the Sensor Node Lamp interaction approach can be used comfortably in typical indoor scenarios even within quite large rooms.

Besides the maximum interaction distance, the size of the area covered by the Sensor Node Lamp is also an important usability factor as it determines the minimum distance among nodes that are to be addressed individually from a given distance. It also shows whether – if desired – multiple neighboring nodes can be selected in a single step.

Unfortunately, we cannot determine such values analytically based on the hardware specification of the Sensor Node Lamp, because it is impossible to create a perfect light beam that does not spread out. The specified cone angle of 8.7 degrees of the lens used in our Sensor Node Lamp prototype refers to the angle at which half of the peak light intensity is reached (e.g, a circular area with a diameter of 15.21 centimeters at a distance of 1 meter) and does neither correspond to the visible size nor the size of the area where the light sensors are able to detect the light signal. Instead, we measured the maximum distance among the light sensors of two nodes at which both are able to detect the same light signal by a Sensor Node Lamp initiating an interaction. Fig. 7.13 (a) illustrates our experimental setup and Fig. 7.13 (b) shows the results of these measurements. It also shows a curve for the practical receiver node distance which we defined as the maximum distance among receiver nodes at which we were able to initiate at least five successful interactions in a row.

The practical receiver node distance only grows up to a little more than 0.5 meters (at a sender-receiver distance of 2.5 meters) and then falls again as the decreasing light level influence of the Sensor Node Lamp is only sufficient for reliably triggering interactions near the center of the light beam. Even the maximum receiver node distance stays below one meter for a sender-receiver distance of 4 meters. Moreover, only very few interaction attempts succeeded at that receiver node distance. Overall, the results illustrate that the Sensor Node Lamp allows an effective interaction with

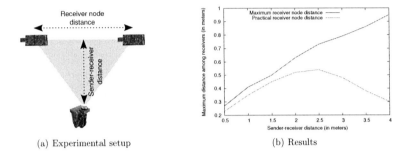

(a) Experimental setup   (b) Results

Figure 7.13: Maximum distance among Sensor Node Lamp receiver nodes

individual nodes even for relatively dense deployments of nodes. Multiple nodes can only be reliably selected at the same time if they are placed at very short distances of each other.

NextOnePlease Interaction

For *NextOnePlease*, the maximum interaction distance is the maximum distance from which the user is still able to determine whether the LEDs on the target node are turned on or off. This clearly depends on the properties of the LEDs used on the node, the specific scenario (i.e., the lighting conditions) and also on the user himself. To get an idea of the distances possible, we set up one indoor experiment in a hallway and one experiment outdoors using TelosB sensor nodes. We measured the maximum distance at which it was still possible to tell whether the LEDs of a node were turned off or on.

For the indoor scenario, we were still able to tell the LED states apart from a distance of more than 50 meters! While the details of the sensor node itself were hardly recognizable at that distance, the light of the LEDs (or the lack of light) was still clearly visible. As expected, the maximum distance in the outdoor scenario depended on the specific settings. In the worst case, bright sunlight shining directly at the node, detection of the LED states was possible up to a distance of three meters. With the sun coming from the side or from behind the node, the maximum interaction distance lay between 8 and 15 meters.

Overall, the experiments have shown that distance is not a real limiting factor for *NextOnePlease* indoors and that interactions over reasonable distances are also possible using this method in outdoor scenarios.

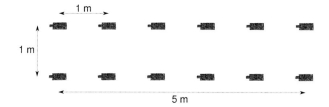

Figure 7.14: Experimental setup of the node interaction user study

7.6.3 User Study

To learn more about how good our approaches support users in interacting with wireless sensor nodes, we performed a small user study in which we asked 12 participants recruited from students and staff at the Universität Bonn to use each of the three systems to execute a set of interaction tasks. Before the experiment started, each participant got an explanation and a short demonstration of how the three interaction mechanisms work.

As the basic experimental setup, we placed 12 TelosB sensor nodes on the wall of a large room arranged in a 6x2 Cartesian grid with an edge length of one meter. The bottom row was placed approximately 90 centimeters above the floor. The experimental setup is illustrated in Fig. 7.14. For each run, we placed colored signs at three randomly selected nodes to mark them as target nodes and asked the participant to select these nodes for interaction using gesture-based interaction, Sensor Node Lamp interaction and *NextOnePlease*. If an interaction attempt failed, we asked the user to try it again until being successful. The participants repeated each experiment three times with different nodes being used as target nodes in each run.

During the experiments we were mainly interested in investigating two aspects: Firstly, we measured the required time for completing each interaction task for assessing the overhead of each method. Secondly, we looked at the success rate of performing the interaction.

Interaction Times

Fig. 7.15 summarizes the results of the measurements of the interaction times in our experiments showing both the average time required by the participants as well as the maximum and minimum times. Interacting with the help of the Sensor Node Lamp clearly outperforms both gesture-based interaction and *NextOnePlease*. With only 6.82 seconds required on average for selecting three nodes, the participants completed the Sensor Node Lamp interactions nearly two times faster than with *NextOnePlease* and 2.8 times faster than with gesture-based interaction. There also do not exist significant outliers for the Sensor Node Lamp approach whereas the longest run with *NextOnePlease* took more than 30 seconds and more than 45 seconds for gesture-based interaction.

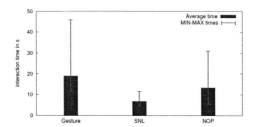

Figure 7.15: Interaction times

Table 7.2: Success rates and rates of false positives

	Success rate	Rate of false positives
Gesture-based interaction	89.4%	4.6%
Sensor Node Lamp interaction	97.22%	0.93%
NextOnePlease interaction	100%	0%

Considering the complexity of the interaction tasks (selecting three nodes in a row), the average interaction times of all three approaches fulfill our expectations and indicate that an efficient use is possible in real-world scenarios.

Success Rate

Table 7.2 provides an overview of the average percentage of successful interaction attempts in our experiments with our three interaction approaches (success rate) and the average percentage of false positives occurring during these experiments.

Failures of gesture-based interactions were mainly due to users moving their hand too quickly over the nodes or keeping too much distance to the light sensors of the nodes. However, some failures were also caused by gesture announcement messages being lost. Here, the reliability of message reception was negatively influenced by the often very small distance between the client device and the receiving node when sending the message. Overall, 89.4% of the interaction attempts succeeded. There was also a small number of false positives (in 4.6% of the cases) due to the small distance among the nodes in the experiment. These false positives were mainly caused by the shadow of users moving to and interacting with neighboring nodes. Our setup with relatively small distances among the nodes and nodes placed one meter above other nodes represents a particularly critical case with respect to the danger of false positives. We expect this rate to be lower in typical real-world deployments.

Only very few interaction attempts with the Sensor Node Lamp failed resulting in a success rate of 97.22%. They were all easily and quickly recovered in a second attempt. Only one participant managed to create a false positive event once activating two neighboring nodes at the same time (0.93% false positives).

False negatives do not occur for interactions with *NextOnePlease* as any target node

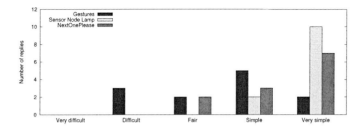

Figure 7.16: User survey – Difficulty of understanding the working principle

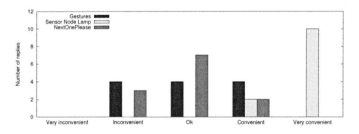

Figure 7.17: User survey – Convenience of use

the user misses while clicking through the list of nodes will be offered again in the next round. This way, if the user makes a mistake in the node selection process, this does not result in a false negative but rather in a higher interaction time. As also no participant falsely selected a node, we achieved a 100% success rate and a 0% rate of false positives for *NextOnePlease*.

As repeating failed interaction attempts is simple and inexpensive, the success rate of all three approaches qualify them for practical use. For gesture-based interaction, our approach with the highest rate of errors, we also expect a higher success rate achievable by experienced users.

User Survey

After completing the experiment with all three systems, we let the participants fill out a short questionnaire asking about their experience with gesture-based interaction, Sensor Node Lamp interaction and *NextOnePlease*. They rated the initial difficulty of understanding the working principle of the mechanisms (from -2 ("Very difficult") to +2 ("Very simple")) and the convenience of using the interaction mechanisms (from -2 ("Very inconvenient") to +2 ("Very convenient")). Fig. 7.16 and Fig. 7.17 show the distribution of responses for both questions.

Our participants were very satisfied with both the ease of understanding and the

Table 7.3: Interaction method selection criteria

	Gesture	SNL	NOP
Hardware required	Light sensors	Light sensors + SNL	LEDs
Interaction distance	$\leq 5cm$	$\leq 5m$	$\leq 8m$
User effort	Medium	Low	Medium
Scenarios	Indoor+Outdoor	Mainly indoor	Indoor+Outdoor
Scalability	Good	Good	Limited

convenience of use of the Sensor Node Lamp interaction (1.83 average rating in both categories). *NextOnePlease* was also easily understood (1.42 points) by the users but was considered more critically in terms of convenience (-0.08 points). Finally, our participants rated gesture-based interaction near the median of the scale both for the ease of understanding (0.5 points) and the convenience of use (0.0 points).

We attribute some of the dissatisfaction of the users with gesture-based interaction and *NextOnePlease* to the prototype status of the client device used. The Zaurus PDA with an attached TelosB sensor node (required as a communication bridge to the sensor network) is not as handy as the self-contained Sensor Node Lamp device. As mentioned before, a much smaller and simpler device only providing two buttons could replace the PDA as the client device both for gesture-based interaction and for *NextOnePlease*.

For *NextOnePlease*, a special difficulty of the interaction task lay in selecting three nodes. We observed that the participants tried to observe all three nodes in parallel in order to perform the complete selection in a single round. While this approach helped speeding up the selection process, it also made the simple task of browsing through the list of nodes much more challenging and exhausting than when concentrating on a single node.

We also learned that gesture-based interaction poses a more difficult initial learning experience than originally expected. While we as expert users were very comfortable and efficient in using gesture-based interaction, the participants of our study struggled with the different errors a user can make in performing gestures (e.g., moving the hand too fast or keeping too much distance to the node).

7.6.4 Comparison of Approaches

Gesture-based interaction, Sensor Node Lamp interaction and *NextOnePlease* focus on different aspects and work best in different scenarios. Table 7.3 summarizes important criteria that help in selecting one of the interaction mechanisms for a specific application scenario.

Based on our experience and the results of our user study, Sensor Node Lamp interaction is the preferable method for interacting with wireless sensor nodes. It works reliably, is simple to use, scales well with the size of the network and is able to cover reasonable distances. Its main limitations are that it works mainly indoors and that it requires additional hardware on the client side. The main strengths of gesture-based interaction are its low hardware requirements and its ability to work both indoors and outdoors. However, the small maximum interaction distance limits the set of scenarios it is usable in. Finally, *NextOnePlease* also sets low hardware requirements (LEDs), works at reasonable distances and can be used indoors and outdoors. Besides the required effort by the user, its main challenge is the scalability in the presence of a very large number of nodes.

7.7 Summary

The focus of this chapter was the problem of initiating interactions between mobile devices and wireless sensor nodes in pervasive computing scenarios. We started the discussion with a motivation of the problem and its relevance in the context of the work of this thesis. Then, we introduced three different solution approaches: a gesture-based approach, a solution using light signals sent from the client device to the sensor nodes and an approach that is based on sensor nodes providing information using their LEDs. We have shown that these solutions cover a wide range of scenarios building on different node capabilities and user actions. In the evaluation we have demonstrated that all three mechanisms are effective in solving the sensor node interaction problem. Sensor Node Lamp interaction, in particular, has been shown to be a very efficient and easy-to-use solution for indoor scenarios.

7.7.1 Future Directions in this Area

There are several potential directions for future work in this area. One question that we would like to have answered is how the solutions developed as part of this work might be applicable to other devices that are part of pervasive computing scenarios like for example small consumer appliances. It would be interesting to see whether new types of pervasive computing applications are possible using our mechanisms.

For *NextOnePlease*, we expect that the scalability and the usability could be significantly improved with more advanced ways of sorting the list of nodes presented to the user, for example based on the role of nodes or based on the history of previous queries by the user.

Another, more radical idea for an interaction approach for wireless sensor nodes is to use the LEDs of the nodes to generate light patterns on the candidate sensor nodes and record and recognize the light patterns generated by the target node with a camera on the client device. As discussed above, we ruled out the use of LED light patterns for *NextOnePlease* after initial experiments mainly due to the high cognitive load on the user. By automating this step using a camera and image recognition software, the task of the user would be reduced to pointing the camera in direction of the target node – transforming *NextOnePlease* into a pointing interaction approach.

For the Sensor Node Lamp, we see the potential of using it as an actuator in various sensor network scenarios. We discuss one such alternative use of the Sensor Node Lamp in the context of security in the following chapter.

8 Securing Sensor Node Interactions

In the previous chapter we have discussed interactions between mobile devices and wireless sensor nodes, more specifically the initiation of such interactions. In this chapter, we are going to discuss an important related topic, namely the security of such sensor node interactions.

We start with a motivation of security in wireless sensor networks in general and for sensor nodes as part of pervasive computing scenarios in particular and show that achieving secure interactions is a difficult but important problem. Based on a short discussion of existing security solutions for wireless sensor networks, we then motivate that the assignment of key information is an important building block of providing secure interactions.

In the main part of this chapter, we introduce a new key assignment approach called *Enlighten Me!* that is applicable to both classic wireless sensor network scenarios and sensor networks forming a part of pervasive computing scenarios. The idea is to transmit key information to sensor nodes using a separate communication channel based on light signals whose set of recipients can be better controlled than for traditional radio communication channels. We describe the *Enlighten Me!* protocol and introduce two different key sender devices for *Enlighten Me!*, one using the Sensor Node Lamp introduced in the previous chapter and another key sender device based on standard PDA hardware.

In the evaluation of our approach, we show that *Enlighten Me!* provides a simple and efficient solution to the key assignment problem that is able to fulfill all relevant security requirements.

8.1 Preliminaries

When wireless sensor networks are to be used for real-world applications outside of closely supervised laboratory environments, then the various security aspects of these systems must be taken into account. For example, malicious entities might eavesdrop the communication in the sensor network in order to record confidential data. They might also try to actively manipulate the message traffic and thereby interfere with the network operation. If the nodes carry mission-critical or sensitive data, then appropriate measures must be taken to prevent such attacks. With wireless sensor networks slowly starting to become used in small and medium-scale commercial deployments, these and similar security considerations become increasingly important.

In our settings, with wireless sensor nodes used as part of pervasive computing scenarios, security is equally important. For example, mobile devices should be able to privately communicate with sensor nodes without others being able to read the messages (confidentiality) or to manipulate the message content (integrity). Both mobile clients and wireless sensor nodes should be able to verify the source of messages they receive (authenticity).

Like for all systems using a wireless communication medium, securing the communication channels between nodes is the primary factor in achieving security in wireless sensor networks. Due to the broadcast nature of the radio communication channel, basically any node can participate passively (by eavesdropping) or actively (by manipulating or injecting messages) in the communication on the channel and extra measures are required to secure the channel.

While it is clear that security is an important aspect of our scenarios, the strong resource constraints of the individual sensor nodes as well as the ad hoc nature of their deployment make achieving security goals in wireless sensor networks a challenging task. Cryptographic algorithms, like algorithms for encrypting or decrypting message data, can only consume a very limited amount of processing time and main memory. This mandates, for example, the use of symmetric encryption over the more costly asymmetric encryption in most scenarios. The ad hoc nature of deployment complicates the setup of secure channels among the nodes.

In this chapter we are looking into a specific part of security in wireless sensor networks, the key assignment to wireless sensor nodes. On the one hand, we have picked this particular problem, because it is very relevant for our scenarios with many independent entities being involved in the communication. On the other hand, our solution is another good example of pervasive computing devices and sensor nodes supporting each other based on their respective strengths – in this case with mobile devices providing key information to wireless sensor nodes.

Let us now argue why the key assignment to sensor nodes is both a very relevant and difficult problem to solve. Nearly all cryptographic algorithms used in wireless sensor networks rely on secret key data that is shared among pairs of nodes or a whole group of nodes. However, assigning secret key information to individual nodes in wireless sensor networks is a difficult problem. On the one hand, this is due to the limited interfacing capabilities of typical sensor node hardware. On the other hand, securely assigning keys to nodes is complicated by the fact that the standard communication method in wireless sensor networks – sending RF messages over the wireless medium – is inherently insecure: Any interested party within communication range can listen to messages or inject its own spurious messages.

Preloading key information at node programming time or transmitting the key data over a wired interface provided by the sensor node (e.g, a USB port or a serial interface) is no alternative, because we expect that future sensor nodes – unlike today's sensor network research platforms – will be delivered preprogrammed from the manufacturer and will not necessarily provide a wired interface. The same will likely be true for other small-scale devices with similar capabilities. The node manufacturers might not be willing to deal with key management and key security for their customers. Moreover, the customers might not trust external entities with creating and managing keys for their applications.

We are going to discuss several key exchange protocols for wireless networks in the related work section of this chapter (e.g., [160, 33, 204]). They allow for an on-demand exchange of key information between arbitrary pairs of nodes. However, they all rely on the availability of a certain amount of initial key data that can be used by such protocols in establishing and securely exchanging dynamic session keys.

In this chapter we describe *Enlighten Me!*, a novel approach to the problem of assigning keys to wireless sensor nodes that is particularly suited for our application scenarios. It supports both the initial assignment of keys during the deployment of a wireless sensor network (which can later be used to create dynamic session keys) and the dynamic assignment of keys from mobile devices to sensor nodes during the normal network operation.

8.1.1 Problem Definition

Let us now provide a more formal definition of the problem of assigning secret key data to wireless sensor nodes.

A secret key consists of k bits of data which are usually randomly generated at some point in time during the system operation. A key is secret in the regard that its k bits of data are (or at least should be) only known to the legitimate owners of the key. To preserve this secrecy, the key data or any parts of it must not be made accessible to outside parties at any time. In particular, secret key information must not be included in messages transmitted over unprotected, open communication channels.

While secret keys are required as part of various security protocols, nodes might not be in possession of all secret key data that they require and are entitled to in the beginning. For that reason, mechanisms for distributing key data to nodes are required. We thereby differentiate between key exchange approaches and key assignment approaches. A key exchange mechanism allows for a symmetric exchange of key data between a pair of nodes (n_1, n_2) in both directions: n_1 can send key data to n_2 but n_2 is also able to send key data to n_1. In contrast, key assignment approaches are asymmetric: A key sender node n_{sender} transmits key data to a key receiver node $n_{receiver}$. The capabilities required for this process can differ significantly between the key sender and the key receiver so that their roles cannot easily be exchanged. In the following, we only consider key assignment approaches. Mobile client devices play the role of key senders and wireless sensor nodes (or similarly constrained devices) act as key receivers.

As part of a key assignment, the key sender n_{sender} transmits a key K to a specific key receiver node $n_{receiver}$. We can assume that the key sender knows the identity of the intended key receiver, for example represented in the form of a node identifier. We also assume that key sender and key receiver are able to communicate with each other directly. However, a whole set of nodes S_{neigh} with $n_{receiver} \in S_{neigh}$ can lie within the transmission range of the key sender and is able to receive all communication exchanged between n_{sender} and $n_{receiver}$. Unlike in previous approaches, we cannot assume that the nodes in S_{neigh} cooperate but have to deal with potential adversaries trying to record the key data. The fundamental problem of key assignment in wireless sensor networks is then to transmit K from n_{sender} to $n_{receiver}$ without any node from $S_{neigh} \setminus n_{receiver}$ being able to receive K as well.

8.1.2 Requirements

The primary goal of *Enlighten Me!* is to provide a secure mechanism for the assignment of keys to wireless sensor nodes. In order to achieve this, *Enlighten Me!* needs to **prevent the overhearing of key data** transmitted from a key sender to a key receiver. Moreover, it needs to prevent attackers from covertly manipulating transmitted key information or injecting spurious keys. We will go into more details of this when we define the attacker model later in this chapter.

Ease and efficiency of use are important secondary goals of *Enlighten Me!*. For being usable in pervasive computing scenarios, the system should require only little user input, provide immediate and easy-to-understand feedback and should be tolerant to user errors.

Finally, our key assignment approach **should not require any special hardware on the sensor nodes** as this would increase the node costs, impede the portability to other platforms and, in general, limit the number of application scenarios for *Enlighten Me!*. We mostly achieve this by only requiring a simple light sensor on the receiver node – a feature found on many sensor node platforms today.

8.1.3 Application Scenarios

With our method for key assignment in wireless sensor networks we support two basic application scenarios: The assignment of keys as part of the initial configuration of a sensor network and the dynamic key assignment in pervasive computing scenarios.

The initial assignment of keys during or after the deployment of wireless sensor nodes is important to provide the nodes with the secret key information required by cryptographic algorithms. These initial keys then allow security protocols to support authentication, encryption and message integrity checks. Most importantly, these initial secret keys are a precondition for dynamically generating new key data for node-to-node communication at a later time. As argued above, one cannot rely on this key information being loaded onto the node at programming time by the node manufacturer. We can close this gap with the help of our key assignment mechanism *Enlighten Me!*.

With the support for an initial key assignment in wireless sensor networks, *Enlighten Me!* provides a valuable contribution to the field of security in wireless sensor networks that is independent of the application scenario it is used in. However, the second way of using *Enlighten Me!* is particularly interesting from the viewpoint of the target scenarios of this thesis: *Enlighten Me!* supports the dynamic assignment of keys to sensor nodes after the nodes have been deployed in the environment. In the context of pervasive computing scenarios this can be used in several ways. The most fundamental one is securing the communication between mobile devices and sensor nodes.

Mobile pervasive computing devices operating in the application area of a wireless sensor network need a way of securely communicating and interacting with nodes in their vicinity. As the set of mobile clients is not likely to be small and fixed, we cannot assume that the sensor nodes already possess matching keys for any client entering the network. Instead, a mobile client can use *Enlighten Me!* to securely assign a key to a sensor node which is then used to secure the following interaction with the sensor network.

It is not necessary that a mobile device separately assigns a key to each sensor node it wants to communicate with. Instead, it is sufficient to "join" the sensor network once by transmitting a key to one of the sensor nodes. This sensor node is then able to securely forward the key information to its peer nodes within the sensor network using an existing security infrastructure.

The fact that *Enlighten Me!* not only requires the key sender to be in the vicinity of the key receiver but also requires a direct line of sight between the two (i.e., both nodes operate in the same area) provides for a special type of authentication that can be useful in pervasive computing scenarios: On the one hand, sensor nodes can limit their exchange of messages with client nodes to mobile devices that have proven their physical presence in the area by assigning a key using *Enlighten Me!*. This effectively excludes nodes trying to eavesdrop and access the sensor network from a distance and can be useful if only local clients should be authorized to access information. On the other hand, *Enlighten Me!* allows the user to explicitly select key receiver nodes based on real-world criteria as he is able to see to which node he assigns the key. The mobile device is then able to check whether subsequent messages really come from the alleged source node.

8.1.4 Overview of Approach

The basic idea of *Enlighten Me!* is to transmit secret key information over a separate communication channel (a side channel) which allows to effectively limit the set of listeners to legitimate receiver nodes. While *Enlighten Me!* exchanges its protocol messages over the normal radio channel, the key data is sent exclusively over the side channel.

For the approach to be implemented on standard wireless sensor nodes, we cannot require additional hardware for this separate communication channel. Our solution is to communicate using light with a controllable light source used to generate the data signal and using the light sensors available on many sensor node platforms to capture and record the signal. Only nodes lying within the sphere of influence of the light signal generated by the key sender are able to receive and store the key information. To securely transmit key information over this light communication channel, we have developed a simple, yet efficient communication protocol that can be implemented on top of the standard operating system abstractions provided by TinyOS.

We have developed two different key sender devices for *Enlighten Me!*. The first device, the Sensor Node Lamp, was already used in the previous chapter to initiate interactions with wireless sensor nodes. Here, we use the integrated LED as the light

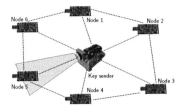

Figure 8.1: Basic communication principle

source for transmitting the key information. The second device, the *Enlighten Me!* PDA, is based on standard PDA hardware and uses the display of the PDA to transmit key information to a sensor node by varying the light level on the display.

Fig. 8.1 illustrates the fundamental working principle of *Enlighten Me!*: They key sender in the middle intends to assign a key to one node (node 5) but a total of six nodes lie within the transmission range of its RF transceiver. While the key sender cannot prevent any of these nodes to overhear and record the radio messages transmitted, it is able to control the propagation of the light signal and make sure that only node 5 is able to receive the key information transmitted as a light signal.

Our solution provides the following set of advantages. Firstly, it effectively prevents eavesdropping in the transmission of key data from the key sender to the key receiver. Secondly, the system is easy and convenient to use and provides meaningful feedback to the user. Thirdly, it allows key assignment both as part of the initial network configuration and in an ad hoc manner during normal system operation. Finally, it is a cost effective solution that does not require additional hardware on the wireless sensor nodes.

One can argue that it would be easier and equally secure to use the wired interface provided by a sensor node (e.g., a USB port or a serial interface) to transmit the key information or to preprogram the nodes with key information. However, we expect that – unlike today's sensor network research platforms – in the future sensor nodes (or devices with similar capabilities) will be delivered preprogrammed from the manufacturer and will not necessarily provide a wired interface. Moreover, *Enlighten Me!* is not only convenient to use but also, as we will show in the evaluation, fast and will outperform attaching a node to a wired interface in many cases.

8.2 Related Work

A growing set of security solutions and protocols is available for wireless sensor networks that have to deal with a diverse set of issues and threats. Examples of fields covered include communication security [160], security of routing protocols [92] or even secure node localization [30]. Common to all of them is their reliance on basic cryptographic mechanisms that in turn require shared secrets or key data as it can be assigned to sensor nodes using the mechanism we present in this chapter.

8.2.1 Key Exchange Mechanisms

Among the existing sensor network security solutions, key exchange and key distribution mechanisms [160, 33, 83, 32, 204] are particularly related to our approach. Their fundamental goal is to allow for a secure communication among any pair of nodes in the network by dynamically exchanging key information.

The simplest solution for the key exchange between arbitrary nodes relies on a centralized, less resource-constrained authority, usually the base station, that acts as a mediator in the key exchange process and shares a secret key with each node in the network (e.g., [160]). To establish a new key with another network node, a node simply contacts the base station and asks it to generate and distribute the key. However, this centralization of all key exchange tasks is also the main disadvantage as the base station is a single point of failure and the communication with the base station can lead to performance bottlenecks in large systems.

To overcome the need for a central authority, several authors have proposed to pre-distribute sets of keys to the nodes in the network either randomly (e.g., [33, 83]) or in a controlled fashion (e.g., [32, 204]). These sets of keys are then used to dynamically create session keys for node-to-node communication.

With random key distribution [33, 83], each node stores a random subset of keys from a key pool. It is then able to form secure links to other nodes sharing one of these keys. Secure paths from node to node can be formed by combining such secure links and session keys can be exchanged over these paths. However, no guarantees can be provided that the key graph is connected. Consequently, the exchange of secret key information among a pair of nodes might fail in some cases.

The idea of controlled key pre-distribution schemes [32, 204] is to construct the key graph deterministically in a way that ensures that keys can be exchanged between arbitrary pairs of nodes in the network. Moreover, it also allows to construct the key graph in a way that prevents individual intermediate nodes that have been compromised from violating the security of the key exchanged over this graph [204].

Note that all key exchange mechanisms discussed here – whether centralized or distributed – require some initial secret key information on the individual nodes in the network. The key assignment mechanism *Enlighten Me!* that we propose in this chapter can be used for this purpose.

8.2.2 Key Assignment Mechanisms

Stajano and Anderson [187] discuss the challenges of security in ad hoc networks in general and the problem of securely associating nodes with each other in particular. They propose the **resurrecting duckling** security policy in which a wireless device associates itself with the first entity sending a secret key to the device after it has been activated much like a duckling recognizes the first moving object making sounds as its mother after emerging from its egg. Unlike for ducklings, Stajano and Anderson propose that such an imprinting could be repeated after some time to start a new lifecycle of the device. For the secure transmission of key data from the parent device, they propose to require physical contact between the devices. They then transmit the key over an electrical contact – requiring special hardware support both on the sender and on the receiver side. With *Enlighten Me!* we are able to easily implement the resurrecting duckling security policy while avoiding the requirement for a key transmission over electrical contacts.

Message-In-a-Bottle [105] is very closely related to our approach in that it also deals with the initial key assignment in wireless sensor networks. The idea is to place the key sender and the key receiver together in a Faraday cage (e.g., a closed galvanized steel pipe) that prevents outside eavesdroppers from overhearing the messages exchanged over the radio channel. The key data can then be sent unencrypted using a simple communication protocol. An additional node placed outside of the cage supervises the protocol and also jams the wireless channel to overshadow any signals from inside not completely blocked by the Faraday cage. The major disadvantage of Message-In-a-Bottle is its need for direct physical access to the nodes as they have to be placed inside of the Faraday cage. Consequently, it is not well-suited for an on-demand assignment of keys after the nodes have been deployed.

Shake Them Up! [31] securely exchanges key information between two entities A and B by sending messages between them over an anonymous channel that hides the identity of the message sender. Both nodes send random sequences of messages in which they claim to be either node A or B. Due to the anonymity of the channel, only the respective communication partner can check the validity of the claim and can convert this into a single bit of key information. To implement an anonymous channel using radio communication, temporal and spatial indistinguishability of message sources must be achieved. Shake Them Up! implements this by randomizing the message send times, by operating both nodes with the same transmission power and by requiring the user to shake the nodes together during the key exchange to prevent determining the sender of a message by analyzing the strength of the received signal. One limitation of the approach in the context of wireless sensor networks is that it might be difficult to provide for identical signal strengths and radio properties with different nodes. Moreover, shaking nodes is an exhausting task and might tempt the user to neglect this important part of the secure key exchange.

Based on our definitions of key exchange and key assignment mechanisms provided in Section 8.1, Shake Them Up! could qualify as a key exchange mechanism, because nodes A and B have equal capabilities and exchange key information with each other. However, we still classify it as a key assignment mechanism as the user is required to actively participate in the key exchange whereas key exchange protocols usually operate in the background without user involvement.

Multiple authors have proposed to transmit key data or authentication data over a privileged side channel. **Talking to Strangers** [10] describes a general protocol that assumes the availability of a "location-limited channel" that allows to identify devices based on their physical context (e.g., the sender must be in the same area as the receiver). The authors do not assume that secrecy is being provided on the location-limited channel. Consequently, they exchange public keys over the normal wireless channel and use the location-limited channel for authentication and to check the key integrity.

If **public key cryptography** can be used, then the secrecy of a key transmission is not important, because everyone is allowed to know the public key of a node without this causing any harm. However, one needs to check that the intended recipient received the key correctly. For receiver nodes it is essential that they are able to authenticate the public key received from another node. Several authors proposed manual solutions for this that involve comparing key hashes on both the key sender and the key receiver represented in the form of readable words or even graphical representations (e.g., [45, 28]). In our scenarios, public key cryptography is often not applicable due to the resource constraints of the wireless sensor nodes. Moreover, the sensor nodes lack the capabilities to show an appropriate representation of key hashes for comparison.

If public key cryptography is used for securing the communication among mobile devices and between mobile devices and wireless sensor nodes in a pervasive computing scenario, then *Enlighten Me!* can be used to securely pair two nodes and to ensure that a public key really originates from the alleged sender.

8.3 Attacker Model

Let us now start the discussion of the *Enlighten Me!* approach by introducing our attacker model and by describing which types of attacks our key assignment scheme is supposed to withstand. We also list the types of attacks that our approach is not able to deal with and justify why this is an acceptable limitation in our scenarios. The basic point of attack that we consider is the wireless communication channel connecting the nodes in the network. However, we also consider the physical integrity of the nodes and the light communication channel used by *Enlighten Me!*.

8.3.1 Passive and Active Attacks

We assume that both passive and active attacks on the wireless communication channel are possible and must be dealt with by the *Enlighten Me!* system.

In a passive attack, an adversary quietly eavesdrops on the message exchange of the nodes in the network and records relevant data. From the viewpoint of our system, passive attacks on the radio channel are not critical as we do not transmit any secret information over the radio communication interface. By listening to the message traffic, the attacker is only able to overhear the key exchange protocol. It cannot record any part of the secret key information this way.

In an active attack, an adversary actively participates in the communication, for example by injecting spurious messages, replaying messages it has received or by forwarding manipulated message content. Active attacks on our system are possible with the help of fake protocol messages. However, as will be shown in the detailed protocol description in Section 8.4.2, all phases of the protocol involve the use of the light communication channel. Fake protocol messages that are not confirmed or followed by the expected signals on the light communication channel quickly lead to timeouts resulting in an abort of the protocol on the receiver side. Consequently, an adversary can only cause short disruptions of the system operation. Sending a very large number of fake protocol messages in a short time interval leads to a denial-of-service attack which we discuss below.

8.3.2 Denial-of-Service Attacks

In the context of key assignments, a denial-of-service attack prevents the successful transmission of key information from a sender node to a receiver node. One possible way for an adversary to do this is to jam the wireless communication medium in the area or to flood the nodes with useless messages or fake protocol messages. Usually, it is easy to detect such kinds of attacks by sampling the wireless communication channel.

If an attacker performs a denial-of-service attack on the wireless communication channel in a pervasive computing environment, this does not only affect key assignment but all operations involving communication. It has also been shown that dealing with denial-of-service attacks in wireless sensor networks is a very complex problem that has to be addressed for all aspects of the system at design time [217, 165]. Consequently, we do not explicitly deal with denial-of-service attacks in *Enlighten Me!* but rely on an underlying system service that ensures communication capabilities among the nodes of our system.

8.3.3 Physical Access to Nodes

It is usually impossible to deal with attackers that have direct physical access to the nodes as they are able to read out the memory of a node including all key information, reprogram the node or even completely destroy or replace the node ("Who has physical access to the hardware owns the hardware..."). However, we are able to deal with adversaries that are operating in the vicinity of the sensor nodes.

An adversary might try to write his own key information to a sensor node using a key sender device and the *Enlighten Me!* key assignment protocol in order to gain access to the encrypted communication of the node or to take over control of the node. We can prevent this by only allowing to freely set the keys once at the beginning of the system operation. If an entity wants to exchange a key later on, it needs to provide the old key first to confirm that it is authorized to perform such a key exchange. During the initial assignment of key data to a node, it is easy to detect if the adversary has managed to assign his key to a node before the administrator. In this case, the node has to be exchanged and reprogrammed.

If we use *Enlighten Me!* to assign keys dynamically on a per-client basis, it is generally acceptable for any mobile client device to assign a key to a sensor node as this key is then only used for securing the communication between this pair of nodes.

The ability of the user to assign a key with *Enlighten Me!* can be considered as a kind of authentication in this case: The user proves that he is actually operating in the vicinity of the node and not just communicating with the node from outside the area.

8.3.4 Attacks on the Light Channel

The fundamental assumption of *Enlighten Me!* is that key information can be securely transmitted over the light channel whereas attackers might have passive or active access to the radio communication channel. This assumption holds if the user has control over the reception area of the light signal. We will discuss the security of the light channel separately for our two key sender devices in Section 8.5.

8.4 The Enlighten Me! Protocol

In this section we describe the details of the functionality and the course of action of the *Enlighten Me!* protocol. We start with a description of our message encoding and decoding method, then explain the individual protocol phases and protocol steps, go into some more detail regarding the key verification and end with a description of the protocol behavior in case of errors. While some aspects of the protocol remind of the Sensor Node Lamp interaction protocol described in Section 7.4 of the previous chapter, the overall differences are significant: The handshake between sender and receiver – the core task of the Sensor Node Lamp interaction mechanism – is only a small first step of the *Enlighten Me!* protocol.

8.4.1 Message Encoding and Decoding

We aim to transmit key data using a light signal emitted by a light source on the key sender device and recorded with the help of a light sensor on the receiver node. The task of the message encoding is to convert the bitstream of the key data into such a light signal. The message decoding then performs the inverse operation, reconstructing the original data bitstream out of the received light signal. We can use two different states of the light signal for encoding information: "light on" and "light off"[1].

For the encoding of our data as a light signal, we use the Manchester code, a relatively simple but robust digital baseband modulation code [188]. Fig. 8.2 illustrates how Manchester encoding works with the help of the example bit sequence "010011". A clock signal controls the encoding of data with exactly one bit being encoded per clock cycle. A one is encoded using a signal level transition from low to high at the middle of the clock cycle whereas a zero is encoded using a signal level transition from high to low.

---

[1]Depending on the properties of the signal sender and the signal receiver, it might be possible to define additional light states based on different light intensity levels or even different wavelengths of the light. However, we have not investigated this possibility for *Enlighten Me!*.

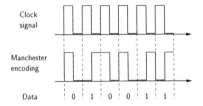

Figure 8.2: Manchester encoding example

An important advantage of the Manchester code in our setting lies in the fact that the phase shift of the clock signal can be directly recovered from the encoded data. This is called the self-timing property of the Manchester code. As Fig. 8.2 illustrates, the Manchester code makes sure that a signal level transition (from low to high or from high to low) occurs at least once per clock cycle independent of which data sequence is encoded. By detecting these level transitions, the receiver can easily synchronize to the clock used by the sender for encoding the signal. This allows us to transmit data from the sender node to any receiver node without having to perform a costly synchronization of their internal clocks first. Moreover, this also provides for a high level of robustness against clock drift on the nodes (i.e., the receiver automatically resynchronizes to the clock of the signal at least once per clock cycle).

There are two parameters that we need to set for the encoding of data with the Manchester code: the period of the clock signal Δ_{clock} and the threshold distance δ_{thresh} used to differentiate between a "light on" and a "light off" signal.

Clearly, the smaller we choose Δ_{clock}, the higher is the throughput of the key transmission. However, limiting factors in this selection include the switching time of the light source, the reaction time of the light sensors, interrupt handling times, times required for processing in software and the limited accuracy of the software timers on the sensor nodes. Note that the communication throughput over the light channel is not that critical for the overall system performance as all normal communication (except for the key transmission) is still performed using the RF channel.

Differentiating between the "light on" and the "light off" state on the receiver node works in the same way as for the Sensor Node Lamp interaction: Before the key transmission starts, the receiver captures its current ambient light level l_{base} which represents the "light off" state. A predetermined threshold value δ_{thresh} is then used to differentiate between the two states as follows: Every light sensor reading l_t at time t is considered to belong to the "light on" state iff $l_t \geq l_{thresh} = l_{base} + \delta_{thresh}$ holds. Otherwise, it belongs to the "light off" state.

An analysis of the clock period Δ_{clock} and the light threshold l_{thresh} can be found in the evaluation section of this chapter.

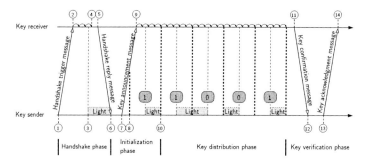

Figure 8.3: Key assignment protocol time diagram

8.4.2 Key Assignment Protocol

The *Enlighten Me!* key assignment protocol consists of four phases. In the first phase, the handshake phase, the key sender advertises the upcoming key assignment, the intended key receiver node is identified and sender and receiver are paired with each other. The key transmission is prepared in the second phase, the initialization phase, during which the key sender specifies parameters of the key transmission. The actual transmission of the key information is performed in the key distribution phase before the correct completion of the transmission is checked in the key verification phase.

The time diagram of the key assignment protocol in Fig. 8.3 illustrates the sequence of events of a successful key transmission for the simple, four bit example key "1001". The example assumes that the key sender n_{sender} and the key receiver $n_{receiver}$ are able to exchange radio messages and that the light source of the key sender is pointed in the direction of the light sensor of the key receiver node. The following explanation of the individual protocol steps refers to events numbered in the time diagram in Fig. 8.3.

The key sender starts the protocol with the handshake phase by broadcasting a *handshake trigger message* (1). This notifies all potential receiver nodes from S_{neigh} including $n_{receiver}$ of the imminent key transmission. The candidate receiver nodes react to the reception of this trigger message by sampling their base sensor value l_{base} (2) used to differentiate between the "light on" and the "light off" state. After the sampling of the base sensor value is finished, the candidate nodes continue sampling their light sensors every $t_{samplePeriod}$ time units.

The key sender meanwhile waits for $t_{hsDelay}$ time units and then activates its light source (3) to provide a sensor stimulus to the key receiver. The key receiver detects this "light on" event (4) and sends a *handshake reply message* back to the key sender (5). All other candidate receiver nodes from S_{neigh} not lying within the light beam of the key sender time out after $t_{hsTimeoutReceiver}$ time units, stop sampling their light sensor and do not participate any further in the key assignment process.

Note that, unlike for the Sensor Node Lamp interaction, the version of the *Enlighten Me!* protocol shown in Fig. 8.3 uses only a simple "light on" event for the pairing of sender and receiver in step (4) of the protocol and not a more sophisticated light signal sequence whose timings the receiver node can check. This might trigger the wrong nodes to send *handshake reply messages* back to the key sender. The protocol then fails during the initialization phase and the key sender needs to restart the procedure. For that reason, we also support the on-off-on-off light pattern used for pairing nodes in the Sensor Node Lamp interaction protocol.

With the reception of the *handshake reply message* at the key sender (6), the handshake phase ends. At this point, sender and receiver know each others identity and are able to start exchanging information over both the radio channel and the light channel.

The key sender starts the initialization phase by sending a *key announcement message* to the key receiver (7). It contains the size of the key to be transmitted and also serves as a notification to the receiver of the beginning of the actual key transmission. Upon receiving this message, the key receiver starts sampling its light sensor again (9) waiting for the key transmission to start. Meanwhile, the key sender waits for a short time interval and then proceeds by sending a 1 on the light channel (8). Remember that a 1 in Manchester encoding consists of a low signal in the first half of the clock cycle and a high signal in the second half. The change from low to high allows the receiver to synchronize itself to the clock of the incoming light signal. By always sending a 1 in the beginning, the key sender provides this synchronization opportunity irrespective of the key data following the 1.

The initialization phase is directly followed by the key distribution phase when the key sender starts transmitting the encoded key data bit by bit over the light channel after it has completed sending out the introductory 1 (10). The key distribution phase then ends when the key sender has sent out all bits of the key data and stops the transmission turning off its light source.

After the key receiver has received all bits of the key data (the size was specified in the *key announcement message*), it stops sampling its light sensor and starts the key verification phase by sending the *key confirmation message* (11). The key sender uses the content of this message to verify the correct transmission of the key (12) and confirms this in a *key acknowledgment message* (13). The key receiver finally assigns the new key when this acknowledgment has been received (14).

The details of the key verification procedure and the structure and content of the last two messages depend on the type of keys and the security protocol used. If symmetric encryption is used, then we propose the following procedure based on the challenge-response principle: The key sender sends a randomly generated number I_{chall} encrypted with the new key K as part of the *key announcement message* to the key receiver.

$$Key\ announcement\ message: \quad n_{sender} \rightarrow n_{receiver} : Keysize, \{I_{chall}\}^K$$

Once the key receiver has successfully received the key over the light channel, it is able to decrypt the message, decrement I_{chall} by one, encrypt it again using key K and send it back to the key sender in the *key confirmation message*.

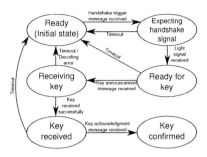

Figure 8.4: *Enlighten Me!* state diagram

$$Key\ confirmation\ message:\quad n_{receiver} \rightarrow n_{sender} : \{I_{chall} - 1\}^K$$

This proves to the key sender that the key receiver has correctly received K. The key sender can now confirm this again using the random number I_{chall} and sending back $I_{chall} - 2$ encrypted by K.

$$Key\ acknowledgment\ message:\quad n_{sender} \rightarrow n_{receiver} : \{I_{chall} - 2\}^K$$

Fig. 8.4 shows the state diagram for the *Enlighten Me!* key reception process on candidate sensor nodes. A node starts in the "Ready" state and switches to the "Expecting handshake signal" state upon receiving a *handshake trigger message*. If the expected light signal sequence is received by the node, then it continues to the "Ready for key" state and waits for the *key announcement message*. Once this message arrives, the node proceeds to the "Receiving key" state. If the node completes the key reception successfully, it switches to the "Key received" state and starts the key verification procedure described above. If the verification also completes successfully, then the node proceeds to the "Key confirmed" state and finally assigns the received key data.

8.4.3 Behavior in case of errors

The description of the *Enlighten Me!* protocol given so far assumed that no errors occur. Nevertheless, the protocol behavior is also clearly defined in case of errors. The most important aspects of this error behavior are explained below.

The most common error occurs during the key transmission over the light channel. Internal or external interferences can prevent the signal from being correctly received by the key receiver node. Due to the properties of the Manchester code, such errors hardly ever cause bit errors in the decoded data but rather a code violation that disrupts the signal detection (i.e., the receiver detects a light signal event that violates the expected Manchester code scheme). The key receiver reports such an abort back to the key sender which repeats the key transmission up to two times starting again with the *key announcement message*. If, however, an error already occurred before the start of the key transmission, then the key sender starts again with the *handshake trigger message*.

The protocol can detect erroneous keys (caused by bit errors) during the key verification phase. For that reason, the key transmission phase does not contain a checksum mechanism like CRC to check the integrity of the received data. We also consider forward error correction too complex for the small number of bit errors expected. Note that such a forward error correction would not be able to deal with the more common code violation errors.

Another type of error occurs if the light source is not pointed in the direction of the key receiver node or if the light signal is too weak. In this case, the protocol fails during the handshake phase as no *handshake reply message* is received within $t_{hsTimeoutSender}$. The key sender device then provides feedback to the user and returns to its initial state waiting for further key assignment requests.

8.5 Enlighten Me! Systems

In this section we describe two different systems that implement the key sender functionality of the *Enlighten Me!* protocol: The Sensor Node Lamp and the *Enlighten Me!* PDA. As the Sensor Node Lamp hardware was already introduced in the previous chapter, we concentrate on implementation details specific to the *Enlighten Me!* approach and discuss the security of the light channel when using the Sensor Node Lamp. For the *Enlighten Me!* PDA, we describe the hardware, our implementation and security aspects of the light channel. At the end of this section, we also introduce the key receiver implementation and describe how it relates to the two key sender approaches.

8.5.1 Sensor Node Lamp

For the Sensor Node Lamp interaction approach discussed in the previous chapter, we use the light signal of the Sensor Node Lamp solely for pairing the Sensor Node Lamp with the wireless sensor node the user is pointing at. For this purpose, a simple on-off-on-off light pattern sent by the Sensor Node Lamp and checked by the receiving sensor node is sufficient. For the *Enlighten Me!* approach, the idea is to use such changes between the "light off" and the "light on" state of the Sensor Node Lamp together with the Manchester code to encode key data that can be recorded and decoded on the receiving sensor node.

As the LED of the Sensor Node Lamp and the timings of its activation and deactivation can be controlled in software running on the integrated TelosB node, the Sensor Node Lamp can be used as a client device for *Enlighten Me!* without hardware modifications and we refer back to Section 7.4.4 for a description of the details of the Sensor Node Lamp hardware. As we will see in the evaluation section, now the maximum switching speed between the "light off" and "light on" states becomes a relevant performance criterion for the Sensor Node Lamp.

Another important aspect of the Sensor Node Lamp that is helpful for the usability of both the Sensor Node Lamp interaction and the *Enlighten Me!* key assignment approach is what we call the flashlight analogy (see Section 7.4.5). For *Enlighten Me!*, assigning a key to a node is as simple as illuminating the node with the Sensor Node Lamp for a few seconds just like someone would do with a flashlight. The visual feedback provided by the light beam of the Sensor Node Lamp not only helps in pointing the device in the right direction, it also gives hints on the size of the reception area and allows the user to adjust this based on the node density or nearby adversaries.

Implementation

We have implemented the key sender functionality on the Sensor Node Lamp in TinyOS 2. All steps of the protocol as well as the Manchester encoding of the light signal are completely implemented in software based on standard TinyOS functionality. We have also developed a simple auxiliary application that allows to generate keys on a PC or a PDA and then upload them to the Sensor Node Lamp over a USB connection.

For the Sensor Node Lamp implementation, we extended the *Enlighten Me!* protocol with an additional phase in the beginning, the **aiming phase**. Just like for the Sensor Node Lamp interaction, the goal of this phase is to support the user in aiming the light beam in direction of the key receiver node. For this purpose, pressing the user button on the Sensor Node Lamp activates the LED and allows the user to direct the light beam in the right direction. When he releases the user button again, the aiming phase ends, the LED is deactivated again and the actual *Enlighten Me!* protocol starts.

To illustrate the functionality of the implementation on the Sensor Node Lamp, Fig. 8.5 shows light levels of a key transmission with the Sensor Node Lamp recorded and collected by a TelosB sensor node acting like a key receiver. In the example the bit sequence "1101010101010101011" corresponding to the 16 bit key value 54613 is transmitted. In the figure one can clearly identify both long and short "light on" as well as "light off" time intervals. Moreover, at the beginning of the recording, it is also possible to identify the aiming phase where the user moved the light beam of the Sensor Node Lamp in the direction of the receiver node before releasing the user button and thereby starting the actual protocol.

Fig. 8.5 also illustrates another issue that we have already seen in the discussion of the Sensor Node Lamp interaction approach: Under seemingly stable external conditions, the light levels recorded by a receiver node oscillate significantly both during the "light on" and the "light off" states of the Sensor Node Lamp. As explained in Section 7.4.3, the reason for these oscillations lies in the properties of the fluorescent tubes used in the environment of the experiment that do not provide a constant light level but rather oscillate with a high frequency (100 Hz or 120 Hz). To deal with the negative impact of such continuous variations of the recorded light values, we use

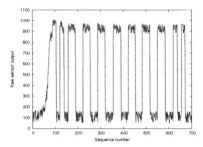

Figure 8.5: Light level example using the Sensor Node Lamp

the same approach as described in Section 7.4.3 and record multiple samples in short order for determining a value of l_{Base} near the upper bound of this oscillation range.

Security of the Light Channel

The primary reason for the security of the light signal sent by the Sensor Node Lamp lies in the fact that the light signal does not penetrate walls, doors and similar obstacles. Unlike for key data sent within radio messages which can be received by any adversary node within the (difficult to control) radio transmission range of the sender, the propagation of the light signal is limited to the physical area the signal is sent in. While eavesdropping is usually easy, observing is not.

To be able to record the key information, the adversary needs to observe the light signal either with the help of a light sensor placed within the area of influence of the Sensor Node Lamp or with a video camera that records images of the destination area. To do this, he needs access to the area where the key assignment is performed. This can be ruled out in many scenarios. In others, it might be possible to see if an adversary has placed a device for recording the light signal in the critical area.

An interesting side note regarding the recording of the light signal with a camera is that special equipment would be required to record a light signal sequence generated by the Sensor Node Lamp: With a minimum clock period of 10 ms as used in our experiments, the state of the light signal can change up to 200 times per second whereas standard video equipment only records between 24 and 30 images per second.

In application scenarios where the user of *Enlighten Me!* needs to deal with adversaries that might have access to the areas where the key assignment is performed, we need to make sure that they cannot record the light signal transmitted by the Sensor Node Lamp. One important factor here is that the user is able to regulate the size of the reception area by himself. By reducing his distance to the destination node, he can reduce the size of the area affected by the light signal of the Sensor Node Lamp. We will take a closer look at the spread of the light cone of the Sensor Node Lamp in the evaluation of *Enlighten Me!*.

In particularly adversary scenarios, we use a black plastic cup with a hole in the bottom to cover the receiver node and prevent any observation of the light signal from the outside. Note that, as mentioned in the discussion of the attacker model in Section 8.3, it is very difficult to provide for the security of individual nodes or the network environment as a whole if an adversary has direct physical access to the deployment area of the nodes.

8.5.2 Enlighten Me! PDA

Enlighten Me! with the Sensor Node Lamp as the key sender requires a dedicated hardware device for the transmission of key information. The motivation of the *Enlighten Me!* PDA approach is to use standard PDA hardware as the key sender. This way, we use hardware for the key assignment process that a user might carry with him anyway.

The idea of *Enlighten Me!* PDA is to place the key receiver node on the display of a PDA with the light sensor oriented towards the display and transmit the key information by varying the light levels shown on the display.

The *Enlighten Me!* PDA displays a rectangle switching its color between black and white representing the "light off" and "light on" states of the Manchester encoding. The underlying assumption is that the difference in the luminance level of the display showing these two colors is large enough to reliably differentiate the two states.

Based on the way it is used, the *Enlighten Me!* PDA approach is mainly applicable during the deployment of nodes and not for dynamic key assignments as it will usually not be possible to place a node on the display of the PDA after is has been deployed in the environment. As the Sensor Node Lamp is able to transmit key information over a significant distance, it does not share this limitation and can also be used for dynamic key assignments during the normal operation of a wireless sensor network in a pervasive computing environment.

Hardware

We have implemented the *Enlighten Me!* PDA approach for the Sharp Zaurus SL-3200 (see description in Section 2.2.2). Fig. 8.6 shows the setup in operation. The key receiver node is placed upside down on a predefined position on the display of the PDA so that the light sensor of the node faces the display. The second TelosB sensor node attached to the PDA over USB acts as a communication bridge to the sensor network.

Implementation

The software running on the PDA has been developed in C++ using the Qt toolkit. In addition to generating the light signal, the graphical user interface also allows the user to define both the key size and the key value to be transmitted to the sensor node

Figure 8.6: The Enlighten Me! PDA prototype

as part of the protocol. Before the protocol is started, a mirrored image of a sensor node helps the user in correctly placing the key receiver node on the PDA.

Despite being a much more powerful device, we cannot necessarily expect the *Enlighten Me!* implementation to work better on the PDA than on the Sensor Node Lamp. An important limitation of the PDA implementation is the switching speed of the LCD display used for the key transmission. Moreover, the low-level, monolithic TinyOS implementation on the Sensor Node Lamp allows for a more precise control of the timings of activating and deactivating the LED as part of the Manchester encoding. Consequently, as is confirmed later in the evaluation, we cannot expect to achieve the same level of precision in the timings of switching between the "light on" and the "light off" states as on the Sensor Node Lamp.

Fig. 8.7 shows the recorded light levels of the same example key transmission for the *Enlighten Me!* PDA as Fig. 8.5 does for the Sensor Node Lamp (also transmitting the bit sequence "11010101010101011"). Interestingly, the recording shows similar levels of noise in the light signal as we could observe for the recordings with the Sensor Node Lamp. In the case of the *Enlighten Me!* PDA, the explanation lies in the illumination of the PDA display which also does not provide a constant light level over time. We deal with the noise in the light signal at the message receiver the same way as described for the approach using the Sensor Node Lamp.

Security of the Light Channel

For the security of the light channel, it is again critical to guarantee that no adversary is able to observe, record and interpret the light signal transmitted between the key sender device and the key receiver node. However, for the *Enlighten Me!* PDA solution, this requirement is easier to fulfill than for the Sensor Node Lamp approach: Our implementation shows the light signal used to transmit the key information only in the area of the display where the light sensor of the key receiver node is placed. This area is completely covered by the sensor node. Additionally, we show bright colors on the rest of the display not covered by the sensor node during the key transmission to outshine any light level differences possibly escaping from under the sensor node.

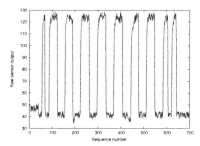

Figure 8.7: Light level example *Enlighten Me!* PDA

This approach makes an external observation of the signal practically impossible.

If the user places the key receiver node incorrectly leaving the send area of the light signal exposed, then the protocol will already fail and abort during the handshake phase – before any secret key information is transmitted over the light channel.

8.5.3 Key Receiver Implementation

We have implemented the key receiver part of *Enlighten Me!* based on TinyOS 2 for TelosB sensor nodes. Due to the modular nature of TinyOS, it is straightforward to combine the *Enlighten Me!* key receiver implementation with application code that realizes the other parts of the security solution and the actual node functionality.

Both the Sensor Node Lamp and the *Enlighten Me!* PDA use the exact same protocol for the key assignment process. Consequently, the basic key receiving mechanism is independent of whether the Sensor Node Lamp or the *Enlighten Me!* PDA is used for sending the key data and we can use the same receiver implementation. Nodes are then able to receive key data from both types of sender devices. The only difference lies in the length of the clock period Δ_{clock} and the light threshold δ_{thresh} used for the Manchester encoding on the Sensor Node Lamp and the PDA. However, the sender node advertises its type as part of the handshake trigger message and the receiver is able to adjust its decoding behavior accordingly.

8.6 Evaluation

In this section we show and discuss our results from the evaluation of the *Enlighten Me!* key assignment mechanism with both the Sensor Node Lamp and the *Enlighten Me!* PDA.

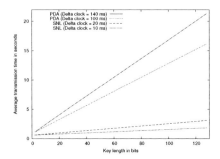

Figure 8.8: Average key transmission times

8.6.1 Key Assignment Performance and Reliability

It is important that the *Enlighten Me!* key assignment process is reasonably fast in order to support the user in quickly assigning keys when configuring the network or when interacting with nodes. To evaluate this, we measured the execution time of the key assignment process with *Enlighten Me!* using different key lengths. We worked with key sizes of up to 128 bits which a current report [146] describes as sufficient for a long-term protection of data when symmetric encryption is used.

The biggest contributor to the overall time is the time required for sending the key as a light signal which depends both on the key length and the clock period Δ_{clock} of the signal transmission. The smaller Δ_{clock} is selected, the more bits can be transmitted per time interval. To minimize this time, we experimented with different values of Δ_{clock} trying to select the smallest value possible.

We found that one important limiting factor for the minimum size of the clock period is the time taken for sampling the light sensor on the receiver nodes. We determined an approximate value for this with an experiment measuring the time taken for sampling the TelosB light sensor 1,000,000 times in a row. This measurement resulted in an estimate of 1.09 ms per sampling. As the sensor must be sampled multiple times per clock cycle, this already gives an idea of a lower bound for Δ_{clock} which is expected to lie in the range of a few milliseconds.

As we have discussed before, another limiting factor for minimizing Δ_{clock} is the switching speed and the timing precision of the light source of the key sender device. Experiments with different values of the clock period for both key sender devices confirmed our expectations that we can operate with much smaller values of Δ_{clock} for the Sensor Node Lamp approach than for the *Enlighten Me!* PDA. Fig. 8.8 summarizes the results of these measurements showing the average time values determined across 200 successful experiments per setting.

As expected, the key transmission time grows in an almost perfectly linear fashion with the key length starting from a small, size-independent base overhead caused by the basic *Enlighten Me!* protocol. Transmitting a 128 bit key with the Sensor Node

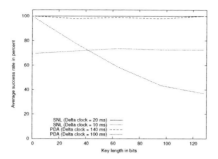

Figure 8.9: Average success rates

Lamp only takes between 1.8 seconds with a clock period Δ_{clock} of 10 milliseconds and 3.1 seconds with $\Delta_{clock} = 20ms$. Due to the necessity of selecting significantly larger values for Δ_{clock}, transmitting the same key with the *Enlighten Me!* PDA takes considerably longer: between 16.2 seconds with a clock period of 100 milliseconds and 21.3 seconds for $\Delta_{clock} = 140ms$. This shows the main advantage of the directly controllable LED of the Sensor Node Lamp over the LCD display of the Sharp Zaurus PDA.

The second important factor besides performance is the reliability of the key assignment with *Enlighten Me!*. Apart from user-induced errors (e.g., moving the light source away from the key receiver during the key transmission), a key assignment can mainly fail due to two reasons. Firstly, noise in the light signal or light level variations caused by external (natural or artificial) light sources can interfere with the light signal decoding at the receiver. Secondly, imprecisions of the signal timings on both the sender and the receiver side can also impede the successful signal transmission.

To evaluate the reliability of the key assignment with *Enlighten Me!*, we measured the success rate for different values of Δ_{clock}. For the Sensor Node Lamp approach, we placed sender and receiver at a fixed distance of 1 meter in a room lit by artificial light coming from fluorescent tubes. Fig. 8.9 shows the results of these measurements.

The Sensor Node Lamp with $\Delta_{clock} = 20ms$ and the *Enlighten Me!* PDA with $\Delta_{clock} = 140ms$ represent the cases of a reliable assignment of keys with both success rates in the range of 100% independent of the key length. However, when further decreasing Δ_{clock}, the behavior of the two approaches differs. On the one hand, for the *Enlighten Me!* PDA with $\Delta_{clock} = 100ms$, the success rate decreases when the key length increases. This is easily explained with the growing window of opportunity for timing errors in the signal or the signal decoding. On the other hand, for the Sensor Node Lamp with $\Delta_{clock} = 10ms$, the success rate remains relatively independent of the key length and lies between 69.5% and 73.5%. We found that almost all protocol errors occurred right at the beginning of the key transmission making the error rate independent of the key length. Either on the key sender or the key receiver timing imprecisions occur right at the beginning of the key transmission in a certain fraction of cases, for example caused by effects of the previous protocol steps. Note that at this very small value of Δ_{clock}, already very small delays caused by one hardware or software component can have a significant effect on the protocol procedure.

We were able to successfully perform key assignments with the *Enlighten Me!* PDA down to $\Delta_{clock} = 80ms$. However, in this case the success rate was only 11% for a key length of 48 bits and we did not observe any successful key assignments for key lengths of 64 bits or beyond. For the Sensor Node Lamp, we were not able to successfully use values of Δ_{clock} smaller than 10ms.

8.6.2 Key Assignment Distance

While the *Enlighten Me!* PDA solution requires the user to place the key receiver node directly on the PDA, it is possible to assign keys with the Sensor Node Lamp from a certain distance. We evaluated the maximum distances for the key assignment in a controlled experiment where we placed the Sensor Node Lamp and the key receiver node at different distances facing each other and measured the success rate across 200 experiments performed with the room lighting turned on. In a second experiment, we placed the receiver node with an angle of 45 degrees to the light coming from the Sensor Node Lamp. This represents the case when the user does not stand directly in front of the key receiver node, for example when it is attached up at a wall.

Fig. 8.10 shows the results of these experiments. Up to a certain distance (3.00 meters in the standard case, 2.40 meters at a receiver node angle of 45 degrees), the success rate is not affected at all. Beyond that "threshold distance", the success rate falls very steeply. Similarly to our experiments with the Sensor Node Lamp interaction approach in chapter 7, this can be explained as follows: With a growing distance between sender and receiver, the impact of the light of the LED on the receiver decreases. Above the threshold distance, the light level difference between the "light on" and the "light off" states becomes too small to compensate the continuous oscillations of the light levels caused by the artificial light in the room – the range of sensor values recorded in the "light on" state begins to overlap with the range of values in the "light off" state. Therefore, a reliable distinction of the states is not possible anymore and the detection of the light signal fails in most cases. Note the much sharper decline of the success rate in these experiments compared to the success rate with the Sensor Node Lamp interaction approach shown in Fig. 7.12 in Section 7.6.2. The main explanation for this is the much longer, more sophisticated light signal sequence in the *Enlighten Me!* key assignment protocol which provides ample opportunity for false positive light events once the threshold distance has been reached.

We were able to achieve higher maximum key assignment distances in experiments with the room lighting turned off (with exact values heavily depending on the current ambient light level). In some sense, the results shown in Fig. 8.10 represent the performance in the worst case scenario.

Overall, with a possible key assignment distance between 2 and 3 meters, it should

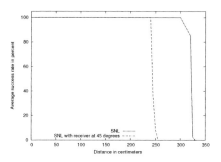

Figure 8.10: Success rate over distance

be possible to reach a large fraction of sensor nodes already deployed in a building or a similar environment. Assigning keys from even larger distances might not be desirable anyway as it reduces the control over which nodes are actually able to receive the light signal.

8.6.3 Security of the Light Channel

Transmitting keys over the light channel effectively prevents the overhearing of key information in neighboring rooms or areas. However, in some scenarios it might also be critical to limit the propagation of the signal within an area. To evaluate the properties of the Sensor Node Lamp in this regard, we measured the impact of the Sensor Node Lamp on light sensors not lying in the center of its light beam. For the experiment, we placed the Sensor Node Lamp and the receiver node 2 meters apart and then gradually moved the Sensor Node Lamp sidewards to move the light beam away from the light sensor. In each position we recorded 1000 sensor values and determined the maximum, minimum and average values for comparison with the base values recorded without the Sensor Node Lamp.

Fig. 8.11 shows the results of these measurements in a room for two situations both recorded at night: In the first experiment, the artificial room lighting was turned on. In the second experiment, the room lay in nearly complete darkness. As can be clearly seen in the graph, when moving the Sensor Node Lamp sidewards, the light level quickly approaches the range recorded without the Sensor Node Lamp in both situations. For the room lighting scenario, already at a sidewards distance of about 30 centimeters no significant difference between the recordings with and without the Sensor Node Lamp can be detected. In the dark room, the average light level recorded with the Sensor Node Lamp remains slightly higher than the average base level even at a sidewards distance of 100 centimeters. However, the range of values recorded with and without the Sensor Node Lamp heavily overlaps starting at a sidewards distance of about 50 centimeters so that a reliable signal detection will not be possible anymore.

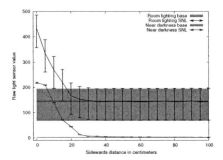

Figure 8.11: Light level over sidewards distance

Note that in the dark room the red light of the Sensor Node Lamp – albeit too weak for the TelosB light sensor – was visible for the human eye over a much larger area, partly due to reflections. Consequently, with specialized equipment it might still be possible to record the signal farther away from the target area. In the room lighting situation, the high ambient light level and the noise present in the ambient light actually help in limiting such an unwanted propagation of the Sensor Node Lamp light signal.

We also performed experiments in daylight scenarios where it showed that the sidewards decrease of the Sensor Node Lamp influence is similar to the room lighting scenario. The main influence here is the comparatively high ambient light level which quickly outshines the Sensor Node Lamp. However, systematic measurements like shown in Fig. 8.11 are difficult to produce as the base light level generated by natural light varies significantly even over relatively short time periods.

As one important result, our measurements have shown that the Sensor Node Lamp allows to effectively limit the reception area of the key signal. In daylight and room lighting scenarios, the high ambient light level and significant variations in this light level help in limiting the propagation of the light signal. If, however, the key assignment has to be performed in a particularly adversary environment, we still recommend to use an auxiliary device like the black cup described before to prevent the light signal from being recorded by other nodes than the destination node.

8.6.4 Memory Overhead

Since the key receiver functionality of *Enlighten Me!* will only form a small part of the application running on a wireless sensor node, its consumption of both program memory and main memory is a very important factor: An auxiliary service like key assignment should only consume a small part of the resources of a sensor node.

With Blink, Oscilloscope and MViz, we have used the same representative applications from the TinyOS source tree as in the evaluation of our node interaction

Table 8.1: Memory overhead analysis

		Blink	Oscilloscope Temperature	Oscilloscope Light	MViz
Original	ROM	2650 bytes	13426 bytes	16592 bytes	28134 bytes
	RAM	55 bytes	394 bytes	438 bytes	1912 bytes
Key	ROM	18820 bytes	20912 bytes	19376 bytes	30558 bytes
Receiver	RAM	556 bytes	666 bytes	632 bytes	2100 bytes

approaches in Section 7.6 and have integrated the key receiver implementation of *Enlighten Me!* with these applications. Table 8.1 summarizes the resulting size values for both program memory (ROM) and main memory (RAM).

Overall, the size values in the table show that the overhead is reasonably small both in program memory and main memory (e.g., only 2424 bytes of program memory and 188 bytes of main memory for the MViz application) and should allow the integration with a variety of applications. Like in similar measurements discussed in chapter 7, the more of the required modules the application already contains, the smaller is the overhead of integrating the key receiver mechanism – ranging from the very simple Blink application that only includes minimal functionality by itself (i.e., no sensor access modules and no communication components) to the complex MViz application which allows reusing large parts of the code.

8.7 Summary

In this chapter we have presented *Enlighten Me!*, a novel approach for the secure assignment of secret keys to wireless sensor nodes that is easy and convenient to use. We have introduced the basic concept of *Enlighten Me!*, discussed the types of attacks it is able to deal with, the details of the protocol and our two types of key sender devices. In the evaluation section we have demonstrated that *Enlighten Me!* achieves its goals and provides an efficient solution for the assignment of keys to wireless sensor nodes – both in classic sensor network scenarios and in more dynamic pervasive computing environments.

8.7.1 Future Directions in this Area

One possible way of improving the performance of *Enlighten Me!* as part of future work is to investigate coding schemes that are more efficient than the Manchester coding we used. However, these schemes might also be more susceptible to timing errors and it could be interesting to investigate which type of solution provides the best compromise between coding efficiency and failure resilience. For the *Enlighten Me!* PDA solution, it might also be possible to improve the efficiency of the data transmission by working with multiple light levels (by displaying different colors) instead of doing the binary "light on" / "light off" encoding.

Another interesting topic for future research in this area is the the integration of our key sender functionality into other commercial off-the-shelf devices. For example, we imagine using the small LEDs which are integrated as a photoflash replacement in some mobile phones today for sending key data. Being able to securely assign key data with mobile phones would provide us with client devices that are nearly ubiquitously available.

We selected the key assignment from mobile devices to static wireless sensor nodes as our contribution to the area of security and privacy in pervasive computing scenarios integrating wireless sensor networks, because we see this as an important building block that was still missing a good solution. For many other aspects of security and privacy, either existing solutions can be used or special solutions tailored to pervasive computing and wireless sensor networks already exist. Nevertheless, we see an important area for future work in the development of a security framework for pervasive computing and wireless sensor networks that integrates all these different aspects, works on various types of hardware with widely different capabilities and helps in making security and privacy a natural aspect of future network deployments.

One big remaining problem of security in pervasive computing that we see and that was also already mentioned in this chapter is the operation in potentially hostile environments. The very assumption that services provided by pervasive computing devices (e.g., wireless sensor nodes) are ubiquitously available requires nodes to be deployed in areas to which both users and malicious entities have access. Providing for a secure operation and secure communication of individual devices or the pervasive computing environment as a whole despite the presence of these malicious entities is a very challenging problem that cannot be solved using standard security solutions. Interesting areas for future research in this direction include intrusion detection systems and tamper proof systems.

9 Code Module Exchange on Sensor Nodes

The ability to update or change the program code installed on wireless sensor nodes is essential to support the flexibility and adaptability requirements of pervasive computing scenarios these sensor nodes are participating in. While application changes and code updates are simple to do in more powerful systems, they present a significant challenge in wireless sensor networks.

In this chapter we describe TinyModules, a novel code update solution for TinyOS-based wireless sensor nodes. TinyModules allows for the exchange of application modules rather than exchanging the complete code image while avoiding most of the computational overhead for integrating the module into the existing code incurred by other module-based solutions. It provides the flexibility and adaptability required by pervasive computing applications as it allows mobile client devices to install application specific modules on nodes in their vicinity.

9.1 Preliminaries

The flexibility and adaptability requirements of pervasive computing applications imply similar requirements for the wireless sensor nodes operating as part of pervasive computing scenarios. If these sensor nodes are to be used as more than mere providers of raw sensor data, then they must be able to adapt their behavior based on varying application and user requirements in the pervasive computing environment. While some of these changes occurring over time can be anticipated and might already be incorporated in the application logic, other changes require an actual adaptation and a modification of the program code executed on the wireless sensor nodes. This is particularly true for cases where new users, new applications or new types of devices enter the scenario. This is a common case in pervasive computing scenarios.

Adapting the behavior of applications, changing the program code of applications or starting the execution of different applications are usually simple tasks on standard computer systems. However, on wireless sensor nodes and devices with similar hardware constraints such adaptations are a significant challenge. Firstly, the strong resource constraints of the nodes set hard limits on the complexity of the operations and the amount of data that can be processed and stored as part of a code update. In sensor networks, it is also important to consider the energy costs of the different update operations – a factor that can usually be ignored on standard computer systems. Secondly, as detailed in chapter 2 of this thesis, operating system and application code are often tightly interwoven which makes replacing one part of the system without also changing the others a challenging task. Moreover, instead of running multiple independent applications in parallel, sensor nodes typically only execute a single application. Thirdly, while more powerful computer systems can store a multitude of applications and different code options in their memory, sensor nodes can only provide a limited amount of storage space. At the same time, transmitting code updates to wireless sensor nodes is a costly operation in itself. Overall, code updates are a significant cost factor in wireless sensor networks and care must be taken in the design of appropriate code update mechanisms.

The problem of updating the code on wireless sensor nodes and in complete wireless sensor networks can be structured into three parts: First of all, we need an efficient mechanism for the distribution of code updates in the sensor network. Secondly, it must be determined what data needs to be distributed in the course of an update and, thirdly, how the update is integrated on the individual sensor nodes. In most cases, the first problem part can be considered separately from the other two and the resulting code distribution mechanism can then be combined with any solution for updating the program code on the individual nodes. The second and the third part of the code update problem, however, are strongly interdependent and must be solved together. In the following discussion, we will concentrate on this part of the problem and will assume that an appropriate code distribution mechanism is in place.

The most basic and simple way of updating and changing the program code installed on wireless sensor nodes is to exchange the complete code image and replace it with the code image of the new program version or the new application. However, while this approach is easy to implement and provides the maximum flexibility in switching between different applications, it can also be very costly in terms of time and energy consumption, because a complete code image must be transmitted to the nodes over the wireless interface for each update. Another problem of this approach specific to our application scenarios might be that a mobile device trying to install application-specific code on wireless sensor nodes in its vicinity does not necessarily have access to the complete configuration and the code image of the sensor nodes.

One goal of more advanced approaches to code updates in wireless sensor networks is to reduce the size of the update data that must be sent to individual nodes involved in the update. Such a size reduction results in a smaller number of update messages and thereby helps to reduce both the time and the energy consumption of the code distribution process. Moreover, a smaller load on the wireless channel reduces the potential for interferences with the normal operation of the application.

One way of achieving a size reduction of the code update data is to partition the application code into modules and to allow exchanging these modules individually. Ideally, only the modules affected and changed by an update then need to be re-distributed in the sensor network resulting in a significantly smaller update size for many update scenarios. One important aspect of such modularized code updates is the process of integrating a new or modified module into the existing code base on the individual sensor nodes. This can be a complex operation with a potentially significant integration overhead which in turn negates some of the advantage of having to distribute less update data.

TinyOS, the widely used operating system for sensor nodes, exhibits another problem with respect to modularization and modularized code updates. It heavily optimizes the program code at compile time and does neither preserve any of the modular structure found in the source code of TinyOS applications written in the nesC programming language nor does it isolate operating system code from application code. While the tight interweaving found in TinyOS is advantageous from the viewpoint of performance, it makes modularized code updates hard to do.

The problem that we aim to solve with the approach presented in this chapter is to perform efficient code updates on TinyOS-based wireless sensor nodes with the goal of providing the flexibility and adaptability required in pervasive computing scenarios. In particular, mobile users should be able to customize relevant parts of the system behavior on sensor nodes in their vicinity. We are looking for a solution that works based on modularization in order to optimize the size of the code updates as discussed above. At the same time, we aim to minimize the costs for integrating the code updates on the individual sensor nodes. One basic way to achieve this is to limit the scope of the updates to cases relevant to the application scenario at hand.

9.1.1 Problem Definition

Let us now define the problem of performing code updates in wireless sensor networks in general and based on that the problem of installing application-specific code modules as considered in this chapter. In this problem definition, we concentrate on the update content and the update integration and largely ignore the code distribution mechanism. Distributing code updates to nodes is an orthogonal problem which can be solved separately and mostly independent of the code update mechanism. We also approach the problem from the viewpoint of a single sensor node and do not consider aspects like the agreement on updates or the coordination of updates among the nodes in a wireless sensor network.

Performing Code Updates in Wireless Sensor Networks

The initial situation each code update starts from is a wireless sensor node running a code image X that realizes an application A. The code image comprises all code parts required for running the application A including both the application logic and the operating system components. Moreover, the code image also has to include the program code of the code distribution mechanism and the program code of the code update mechanism.

A code update process is triggered by a user requesting a transition from the current application A to a different application B (which can also be an updated version of A). Alternatively, such a change request can also be triggered automatically, for example by an adaptation mechanism. In the following, we assume the required code update data has already been transmitted to the sensor node and stored in its external flash memory. This transmission can usually be done in parallel to the normal execution of

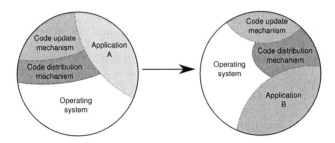

Figure 9.1: Schematic overview of a code image before and after a code update

the application A. The actual code update process is then started once the complete update data is available in the memory of the node.

As part of the code update process, the sensor node needs to prepare the code update data and then update or exchange the code image installed in its program memory. It thereby generates a new code image Y that realizes application B and again includes the program code of the code distribution mechanism and the program code of the code update mechanism.

Fig. 9.1 illustrates the changes to a code image in the course of a code update in a schematic representation. Since the four parts application code, operating system, code distribution mechanism and code update mechanism are not separated from each other, the layout of the code image after updating to application B does not have to show any structural similarity to the code image X from before the update.

Another way of looking at the problem of code updates in wireless sensor networks is to consider the individual steps that need to be performed in the course of a code update. Here, one can distinguish between steps required for preparing a system for code updates and the different steps of actually performing a code update.

In preparing a system for code updates, the first steps need to be performed before the deployment of the network. Most importantly, the program code for the sensor nodes must be prepared for future code updates and needs to include both the code distribution mechanism and the implementation of the code update algorithm itself. Depending on the code update solution used, it also needs to adhere to special requirements, for example a special structure of the code. The second part of the preparation then pertains to the deployment of the initial code image on the sensor nodes. This initial code image can either realize the first incarnation of the sensor node application or it can be a purely generic base implementation with the real application being installed using the code update mechanism.

After the first two preparatory steps, a valid code image is executed on the wireless sensor nodes and the sensor network is ready to receive code updates. The first step of such an update is the preparation of the code update data on the base station or on a client device initiating an update. The required procedure heavily depends on the code update mechanism used and has to ensure that the update data is compatible to the program code currently installed in the sensor network. The second step is then the injection of the code update data into the network and the code distribution to all affected nodes in the network. The third step is a direct consequence of the second step and encompasses the reception and storage of the code update data on the individual nodes. The fourth and final step, the installation of the code update, is then performed locally on the individual nodes. This step usually consists of the preparation of the code update and the transfer of the code to the program memory of the node.

Code Module Exchanges on Wireless Sensor Nodes

After describing the general code update problem above, let us now introduce a formal definition of a constrained version of this problem, the code module exchange on wireless sensor nodes, that we solve as part of this chapter. While the definition of this problem appears similar to the general code update problem, we will later see how the additional constraints allow for efficient code module exchanges.

As before, we start with a wireless sensor node running a code image X that realizes an application A. However, now we assume that the code image adheres to a given internal structure consisting of two separate parts: a static base implementation $CodeImage_{static}$ and a dynamic module part $CodeImage_{module_A}$. For the code update process, the major difference is that only the dynamic module part $CodeImage_{module_A}$ can be updated or exchanged during a code update whereas the static base implementation remains unchanged.

As part of the code update, the sensor node switches from code image X to a new code image Y that realizes the new application B. Y again consists of two parts, the original static base implementation $CodeImage_{static}$ and a new dynamic module part $CodeImage_{module_B}$.

Analogously to Fig. 9.1 for general code updates, Fig. 9.2 provides a schematic representation of the changes to a code image when exchanging a code module. Now, the operating system, the code distribution mechanism and the code update mechanism remain unchanged and only the part of the code image storing the code module needs to be modified. In this way, the structure of the code image is preserved.

9.1.2 Requirements

Like for the other solution approaches discussed in this thesis, the **correctness** of the solution is also the most fundamental requirement when considering code updates and the exchange of code modules. In this context, correctness means that the update mechanism must preserve the integrity of the code image installed on the sensor node and must correctly transform the previous version of the code image X into the new code image Y realizing the new version of the sensor node application B.

Another important factor is the **efficiency** of the code update. Here, efficiency concerns two aspects: the time required for the update and the energy consumption of the update operations. The code update time is relevant, because the user expects a

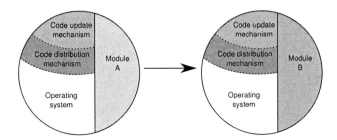

Figure 9.2: Schematic code image overview before and after a code module exchange

timely reaction to his update requests. Moreover, as the update process often interferes with the normal operation of the node to some extent (e.g., interrupting the program execution), a shorter duration of the update helps in limiting the negative effects of such interferences.

Minimizing the energy consumption of code updates is important, because energy usually is the most limited resource on wireless sensor nodes that constrains the lifetime of the sensor node and the sensor network as a whole. The energy consumption is closely linked to the time requirements with longer running updates consuming more energy. However, the energy-related properties of the operations used also have a significant impact. For example, message send and receive operations or operations accessing the external flash memory of the node are much more expensive than computations performed by the processor.

In wireless sensor networks, there often exists a tradeoff between the efficiency of the code update and the efficiency of the normal sensor node operation. For example, the use of byte code interpreted by a virtual machine running on the wireless sensor node provides for very simple and efficient updates of code but results in a comparatively low performance in the execution of the application code. In general, it is important to find the **right balance between code update efficiency and code execution efficiency** based on the requirements of the respective application scenario (e.g., the expected update frequency).

There are two fundamental aspects that must be considered for achieving efficiency in code updates: the size of the code update sent to the nodes and the overhead for integrating updates on the wireless sensor nodes. The smaller the size of the code update, the fewer messages need to be sent within the sensor network to distribute the update to all affected nodes. Fewer messages both result in a shorter update time and save on energy as sending and receiving data over the wireless interface consumes significant amounts of resources. The amount of effort required for integrating a code update into the existing code image on the sensor nodes similarly affects the time and energy consumption of the code update with fewer and less costly integration operations reducing the time and energy requirements. As both aspects are particularly relevant for the code module exchanges considered in this chapter, we add **mini-**

mizing the size of the update code sent to the nodes and minimizing the overhead for integrating code modules on the wireless sensor nodes to the list of requirements for our code module exchange mechanism.

Besides correctness and efficiency, **flexibility** is a third important requirement for code update solutions in wireless sensor networks. The code update mechanism should support any type of update required by the user in the application scenario at hand. In general, it should be possible to replace the current code image A with any other code image B. However, as detailed in the problem definition above, the update needs of an application scenario can often be met by a less general solution supporting a specific subset of updates. In TinyModules we optimize the efficiency of code module exchanges but also support complete code exchanges as a fallback solution.

9.1.3 Application Scenarios

The main application scenario for the TinyModules code update mechanism presented in this chapter are mobile pervasive computing devices operating in areas equipped with wireless sensor nodes or similar resource-poor devices. As described in detail in chapter 3, pervasive computing scenarios require a high level of flexibility and adaptability from participating devices to deal with changing application requirements. Providing the ability to update code parts is an important aspect of adaptability on wireless sensor nodes and we envision two ways of using TinyModules in this context.

Firstly, mobile client devices can use the code module exchange mechanism to install an application-specific module on sensor nodes in their vicinity. This module can then support the provision of pervasive computing services to the user of the mobile device. By allowing the installation of such application-specific code modules, the sensor nodes can adapt to the varying needs and requirements of the applications run in their environment. One example usage of such application-specific modules could be the detection of events where the module installed on the sensor nodes triggers exactly the set of sensor events required by the user application.

The second application scenario for TinyModules in the context of pervasive computing relates to the setup and configuration of nodes in smart environments. We expect that sensor nodes are delivered with a generic base installation and the code module exchange mechanism could be used to customize the behavior of sensor nodes during the setup and configuration of a smart environment by plugging in custom modules through well-defined interfaces as required by cooperating devices and the applications running in the smart environment.

While the main target scenario of our work is the installation of application modules on resource-constrained nodes from mobile pervasive computing devices, TinyModules can also be used as a code update mechanism in standard wireless sensor networks. However, due to the specific focus in the design of TinyModules, it is not well-suited for performing arbitrary code updates. It should mainly be used to exchange specific code modules prepared for this kind of update process.

There are two main ways of using TinyModules in wireless sensor networks. Firstly, it can be used to switch between different applications building upon a generic base implementation. The base implementation provides common functionality like sensor access, timers or communication used by all applications. The exchangeable code module building on top of that base then only needs to provide the application specific functionality. This allows switching between highly different applications by only exchanging a small part of the code image. We use such a scenario in the evaluation section of this chapter to illustrate the capabilities and the performance of TinyModules.

The second type of application for TinyModules in wireless sensor networks is switching between different implementations of an algorithm or a protocol that keep the same external interface. As an example, a sensor node application could use TinyModules to quickly and efficiently switch between different routing protocols or different data processing algorithms when triggered by external commands or for adapting and optimizing its own behavior given the current external conditions.

9.1.4 Overview of Approach

The idea of TinyModules is to divide the code image installed on wireless sensor nodes into a static part, the *ModuleFrame*, and an exchangeable part, the so-called *TinyModule*. While the static part of the code image remains unchanged throughout the lifetime of the sensor node (or until a complete code exchange is performed), the *TinyModule* can be dynamically exchanged in an efficient manner at any time of the system operation.

The developer can freely define which parts of the application and system code should be part of the *ModuleFrame* or the *TinyModule* giving him the flexibility to define which parts of the code TinyModules should be able to update. *ModuleFrame* and *TinyModule* then interact through a well-defined, static interface that ensures that the *ModuleFrame* can interact with different *TinyModule* instances.

The main concept of TinyModules is to prepare a special memory layout for the code both in program memory and in the main memory of the sensor nodes. The special memory layout is responsible for two things. Firstly, it cleanly separates *ModuleFrame* and *TinyModule* from each other so that the *TinyModule* can be exchanged without affecting the code of the *ModuleFrame* in program memory and without having to change the location of *ModuleFrame* data objects in main memory. Secondly, both parts of the code image are structured in a way that ensures that the memory addresses for calls from the *ModuleFrame* to the *TinyModule* remain constant irrespective of the current *TinyModule* instance.

Based on the preparations of the code image and the memory layout described above, the actual code update process on the individual sensor nodes is relatively simple and can be performed in an efficient manner. The main task to perform is to copy the code of the new TinyModule to the program memory. After that, only a small number of simple adjustments are necessary to generate a valid code image before restarting the node.

We have integrated TinyModules with an established code distribution mechanism that allows distributing and installing TinyModules code updates in a multihop wireless sensor network.

9.2 Related Work

Related work in the area of code updates in wireless sensor networks can mainly be classified in two groups: Code distribution mechanisms (e.g., [104, 121]) and code exchange and integration mechanisms on the sensor nodes (e.g., [82, 166]).

Code distribution mechanisms are concerned with efficiently distributing code update data within a wireless sensor network. On the one hand, they need to ensure that updates are distributed in a timely fashion to all affected nodes after new updates become available. On the other hand, they need to minimize the number of messages exchanged between the nodes, especially during time periods without new update data. An additional challenge is keeping the code versions available to the nodes largely consistent in the whole network despite message loss and temporary network partitionings.

The mechanisms for code exchange and integration assume that code updates are being distributed to the sensor nodes by some code distribution mechanism and deal with the question of what data needs to be transmitted to the nodes as part of an update and how this data is then used to actually update the program code installed on the nodes.

Both areas of code distribution and of code exchange and integration have received considerable attention in recent years [205, 73]. Since TinyModules concentrates on code exchange and integration and can be combined with any code distribution mechanism, we concentrate on the second group in the following discussion.

9.2.1 Code Exchange Mechanisms

There are different basic mechanisms available for exchanging code on wireless sensor nodes. Each of them builds upon different assumptions and requires different preparations before deployment and before injecting an update into the network.

Complete Code Exchanges

The basic way of performing code updates in wireless sensor networks is to distribute the complete code image of the new program version in the sensor network and then to install this code image on the individual nodes. The obvious advantage of these complete code exchanges is their simplicity: The required processing on the sensor nodes is mainly concerned with the code distribution whereas the code update procedure only needs to buffer the code image and then transfer it to the program memory once it has been completely received. However, the main disadvantage is the large volume of data of the code images distributed with each update. This entails a high overhead in terms of update time and energy consumption. Deluge [82], which is part of the standard TinyOS releases, is the best known representative of this class of update mechanisms. One of its features is an advanced code distribution mechanism that aims to minimize the amount of communication among the nodes while providing for reliable and timely distribution of changes.

Stream [151] implements a variation of the concept of complete code exchanges building upon Deluge. Its idea is to segment the program code into two images, the application image and the code update image. The sensor nodes reboot from the application image to the code update image whenever a code update is triggered. Code updates only exchange the application image thereby saving the overhead for transmitting the code update program code. The authors show that this provides for significant savings in the size of the code updates. A clear downside of Stream is the strong division between application phase and code update phase: Nodes always have to reboot and reprogram themselves first to perform code distribution or code update operations – even when they are only required to forward program code to a newly joined neighbor node. TinyModules provides the same advantages as Stream in that it does not transmit the code distribution program code as part of its code updates. At the same time, TinyModules is not subject to the described limitations of Stream.

Diff-based Approaches

Diff-based approaches [166, 86, 119] aim to reduce the amount of data to be transferred to the wireless sensor nodes by calculating the changes between the code image installed on the nodes and the new code image. Only these modified parts of the code need to be transmitted in the form of a change script which can then be used to construct the new code image on the nodes.

Reijers and Langendoen [166] use a diff-like approach to compute a diff script that transforms the installed code image into a new one. Likewise, the incremental network programming protocol presented by Jeong and Culler [86] uses the Rsync algorithm [199] to find variable-sized blocks that exist in both code images and then only transmits the differences. However, both of these approaches just compare the code image using very limited knowledge about the application structure, if at all.

The main challenge for diff-based code updates is that already small changes to the source code of a program can result in heavy changes in the compiled binary code. For example, a single command added to a function increases the size of the function code and might shift the complete program code placed behind this function backwards. This, in turn, entails changes to all code locations referencing the moved code. Consequently, such a small change can result in a large change script and many adjustment operations for reconstructing the new code image on the individual nodes. A variety of optimizations are required to deal with such problems and to keep the size of the change scripts small and the integration operations efficient.

Koshy and Pandey [99] describe a scheme that uses incremental linking (on a PC) to reduce the number of changes in the code and transmit the code update with a diff-like algorithm. They leave most parts of the previous program image unchanged and modify only those functions that actually change. In order to avoid address shifts when the size of a function changes, they add empty space behind each function.

UCC [119] also prepares diff-based code updates already at compile time and generates binaries in a way that later minimizes the number of required update operations in the change script. The authors concentrate on two areas, the placement of variables and the allocation of registers for variables. They aim to place new variables at the location of old, deleted variables and – up to a certain limit – leave space empty if variables are deleted in order to avoid moving other variables. For the allocation of registers, they try to avoid moving variables to other registers due to a code update. Up to certain limits, they even add additional commands for this purpose.

Overall, diff-based approaches can be an efficient solution for code updates, particularly when the changes to the code remain rather small. They are not well-suited for updates exchanging significant parts of the functionality or restructuring the code image. Moreover, when considering diff-based code updates, one has to be aware of the fact that updating the code based on a change script entails considerable processing overhead on the sensor nodes which can be a significant cost factor of the overall update procedure.

Virtual Machine Approaches

A popular alternative to performing code updates on wireless sensor nodes is to use virtual machines [117, 100]. Instead of installing and executing machine code, these virtual machines interpret byte code which can be directly read in from main memory or external flash memory. This saves the cost for transferring data to the program memory and often allows a more compact representation of the application logic which saves transmission costs. However, the expressiveness of these small VM languages is necessarily limited and the execution performance lies well below the performance of native code. Consequently, virtual machines are mainly used in scenarios with a very high update frequency.

9.2.2 Operating System Support

As already discussed in chapter 2, some sensor network operating systems other than TinyOS already provide support for exchanging modules in the running system as a core operating system service, for example Contiki [43], SOS [72] and MANTIS [3]. They achieve modularization and the exchangeability of modules at the cost of additional levels of indirection and some runtime overhead. Refer to chapter 2 for a short description of how these operating systems realize these update mechanisms.

9.2.3 FlexCup

As part of previous work [54, 131], we have developed **FlexCup**, a code update mechanism for wireless sensor networks running the TinyOS operating system. Our experiences with both the development and the use of FlexCup have strongly influenced the design and development of the TinyModules code module exchange approach that is presented in this chapter. For that reason, we discuss FlexCup in a little more detail in the following paragraphs.

Unlike other code update solutions previously available for TinyOS, the design of FlexCup is based on the concept of code modularization. FlexCup aims to support the exchange of individual code modules (also often called components) rather than exchanging the complete code image. The goal of this approach is to only have to exchange the code of the modified components in the course of a code update thereby minimizing the amount of data that has to be distributed within the network. Since TinyOS does not support such a modularization of its compiled code by itself, FlexCup needed to introduce a module concept and FlexCup's main responsibility then is the dynamic integration of updated code modules into the existing code image on the individual sensor nodes.

FlexCup Concepts

Like TinyModules, FlexCup is based on the concept of binary components. Binary components are a feature of the nesC compiler that allows to compile a set of TinyOS modules separately from the rest of the application code into a standard object file called binary component. This standard object file is then only combined with the rest of the application code by the linker when assembling the code image. By generating a binary component for each code module defined by the application programmer, FlexCup is able to clearly separate the different code parts from each other in the binary code image. Such a separation is essential for being able to exchange individual code modules independently from each other.

To perform its tasks, FlexCup needs to be involved in compiling the components on the base station: During the code generation process, it generates meta-data that describes the compiled components. This meta-data consists of three parts: generic program information, a program-wide symbol table and a relocation table for each binary component in the program code. The symbol table contains information on the global data and function symbols used by the different components. The relocation tables list the references from inside the component code to data or function symbols specified in the symbol table. The program meta-data is then stored on each sensor node and component meta-data is also transmitted with each code update to provide information about the updated components. FlexCup uses this meta-data during a code update to place the new components inside the existing application code, relink function calls to the appropriate locations and perform address binding of data objects.

FlexCup does not deal with the distribution of code updates in the network but concentrates on the code update part. It can be combined with any code distribution mechanism and the basic implementation used, just like TinyModules, the established code distribution mechanism from Deluge.

The core part of FlexCup is a dynamic linker operating on the individual sensor nodes. It is responsible for integrating new or updated code components into the existing code image. After the components have been received over the wireless communication interface and have been stored in the external flash memory of the node, the FlexCup Linker starts the integration process. As a first step, it copies the new component code into a copy of the code image maintained in the external flash memory. If necessary, it moves other components within the code image to clear space for the updated components. Following this, it updates the meta-data of the program to reflect updated locations of symbols both within program memory and data memory and overwrites the relocation tables of the updated components with the new versions. Next, the linker goes through the relocation tables of all components and checks whether any of the references need to be updated. An update is required for all references coming from new component code and for all references to data symbols and function symbols that changed their address during an update. After performing these changes where required, the code image is ready for installation. As the final step of the update process, a bootloader copies the new version of the code image from the external flash memory to the program memory of the nodes and restarts the application.

Results

For evaluating the performance of FlexCup, the approach has been compared to two other basic code update solutions: Deluge [82] as a representative of approaches implementing complete code exchanges and MOAP-Diff [191] as a representative of the diff-based approaches. In addition, a second version of FlexCup was considered where the MOAP-diff algorithm was used to compute a diff of old and new versions of a binary component and to only transmit this diff script (FlexCup Diff).

Fig. 9.3 and Fig. 9.4 summarize experimental results for the four approaches showing the time and energy consumption of Deluge, MOAP-Diff, FlexCup and FlexCup Diff in six different scenarios. FlexCup is clearly superior to both Deluge and MOAP-Diff both in terms of update time and energy consumption. Due to the smaller update size, it requires significantly less time and energy than Deluge for transmitting the update data in the network. The additional overhead for preparing the code image on the nodes does only take up a small part of these savings. Compared to MOAP-Diff, FlexCup generates less integration overhead which overcompensates the sometimes slightly higher cost for transmitting the code to the nodes. Comparing FlexCup with FlexCup Diff nicely illustrates that the integration operations on the sensor nodes can be a critical factor causing FlexCup Diff to perform worse in some cases despite significantly lower update data volumes.

Limitations

Despite the very good results FlexCup showed in comparison to other code update approaches for TinyOS, our experience with its use also showed a set of limitations which motivate the work on alternative approaches like the TinyModules code update solution discussed in this chapter. This is particularly true for scenarios with specific needs like sensor networks being deployed as part of pervasive computing scenarios as discussed in this thesis.

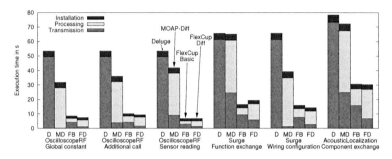

Figure 9.3: Execution times of code updates with FlexCup (from [131])

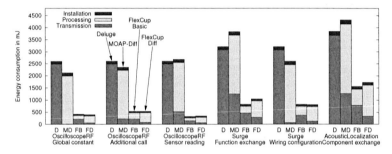

Figure 9.4: Energy consumption of code updates with FlexCup (from [131])

One of the strengths of FlexCup, the complete flexibility in defining the partitioning of the application and operating system code into separate modules, proved to also be one of FlexCup's main weaknesses: Partitioning a large application into a reasonable set of binary components is a lot of work as not only the application modules but also all TinyOS modules and library modules used by the application need to be considered. Unfortunately, the concept of binary components did not get widely recognized by the TinyOS community and a clean structuring of the TinyOS operating system into parts suitable for binary components never happened. Moreover, defining meaningful, stable interfaces between different parts of the system is very difficult (e.g., an interface for the routing module that fits all possible types of routing algorithms). However, without such preparatory work, the partitioning has to be done over and over again for each type of application which is in general too much overhead for a code update mechanism.

Another limitation of FlexCup is its strong hardware dependence. FlexCup was implemented for the MICA family of sensor nodes which use processors based on the AVR RISC architecture. Changing the processor or other central elements of the system (e.g., the compiler) would entail a reimplementation of large parts of the

FlexCup code. This is mainly due to the relinking approach taken by FlexCup which is highly processor-specific and compiler-specific.

Related to the hardware dependence of FlexCup is another limitation, the strong requirements on the properties of the external flash memory used for storing and preparing code updates. As part of relinking the code image, FlexCup needs to be able to change small pieces of code (i.e., the relocation addresses) at individual locations in the flash memory. While this does not constitute a significant problem on the MICA sensor node platform (except for wear levelling and the energy cost for accessing the flash memory), the flash memory on the TelosB sensor nodes, as an example, does not support such random access write operations well. This limitation effectively prevented us from porting FlexCup to the TelosB sensor nodes and several other sensor node platforms.

Even on sensor node platforms that support the operations on flash memory performed by FlexCup, the update data and the update operations consume a significant amount of the flash memory which is then not available for storing application data. This limits the scope of applications of FlexCup to scenarios where the remaining available flash memory is sufficient for the application.

A final limitation of FlexCup is the difficulty of applying the solution approach to TinyOS 2. FlexCup was originally developed for TinyOS 1.1 and would have to be adapted to work with a current version of TinyOS. However, changes in the core architecture of TinyOS make this very difficult. One major problem for FlexCup in TinyOS 2 is the scheduler. It works with a static set of tasks that must be allocated at compile time. Such an allocation does not work across boundaries of binary components. As we will see below, there exists a simple workaround for that problem for TinyModules but not for FlexCup.

Overall, our experience showed that FlexCup – despite its performance advantages compared to related work – is a rather heavyweight solution that requires considerable preparatory work and cannot be applied in all scenarios.

Lessons Learned

Our experiences with FlexCup and particularly with the limitations of FlexCup listed above had a strong influence on the design of TinyModules. In the following paragraphs, we summarize the most important lessons learned from FlexCup and sketch how we have built upon these lessons with TinyModules.

One important lesson learned from our experience with FlexCup is that a code update solution should avoid – as far as possible – extensive and expensive computations on the wireless sensor nodes. While FlexCup's operation on the sensor node was significantly more efficient than the diff-based approach it was compared to, the computations required for preparing the code image still lost a noticeable part of the energy and time savings achieved by reducing the amount of code update data sent to the nodes. For TinyModules we avoid many of these costly operations by preparing the code image installed on the sensor nodes and the update data of the code module in a way that ensures that the update process requires little more than just copying the new code module to the program memory of the nodes.

Simplifying the operations required on the individual sensor nodes is also related to another lesson learned from FlexCup: A code update solution should preferably avoid a strong dependence on the hardware it is implemented on in order to facilitate the support of different hardware platforms. The FlexCup Linker running on the sensor nodes is inherently hardware dependent and would have to be largely reimplemented for every sensor node architecture. In TinyModules we avoid that by using a simple integration mechanism on the sensor nodes mainly copying the new code to program memory. Another positive effect of the simple integration is that TinyModules does not rely on special features of the flash memory and can basically be used on any sensor node platform that supports dynamic code updates. Note, however, that some dependence on the individual hardware platforms is unavoidable and must be adapted when porting the implementation. For TinyModules this mainly affects the compiler-dependent code preparation mechanism used before deploying code to the sensor nodes.

As mentioned above, one problem of FlexCup is the high initial cost for preparing the program code of a sensor node application for future modularized code updates. As this is a considerable obstacle to the adoption of the mechanism, TinyModules aims to avoid this: The developer does not have to provide a module structure for the complete code image with well-defined interfaces between all connected code parts. Instead, only a single interface between the static part and the exchangeable part must be defined. The scope of this interface can be freely defined by the developer.

Finally, a general insight resulting from our experience with FlexCup is that there is a tradeoff between the flexibility and generality of a code update solution on the one side and the simplicity and efficiency of its implementation on the other side. With FlexCup we aimed for a general solution that can basically perform any kind of code update task in an efficient manner. However, it is possible to simplify the code update implementation by narrowing the scope and only supporting a specific type or a specific way of code updates as required in the respective application scenario. In TinyModules, we realize this by supporting the exchange of one specific application module instead of providing a generic code update solution based on modularization. Nevertheless, TinyModules provides a significant amount of flexibility as it allows the system developer to freely define the border between the static part and the dynamic part of the code image.

9.3 Code Modularization With TinyModules

In this section we introduce the basic concept of code modularization with TinyModules and the exchange of such modules as part of a code update operation. We start with a short discussion of modularization in TinyOS and its implications for our mechanism before we continue with the various aspects of modularization in TinyModules.

9.3.1 Modularization in TinyOS

In Section 2.1.2 of Chapter 2 we have given a high-level overview of the concepts of the TinyOS operating system and its approaches on providing suitable operating system services on resource-constrained sensor node platforms. As mentioned there, modularization of source code is one of the core features of nesC [65], the programming language underlying the TinyOS operating system: TinyOS and the applications building on top of the operating system are structured in are large set of components that are wired together based on the application requirements. Unfortunately, this clean modularization is given up at compile time when the nesC compiler combines both application and operating system components into a single C file which is then compiled to binary code using a standard C compiler. The advantage of this approach taken by TinyOS is that considering the complete program in one piece facilitates performance optimizations and whole program analysis. The downside is that the lack of structure in the binary code complicates other tasks, like for example efficient code updates.

In the description of FlexCup in Section 9.2.3, we already mentioned the concept of binary components introduced in version 1.2 of the nesC compiler. Binary components support the preservation of some of the module structure from the nesC source code in the the binary code image by allowing the programmer to group together a set of TinyOS components and compile them separately from the rest of the program. Internally, a standard object file is then created for each binary component and these object files are assembled by the linker to create the executable. To the outside world, a binary component is specified by its component description – an interface which contains all nesC interfaces, commands and events which the binary component provides or uses.

Binary components as a feature of the nesC compiler originally did not aim at modularized code updates. Instead, the main idea was to allow developers to provide binary code libraries that others can integrate into their sensor node applications without having access to the library source code. Consequently, support for code updates using binary components has to be built as an additional feature on top of the basic concept – an approach taken by both FlexCup and TinyModules.

9.3.2 Modularization in TinyModules

Given the requirements detailed in Section 9.1.2 and the given properties of TinyOS, we designed TinyModules based on the concept of modularization in a way that allows a simple and efficient integration of modules on the individual sensor nodes. The idea is to divide the program code installed on the sensor nodes into a static part, the *ModuleFrame*, and an exchangeable part, the *TinyModule*. The two parts interact through a well-defined interface, the *TinyModule Interface*.

Like FlexCup, TinyModules builds upon the concept of binary components in nesC and uses it to implement modularized code updates. The exchangeable part of the code image – the TinyModule – is implemented as a binary component. The TinyModule

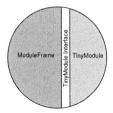

Figure 9.5: Schematic overview of a code image using TinyModules

Interface constitutes the external interface of this TinyModule binary component and describes how the TinyModule interacts with the rest of the program. The Module-Frame is implemented as a standard TinyOS application that integrates a TinyModule through its binary component interface (i.e., the TinyModule Interface).

Following the schematic display of code updates in Fig. 9.1 and code module exchanges in Fig. 9.2, Fig. 9.5 shows a schematic overview of the code image on a sensor node using TinyModules with the two code parts ModuleFrame and TinyModule and the TinyModule Interface in between governing their relationship.

TinyModule Interface

The *TinyModule Interface* specifies the interface between the ModuleFrame and the TinyModule in both directions: It defines which TinyOS interfaces, commands and events the ModuleFrame provides to the TinyModule und which are to be provided by the TinyModule for use by the ModuleFrame.

The TinyModule Interface remains fixed over the lifetime of the ModuleFrame. While it is possible to switch between different TinyModule instances, the external interface of these TinyModules cannot change without also changing the TinyModule Interface and the ModuleFrame.

ModuleFrame

The *ModuleFrame* provides services statically installed on the sensor nodes as specified in the TinyModule Interface. This means that the nesC components included in the ModuleFrame cannot be exchanged by the TinyModules code update procedure.

There are two basic ways of designing the ModuleFrame. As a first option, it can provide generic functionality through the TinyModule Interface that is able to support a variety of applications. In this case, TinyModules can be used to switch between very different types of applications that only share the basic operating system abstractions provided by the ModuleFrame. As an alternative option, the ModuleFrame can provide a very specific TinyModule Interface that encapsulates one specific part of the node functionality into the TinyModule (e.g., data preprocessing modules) that is expected to be exchanged on a regular basis. In this case, changing the TinyModule does not change the complete application but only the part or the algorithm specified in the TinyModule Interface.

The ModuleFrame also contains the code distribution mechanism and provides abstractions for accessing TinyOS internal information specific to each node (e.g., the node identifier).

Most parts of the ModuleFrame implementation are relatively simple to prepare as they only require wiring the commands and interfaces specified in the TinyModule Interface to the specific implementations provided by the TinyOS operating system and hardware specific system components also provided by TinyOS.

TinyModule

The *TinyModule* contains the application logic that implements the specific functionality of the sensor nodes. While the ModuleFrame can be considered the "generic" base implementation that is statically available on all nodes and for all applications, the TinyModule contains the code that distinguishes individual applications or individual program versions.

It is essential that all external dependencies of a TinyModule implementation are expressed by the TinyModule Interface it is building on irrespective of whether these dependencies refer to other application-level components included in the ModuleFrame or to TinyOS operating system components. If the TinyModule was allowed to directly access operating system or hardware functionality (through their TinyOS implementations) not specified in the TinyModule Interface, this could lead to a dangerous duplication of functionality in the ModuleFrame and in the TinyModule: If both code parts contain the same code components accessing the same resources without a controlling instance, this can cause an unplanned, arbitrary behavior of the overall system.

TinyModules ensures that the TinyModule part of the application can be exchanged dynamically without requiring expensive integration operations on the individual nodes. As described below, this is achieved with the help of a special memory layout both for the program memory and the main memory. Moreover, the TinyModule integration is facilitated by a static layout of the external function entry points that avoids the relinking of program code.

9.3.3 Memory Layout

To divide the code of a sensor node application into ModuleFrame and TinyModule and to provide for a clean separation of the two parts, we have to consider both the structure of the code image in the program memory of the nodes as well as the memory layout used for storing data in the main memory of the nodes. The following discussion concentrates on the structure and layout generated by the MSP-GCC compiler for the MSP430 family of microcontrollers from Texas Instruments that is used, for example, on TelosB sensor nodes. However, the basic memory layout is identical or very similar for other architectures like the AVR processor architecture used in the MICA family of sensor nodes.

Code and Data Placement

The compiler normally generates three main sections in the program memory as illustrated by Fig. 9.6 (a): The *.text* section contains the program code executed by the program. The *.data* section contains the initialization data for the variables which is copied to the *.data* section in main memory at node startup time. The *.vectors* section contains the interrupt vector table which consists of pointers to the routines that handle interrupts.

If TinyModules used the standard compilation procedure, the program code of the TinyModule would be placed somewhere in the *.text* section together with the other parts of the application code. In this case, any update of the TinyModule code (which potentially might increase the code size of the TinyModule) could directly affect other code in this section and might overwrite data. To avoid this problem without having to move and relink parts of the *.text* section dynamically, we place the TinyModule program code in a separate section called *.module_text* and the TinyModule initialization data in the section *.module_data*. We can safely place the two TinyModule sections directly following the *.text* and the *.data* sections as these two sections now only contain code and initialization data of the static ModuleFrame, do not change in the course of an update and therefore keep a constant size. The resulting layout of the program memory is shown in Fig. 9.6 (b). In this layout the program code and the initialization data of the TinyModule can change in an arbitrary manner without these changes affecting the code and data in *.text* and *.data*.

While the exchange of a TinyModule directly influences the code structure in the program memory, it can also affect the layout of the data structures used by the program in the main memory. A compiler typically prepares two or three types of sections in main memory illustrated in Fig. 9.6 (c): The *.data* section which stores the values of initialized global variables, the *.bss* section which stores the values of global or static variables initialized to zero at startup time and optionally the *.noinit* section which holds variables not initialized at startup time. The remaining part of the memory is available to the stack.

To avoid that changes to the set of variables used by the TinyModule interfere with the structure and the location of the variables used by the ModuleFrame, we create separate *.module_data*, *.module_bss* and *.module_noinit* sections analogous to the separation of TinyModule and ModuleFrame in the program memory. The resulting main memory layout is shown in Fig. 9.6 (d). If a code update now changes the amount of main memory consumed by the TinyModule, this cannot affect the variables used by the ModuleFrame code anymore as these are placed in front of the TinyModule memory sections.

At node startup time, it is the responsibility of the reset vector to load the initialization data from the program memory of the node to the *.data* section in main memory and to initialize the values in the *.bss* section with zero. Due to our changes

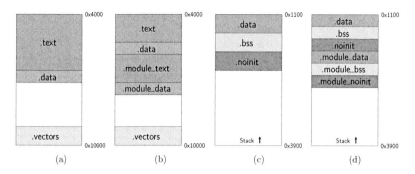

Figure 9.6: Layout program memory original (a) and proposed (b); main memory original (c) and proposed (d)

to the memory layout detailed above, TinyModules requires a custom reset vector implementation that takes care of correctly initializing the *.data* and *.bss* sections of both ModuleFrame and TinyModule.

Code Structure

For being able to integrate different TinyModules without relinking the code image, the layout of all parts of the code where the TinyModule is calling the ModuleFrame or vice versa has to remain constant. Note that it is sufficient to place function entry points at fixed locations as ModuleFrame and TinyModule do not share any state in the form of shared variables.

The set of functions in the ModuleFrame that are callable from the TinyModule is defined by the set of commands provided to the TinyModule and the set of events coming from the TinyModule that the ModuleFrame is connected to. Both are specified in the TinyModule Interface. In addition, the TinyModule can also call any system library function included in the ModuleFrame. Fortunately, keeping all these function entry points at constant locations is simple as the ModuleFrame does not change during code updates. Consequently, a TinyModule can be linked to these fixed addresses using standard linking mechanisms.

The situation is different for the function entry points in the TinyModule callable from the ModuleFrame. The set of function entry points is completely defined by the TinyModule Interface and can easily be derived during the compilation process. It also does not change between different TinyModule instances as this would require changing the TinyModule Interface and, as a consequence, also the ModuleFrame. However, to allow linking the ModuleFrame with static destination addresses for these function entry points, a mechanism is required that ensures that all relevant function entry points are placed at constant locations independent of any changes to the program code of the TinyModule. This is not trivial to do, because the code and the code size

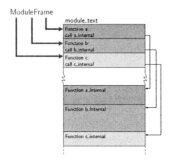

Figure 9.7: Function entry points in the TinyModule

of the individual functions can change as part of the code update which can trigger the compiler to place the functions differently in the object file (e.g., moving code backwards to free space for a function that has increased in size) which determines their addresses within .module_text.

Our solution to the TinyModule code placement problem is to place all externally accessible function entry points at the beginning of the TinyModule section. Since the size of the functions itself is not fixed, we cannot place the code of the functions there. Instead, we add a level of indirection calling the actual functions from this place which results in a small additional cost for each call.

Fig. 9.7 illustrates the layout of the TinyModule program code resulting from the additional level of indirection. The size of the functions a, b and c is now fixed as they only consist of calls to the actual functions $a\_internal$, $b\_internal$ and $c\_internal$. Due to their static size, the functions can be placed at fixed locations at the beginning of .module_text. When the TinyModule is exchanged, the structure of a, b and c remains unchanged. The only possible difference are the addresses used for calling $a\_internal$, $b\_internal$ and $c\_internal$ if these functions have moved within the TinyModule code.

9.3.4 TinyModule Integration

One important goal of TinyModules is to avoid any complex computations on the sensor nodes required by other approaches to prepare the code update data (e.g., by executing a diff-script or by dynamically linking object files on the nodes). The integration of a new TinyModule into the existing code image installed in the program memory of a sensor node should mainly require copying the module code from the external flash memory (where it is buffered by the code distribution mechanism) to the program memory.

As we have shown above, it is possible to arrange the program code in a way that allows the integration of a new TinyModule without moving relevant function entry points and hence without relinking the code. However, there is one exception: The reset vector code executed at node startup time needs information on the size of the *.data* and *.bss* sections for being able to initialize the main memory correctly at node startup time. In the case of TinyModules, such information is required for both the ModuleFrame (*.data* and *.bss*) and the TinyModule (*.module_data* and *.module_bss*). For the ModuleFrame this information is available at linking time and does not change later, because the ModuleFrame is not modified by TinyModules. However, each TinyModule can have different *.module_data* and *.module_bss* sections with different sizes which impedes a static configuration of the reset vector implementation.

One possible solution would be to assume static maximum sizes for *.module_data* and *.module_bss*. The linker could place the sections accordingly and the reset vector could operate with these maximum sizes. However, to work for all possible TinyModule instances, the estimation of the maximum size values would have to be pessimistically high producing an unnecessary fragmentation of the main memory and thereby consuming space otherwise available to the stack.

To avoid this memory fragmentation, TinyModules performs a small amount of dynamic linking on the nodes and adjusts the affected address values in the reset vector. Fortunately, this linking is very simple and generates little overhead: Only four relocations need to be adjusted and the source addresses of these relocations are well-known, because the reset vector code does not move. We specify the required size information of the data sections in the module properties delivered to the nodes together with the TinyModule code.

9.4 TinyModules Implementation Details

After the description of the TinyModules concept in the previous section, let us now describe important details of realizing the concept in a concrete implementation. We start with a description of specific challenges resulting from the properties of TinyOS and their solution in TinyModules. We then continue by describing the overall procedure, describe the implementation on the sensor nodes and finally provide a short discussion of the use of TinyModules in pervasive computing scenarios.

9.4.1 Challenges

As explained before, the nesC compiler supports partitioning a program into multiple parts, the so-called binary components, and allows to compile these parts separately from each other. Unfortunately, some of the special characteristics of TinyOS complicate such a clean division of programs into separate parts.

Compile-Time Allocation of Resources

One of the key features of TinyOS together with nesC lies in the optimization of the sensor node application code at compile time. The nesC compiler generates a code image that only contains the set of operating system and application level components actually needed by the respective application. This way, no generic operating system implementation including standard components is used. Instead, the code image is fully customized to the application and its needs. Moreover, the compiler is also able to statically allocate the set of resources required by the application. As an example, it is known at compile time how many timer instances are required by the application and the timer component only allocates resources for exactly this number of timers.

While the static allocation of resources is optimal from the point of view of a static TinyOS application, it complicates the approach of TinyModules where we aim to exchange a single code module. In the general case, the set of required resources might change between different instances of the TinyModule installed on the sensor node. For example, one TinyModule instance might use three timers whereas the previous instance only needed two timers to perform its tasks. To conform to the TinyOS resource model described above, TinyModules needs to make sure that this does not happen. The set of required resources is not allowed to change in the process of exchanging the TinyModule code or such changes should at least not be noticeable to the outside.

As we have discussed above, the *TinyModule Interface* is the basic abstraction for connecting ModuleFrame and TinyModule that ensures that different TinyModule instances are compatible with the resources provided by the ModuleFrame. However, there are a few subtleties to consider in the context of generic modules that can be illustrated with the help of the timer example.

If a module in a TinyOS application requires a timer, it specifies this requirement in its module header. The configuration wiring the module to the rest of the application then provides the requested timer by creating a new timer instance and wiring this timer instance to the module. The nesC compiler determines the number of timer instances created in the different parts of the application and allocates the resources in the timer component accordingly. For example, it creates data structures with one entry for each timer in the system. However, this static allocation of resources as part of the compilation process is not possible when compiling ModuleFrame and TinyModule separately, because the timer component in the ModuleFrame has no way of determining how many timers the TinyModule is going to allocate.

Our solution to this problem is simple and corresponds to the requirement already given above: **All** external dependencies of the TinyModule must be specified in the *TinyModule Interface*. For our timer example this means that we need to decide beforehand how many timers a TinyModule needs at maximum and need to explicitly state this in the interface specification. The timers are then allocated in the Module-Frame and provided as separate resources in the TinyModule Interface. Fig. 9.8 (a) illustrates this with an example TinyModule Interface where three timers are made available to the TinyModule as *TimerOne*, *TimerTwo* and *TimerThree*. The Tiny-Module can use these three timers in an arbitrary fashion but is not allowed to create additional timer instances itself.

Note that not all resources provided by the ModuleFrame must actually be used by the TinyModule implementation. For example, the TinyModule does not need to wire all timers. The penalty for allocating resources in the ModuleFrame that are not

```
                                     component TinyModuleInterface {
component TinyModuleInterface {        [...]
  [...]                                provides command error_t postTaskOne();
  provides interface Timer<TMilli> as TimerOne;    provides command error_t postTaskTwo();
  provides interface Timer<TMilli> as TimerTwo;    provides event void runTaskOne();
  provides interface Timer<TMilli> as TimerThree;  provides event void runTaskTwo();
  [...]                                [...]
}                                    }
```

(a) Timers   (b) Tasks

Figure 9.8: TinyModule Interface examples

used by the TinyModule is usually relatively small – often only a few bytes of program memory and main memory.

TinyModules and Tasks

A task in TinyOS is a deferred procedure call that can be posted in the context of an event or as part of a command execution. A task is not immediately executed but is scheduled for execution by the task scheduler at a later point in time. The TinyOS 2 task scheduler allocates a separate slot (a small amount of main memory) for each task at compile time. Similar to the resource allocation problem described above, it is impossible to determine the number of tasks used in a TinyModule at compile-time if the TinyModule is compiled separately from the ModuleFrame and if the ModuleFrame is supposed to work with different TinyModule instances. What sets the problem of tasks in a TinyModule apart is the fact that tasks are a language concept of nesC whose dependencies are not expressed with the help of interfaces but hidden from the programmer[1].

To allow the use of tasks in a TinyModule, we use the same approach internally used by the nesC compiler and explicitly specify the tasks used by the TinyModule in the TinyModule Interface. This is illustrated in Fig. 9.8 (b).

Instead of posting a task itself, the TinyModule calls a `postTaskX` command from the TinyModule Interface. As a reaction to this call, the ModuleFrame posts a task and – once this task is executed by the task scheduler – calls back to the TinyModule using a `runTaskX` event. Now the TinyModule can execute its task code within this context. Again, the only (inevitable) limitation of this solution is that the maximum number of tasks available to a TinyModule must be defined when the TinyModule Interface and the ModuleFrame are created. Using additional tasks within the TinyModule is not allowed.

Integration of System Libraries

The TinyModule Interface expresses all external dependencies of the TinyModule on the level of TinyOS and its components. However, in addition to the commands and

---

[1]The nesC compiler internally implements tasks using interfaces. However, this remains transparent to the programmer.

events defined there, the implementation of a module can also use functions from C system libraries. One example are the math functions provided by the GCC support library *libgcc*. Since the requirements of individual modules on such system library support will generally differ, we expect different TinyModule instances to reference different sets of library functions. For TinyModules, the problem to solve is making sure that all system library functions required by a TinyModule are available on the sensor node.

A simple solution would be to include all possible system library functions in the program code of the ModuleFrame. However, this would consume enormous amounts of program memory not available on the nodes. Moreover, in heterogeneous environments it might even be impossible to determine the set of libraries available to the programmer. The other extreme, not including any system libraries in the ModuleFrame and including all required libraries in the TinyModule, would significantly increase the transmitted code size of updates as shared library functions would have to be transmitted repeatedly with each update.

For our implementation of TinyModules, we opted for an approach that achieves a good compromise between the two extreme solutions described above. We statically include a set of common library functions that are likely to be used by many modules. If a module references one of these library functions, it is able to use the implementation in the ModuleFrame. If, however, it uses additional library functions not included in the ModuleFrame code, then these library functions are placed in the module section of the program memory and transmitted to the sensor nodes together with the code of the TinyModule. This is achieved with the help of a custom-made tool that analyzes the module as part of the linking process and prepares a suitable layout by modifying the linker script accordingly.

9.4.2 Overall Procedure

Using TinyModules to install custom code modules on wireless sensor nodes requires preparing the nodes for such updates before deployment. New TinyModule instances can then be installed as part of a module update procedure.

Preparation of Deployment

Irrespective of whether TinyModules is used to exchange a small specific part of the node functionality or whether a generic ModuleFrame is used upon which a variety of applications can build, the first step of preparing the deployment of nodes is to **define the TinyModule Interface**. This step requires careful consideration as the interface not only defines the relationship between ModuleFrame and TinyModule but also the basic functionality available to the module developer.

Based on the definition of the TinyModule Interface, the next step is to prepare the ModuleFrame implementation which contains the actual functionality provided through the TinyModule Interface. If the TinyModule Interface mainly exposes functionality provided by TinyOS system components (timers, radio communication, sensor access), then implementing the ModuleFrame is very simple and essentially requires wiring the respective functionality of the TinyModule Interface. If, however, specialized functionality is provided through the TinyModule Interface that is not part of TinyOS, then its implementation must be provided by the system developer and integrated in the ModuleFrame.

The ModuleFrame can be compiled without an accompanying TinyModule generating the ModuleFrame object file which forms the basis for all future code images irrespective of the current implementation of the TinyModule. For generating the code image, the ModuleFrame is either linked with an initial version of the TinyModule implementing the desired application functionality or with a simple, generic TinyModule called *EmptyModule* which can later be replaced with an actual application module. Once the code image has been generated, the final step of preparing the node deployment is to install the code image and to distribute the sensor nodes in the deployment area.

Module Update Procedure

The procedure of exchanging the TinyModule on the sensor nodes starts with the implementation of the new module version. The new TinyModule has to use the exact same TinyModule Interface to be compatible with the ModuleFrame already installed on the sensor node. To ensure its binary compatibility, it is also linked against this version of the ModuleFrame.

After the new TinyModule instance has been compiled and linked against the ModuleFrame, the next step is to inject the module into the network at the base station. The data to inject consists of the module code and a small set of metadata describing the module. The TinyModule is then distributed to the nodes in the network using some code distribution mechanism – in our case we use the code distribution mechanism from Deluge. When a sensor node receives the TinyModule, it buffers the code and the metadata in its external flash memory.

Once a sensor node has completely received a new TinyModule instance, it initiates a reboot to enter the bootloader. The bootloader is then responsible for transferring the new module code from the external flash memory to the program memory and for the adjustments needed in the reset vector that we have described above. After that, the bootloader restarts the mote application and the sensor node resumes its normal operation using the new TinyModule instance that either implements a modified version of the previous application or even completely new application functionality.

9.4.3 Sensor Node Implementation

We have implemented TinyModules for TinyOS 2 using TelosB sensor nodes. However, as TinyModules does not set special requirements on the properties of the sensor hardware, porting TinyModules to other platforms is straightforward.

The concept of TinyModules is independent of the code distribution mechanism used to distribute the updated or new TinyModule images in the sensor network. For our implementation we decided to integrate TinyModules with the code distribution mechanism from Deluge [82], more specifically with the Deluge T2 implementation for TinyOS 2, because Deluge is a mature project that is well-established in the TinyOS community and has been ported to various node platforms that are also target platforms for TinyModules. It provides the complete toolchain including software to inject a code image at the base station, the code distribution mechanism and a bootloader to install code images in the program memory of the individual sensor nodes. From the point of view of the user, the only difference our implementation provides to what he knows from Deluge is that he injects a TinyModule instead of a complete code image.

The tight integration with Deluge provides us with another advantage: While a typical TinyModules code update should only exchange the code of the TinyModule, we also have the option to fall back to the original Deluge mechanism and exchange the complete code image including both TinyModule and ModuleFrame. This fallback code update solution provides the full update flexibility and allows to install any code update at the cost of a significantly larger update volume. This way, it is possible to also adapt the TinyModule Interface in the rare case where the requirements on the provided functionality change.

9.4.4 TinyModules and Pervasive Computing

While TinyModules can be used as a code update mechanism in wireless sensor networks, our main interest in this thesis lies in the use of TinyModules for operating wireless sensor nodes in pervasive computing scenarios. Here, the motivation is to allow mobile pervasive computing devices to adapt the behavior of the wireless sensor nodes operating in their vicinity and to allow them to install custom application modules that support the applications running on the client device.

On the implementation level, we expect the sensor nodes to run a ModuleFrame implementation that not only contains components for fundamental functionality like communication or sensor access but also directly implements basic functionality like routing, duty cycling or answering simple queries. The TinyModule Interface then exports commands and events for implementing advanced functionality on top of that. One motivating example is the detection of complex events: A client device can upload an event detection TinyModule to the relevant nodes in the neighborhood which then controls the sensor nodes as needed, performs a distributed event detection and only notifies the client device once such an event has been detected.

Referring back to the example scenario describing Bob's world in Section 3.4.2, TinyModules could be used to customize the behavior of the smart devices embedded in Bob's environment. For example, the new television set Bob has bought and installed in his living room could install a custom TinyModule on the light and noise sensors in the living room to help in optimizing Bob's television experience.

9.5 Evaluation

In this section we show results from our experiments performing code updates with
TinyModules and also discuss potential sources of overhead when using TinyModules.

9.5.1 Experimental Analysis

For our experiments we implemented a generic ModuleFrame and used it as a basis
for different applications building on top of it. Our exemplary ModuleFrame provides
three timers, the interfaces for sending and receiving messages, the Leds interface used
to control the three LEDs integrated on the nodes and access to the two light sensors,
the temperature sensor and the humidity sensor of the TelosB sensor nodes. This set
of functions is made available to the TinyModule instances through the TinyModule
Interface. Since we cover all basic functionality of the TelosB node hardware, our
TinyModule Interface provides for a high degree of flexibility in implementing various
kinds of applications on top.

It is worth noticing that the effort for implementing such a generic ModuleFrame
is minimal: The complete ModuleFrame implementation consisted of only one configuration file wiring the TinyModule Interface to TinyOS system components providing the respective functionality (e.g., `TinyModuleInterface.ReadTemperature ->`
`SensirionSht11C.Temperature;`) and a small TinyOS module that exports access to
the node identifier to the TinyModule.

We used four different applications in our experiments: The **Empty** application
does – as the name suggests – nothing at all. It mainly consists of implementations
of the functions specified in the TinyModule Interface. We use it to determine the
basic overhead of both Deluge and of TinyModules. **Blink** and **Oscilloscope** are
two well-known applications from the TinyOS source tree that we already used in
the evaluations in Chapters 7 and 8. The **EventDetector** application compares
time series of sampled sensor values to detect events based on predefined criteria and
announces these events to the base station. We originally developed this application
as part of our work on gesture recognition with wireless sensor nodes discussed in
Chapter 7. We modified the implementations of all four applications to allow building
them as TinyModules on top of our generic ModuleFrame.

The basic goal of TinyModules is to save on the amount of data to be transmitted
to the individual sensor nodes in the course of a code update. So the first step in our
evaluation was to analyze the savings in the update volume achieved by TinyModules.
Fig. 9.9 (a) shows a comparison of the amount of data to be transmitted to a sensor
node when using Deluge and TinyModules for installing one of our four example
applications. In our code size analysis, we distinguish three parts: the raw code size
of the application code, the overhead incurred for transmitting the code distribution
mechanism with each update (only for Deluge) and the encoding overhead.

As expected, the TinyModule code updates are drastically smaller than the Deluge
code updates requiring only between 5.5% and 8.0% of their volume. One important contribution to these savings comes from the Deluge code distribution and code

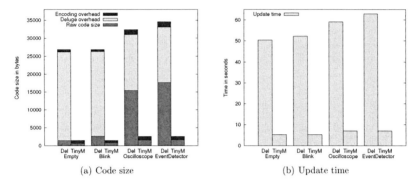

(a) Code size   (b) Update time

Figure 9.9: TinyModules experimental results

update mechanism that does not have to be transmitted to the nodes with each update. Note that this is particularly true for the *Empty* and the *Blink* applications that do not contain many of the components required for code updates (e.g., the radio communication components) in their application code. The *Oscilloscope* and the *EventDetector* applications also exhibit significant savings in their raw code size as many of the TinyOS components they require (e.g., the sensor access components) are part of the ModuleFrame and do not have to be transmitted with an update of the TinyModule.

We confirmed the promising results TinyModules showed with respect to the update size with the help of practical experiments with TelosB sensor nodes in which we measured the time for transmitting and installing code updates with both TinyModules and Deluge. We measured the update time over a single hop between the base station and a second node placed at a distance of 1 meter from the base station. Each result shown in Fig. 9.9 (b) represents an average value determined across 25 runs of the experiment. The results show that updates with TinyModules only take between 10.1% and 11.2% of the time required for the same updates performed with Deluge. These results do not completely match the ratios concerning the update size. However, this was to be expected due to some constant update overhead, like for example the time required for rebooting the node. This constant overhead has a stronger influence for the small TinyModules updates than for the large updates with Deluge.

We expect the relationship of the energy consumption of code updates with TinyModules and Deluge to closely follow the results shown for the time consumption of the code updates as none of the two approaches uses particularly energy-expensive operations (e.g., repeated read and write accesses to the external flash) that are not used by the other approach as well.

To get a better understanding of the factors contributing to the savings provided by TinyModules, Table 9.1 shows the size of the four applications implemented as TinyModule instances in the program memory and the contributions of the individual

Table 9.1: TinyModules size analysis

	Empty	Blink	Oscilloscope	EventDetector
TinyModule	659 bytes	863 bytes	1571 bytes	1702 bytes
ModuleFrame general			22624 bytes	
ModuleFrame Deluge-specific			15142 bytes	
Total	38425 bytes	38629 bytes	39337 bytes	39468 bytes
Total size Deluge version	26200 bytes	26314 bytes	30998 bytes	33130 bytes

parts to this size. The goal of using the static ModuleFrame to collect standard node functionality that is used by many different applications including the Deluge code distribution components is obviously very effective: Only between 1.7% and 4.3% of the code end up in the TinyModule that is transmitted as part of code updates. These low percentages are remarkable considering the fact that the four applications implement widely different functionality. Clearly, the more sophisticated the applications building on top of the TinyModule Interface get, the larger is the size of the TinyModule code. However, the savings should remain significant – particularly due to the fact that the size of the Deluge version of an application is also growing with an increasing complexity of the application.

The last two lines of Table 9.1 compare the overall space consumption in the program memory of the TinyModules version and the Deluge version for the four programs. As expected, the TinyModules version consumes significantly more space (between 19.1% and 46.8%) with a larger overhead for the small applications which only use a small part of the functionality included in the ModuleFrame. Besides ModuleFrame functionality not used by the TinyModule, system libraries included by default are another major contributor to this space overhead. In our generic ModuleFrame implementation we enforced the default integration of 17 system library functions, most of them providing mathematical calculations. The code of these default system library functions contributes 3712 bytes to the ModuleFrame code size. Most of this code would not be required in a minimal implementation. This provides significant potential for savings if the size of the program memory is a limiting factor.

We could not compare the performance of TinyModules with our older code update approach FlexCup [131] or the other solutions based on TinyOS 1.x since there are no implementations of these update solutions available for TinyOS 2. However, TinyModules has a speedup of up to a factor of 10 with respect to Deluge (version 2). FlexCup, which happens to be the best of TinyOS 1.x related work, only reports improvements by a factor of 8 compared to Deluge. This performance advantage makes TinyModules a very viable alternative for code updating in TinyOS 2.

9.5.2 Module Integration Overhead

Deluge and similar approaches implementing complete code exchanges constitute the optimal case concerning the overhead of integrating a code update on the sensor nodes as the only step required after receiving an update is copying the update data from the external flash memory to the program memory of the node. No processing of the

Table 9.2: Average overhead for TinyModule operations

Issuing a command	$12.73\mu s$
Receiving an event	$10.42\mu s$
Posting and scheduling a task	$23.02\mu s$

update data is required beforehand.

TinyModules approximates the optimal case with the main update operation consisting of copying the new TinyModule code to the program memory. The only additional operation required is updating the value of the four relocations in the reset vector. Consequently, the TinyModules bootloader is only slightly more complex than the TOSBoot bootloader used by Deluge. In addition to small changes, the additional operations added less than 20 lines of code. The resulting bootloader binary comprises 2344 bytes compared to 2112 bytes for the original TOSBoot bootloader.

9.5.3 Runtime Overhead

Besides the performance of the code update operations themselves, the influence of the code update mechanism on the performance of the normal node operation is also important for evaluating TinyModules. An extreme example motivating this are the virtual machine approaches that we discussed in the related work section: They provide a small update volume and very low update integration costs but generate an extremely high overhead in the execution of the application code during the normal node operation.

The overhead of TinyModules during the normal runtime of an application is minimal. Its only source is the additional level of indirection introduced by partitioning the code into binary components that is required for calls between the ModuleFrame and the TinyModule.

To evaluate the effects of these indirections on the runtime of relevant code parts, we measured the time required for 1,000,000 iterations of the three basic interactions between the TinyModule and the ModuleFrame: Issuing a command, receiving an event and posting and scheduling a task. To determine the overhead, we then compared these values with the corresponding values measured using a monolithic TinyOS version of the same test program. Table 9.2 shows the results of this analysis.

The results confirm the expected low overhead in the range of a few microseconds per interaction. Note that these small overhead values are facilitated by the fact that no dynamic lookup procedures are required for the connection of ModuleFrame and TinyModule. Also note that this overhead can be found in any solution building on modules (e.g., FlexCup) and is significantly lower than for solutions requiring dynamic lookups. The higher cost for posting and scheduling a task reflects that this operation involves both issuing a command and receiving an event from the ModuleFrame once the task is scheduled. Hence, the cost approximately corresponds to the sum of the costs of its two parts.

9.5.4 Programming Overhead

The required effort for a programmer to integrate his application code with Tiny-Modules is difficult to measure. In the optimal case, the application is developed for a predefined TinyModule Interface. This way, the additional overhead should be minimal and a given ModuleFrame could even simplify the task of unexperienced developers.

If an existing application is to be ported to TinyModules, an important factor for the cost is whether the module interface provides all services required by the application. The experience with our generic TinyModule Interface and the applications used in our experiments provides some anecdotal evidence for the ease of portability. As an example, porting the Oscilloscope application to TinyModules using our generic TinyModule Interface only required wiring the main application component to the TinyModule Interface and changing two lines in the original program code. This required change was due to the fact that program code in the TinyModule needs to query the local node identifier through the TinyModule Interface whereas it can be directly inferred from the compile-time constant "TOS_NODE_ID" in the original implementation.

9.6 Summary

In this chapter we have presented TinyModules, a novel approach to the problem of exchanging code modules on wireless sensor nodes running TinyOS as part of code updates or for installing application-specific modules in dynamic pervasive computing scenarios. Instead of exchanging the complete code image with each update, Tiny-Modules limits the changes to a predefined module section that is isolated from the rest of the application. This provides for a simple and efficient integration of code modules into the running code on the nodes.

We have shown that TinyModules is able to achieve significant savings in terms of transmitted code size and update time while generating negligible processing overhead on the individual sensor nodes. At the same time, the application developer hardly loses any flexibility as a complete exchange of both ModuleFrame and TinyModule using Deluge is available as a fallback solution. All that makes TinyModules a worthwhile alternative to existing code update approaches in wireless sensor networks and a prime option for dynamically installing client-specific application modules on sensor nodes in pervasive computing scenarios.

One can argue that TinyModules reintroduces the traditional division between application and operating system missing in TinyOS. However, TinyModules is more flexible: It is the system developer who decides which parts of the application should be part of the static ModuleFrame and which should be exchangeable as part of the TinyModule.

9.6.1 Future Directions in this Area

One important area of future work for advancing the TinyModules approach is to develop more advanced tool support for creating modules and a ModuleFrame with a customized module interface. The goal would be to facilitate the creation of domain-specific versions of TinyModules that optimally support the requirements of specific application fields.

From the viewpoint of pervasive computing, an interesting extension to the Tiny-Modules approach would be the support of multiple exchangeable modules within one code image. This would, for example, allow multiple client devices to install their client-specific code modules in parallel. An interesting question to consider in this context is how to arbitrate between conflicting interests of code modules installed by different clients. For supporting multiple code modules within a code image in general, it will be important to investigate the balance between the additional flexibility of being able to exchange different modules with different parts of the node functionality and the additional overhead induced by multiple module interfaces.

Another possible improvement for TinyModules would be support for exchanging the TinyModule without having to reboot the node as part of this process. On the one hand, this depends on adequate hardware support of the sensor node platform. On the other hand, this requires a careful consideration of how state is handled on the sensor nodes to avoid inconsistencies caused by the update of a TinyModule.

Generalizing from the code update problem to operating system design, we still see the need for more research in the area of operating systems for wireless sensor nodes and other embedded devices in pervasive computing scenarios. Based on experiences from the last years, it might be useful to reconsider the issues and requirements for operating systems in this area again. With respect to code updates, we currently have the monolithic TinyOS on the one side and the modularized operating system approaches (e.g., Contiki) on the other side of the spectrum. With TinyModules we have shown that there is a useful middle course that provides the system developer with the control over the border between operating system part and application part. It might be interesting to reconsider this in the design of a new operating system.

10 Conclusions and Future Work

This chapter provides a short summary of the various topics discussed in this thesis. It also gives a brief outlook on possible future work and future research directions in this area and then ends this thesis with some concluding remarks.

10.1 Summary

In this thesis, we have investigated the problem of integrating wireless sensor nodes and wireless sensor networks in pervasive computing scenarios. We have motivated why such an integration is useful and important for pervasive computing applications and have also shown why the integration is a challenging problem. The main goal of our work then was to develop solutions that facilitate the integration of wireless sensor nodes and other devices with similar constraints into pervasive computing scenarios by addressing the various problem fields that we have identified.

An important first part of our work was a thorough analysis of both the area of wireless sensor networks and the area of pervasive computing. We identified the respective system properties as well as the various commonalities and differences and discussed typical application scenarios. Based on this analysis, we identified a set of five fundamental problem areas that require attention when working on integrating sensor networks in pervasive computing scenarios: communication, network setup and configuration, user experience, security and flexibility and adaptability. We have shown why finding solutions for these five problem fields is essential for many pervasive computing scenarios integrating wireless sensor nodes.

As the main contribution of this thesis, we have developed six different solution approaches that cover different aspects of the complex problem of integrating sensor networks and pervasive computing. Each solution approach deals with one of the five problem areas identified in our problem analysis. In our first solution approach, we have shown how symbolic coordinates can be used to implement an efficient routing of messages between mobile devices and resource-constrained wireless sensor nodes. With our second approach, we have presented a solution for assigning symbolic coordinates to nodes as part of configuring a smart environment during the network setup. Our third solution approach also deals with the initial network configuration and is a representative of the group of self-organization solutions. It autonomously determines a grouping of nodes where nodes in the same area are placed in the same group and vice versa. In our fourth solution approach, we have dealt with the problem of proactively interacting with wireless sensor nodes and have devised three solutions that allow the user to interact with specific nodes in his environment in a simple and efficient manner.

For our fifth solution approach, we have investigated an important subproblem of the problem of providing security in pervasive computing scenarios integrating wireless sensor nodes and have developed a solution for the secure key assignment to sensor nodes. Finally, in our sixth solution approach we have dealt with code updates on wireless sensor nodes with the specific goal of providing a flexible way for pervasive computing devices to customize the code installed on sensor nodes in their vicinity.

A central element in our work has been the idea of providing mutual support between wireless sensor nodes and pervasive computing devices with each type of device contributing to the solution of a joint problem based on its respective capabilities. As we have discussed, mobile pervasive computing devices benefit from the environmental data provided by wireless sensor nodes. Sensor nodes, in turn, can benefit from input provided by the mobile devices like for example in our solution for the assignment of symbolic coordinates or in our key assignment solution. Our solution for a routing based on symbolic coordinates is a good example of a solution exhibiting real cooperation of the two device types in achieving the common goal of routing messages between a mobile client device and wireless sensor nodes.

10.2 Future Work

We have already provided ideas for potential future work and future research related to our six solution approaches in the individual chapters describing these approaches. In this section we want to discuss potential future research related to the overall thesis topic and want to introduce several possible directions for future work going beyond our basic goal of integrating wireless sensor nodes and wireless sensor networks in pervasive computing scenarios.

We have identified four different research directions that arise out of the work presented in this thesis or that would form a consequential continuation of the work: The development of a communication middleware for heterogeneous environments including both mobile devices and resource-constrained wireless sensor nodes, more work on the mutual support between mobile devices and wireless sensor nodes, continuing the investigation of self-organization of wireless sensor networks in the context of pervasive computing and an exploration of the use of heterogeneous sensing devices.

10.2.1 Communication Middleware

One research area that we perceive as particularly interesting and promising for future research is the communication between devices of widely different capabilities and communication abstractions governing such a communication. In particular, we see the need for a communication middleware that integrates resource-poor with more powerful devices.

The communication with very resource-poor devices requires paying attention to many details like for example their activity and sleep cycles or limitations on the size of their message buffers. At the same time, with a growing diversity of devices and the dynamics of pervasive computing scenarios, the details of the communication among nodes cannot be managed by the application anymore. One reason for that lies in the difficulty of anticipating all different scenarios and situations the application will be used in. Moreover, the application programmer is not always aware of the properties of the devices participating in providing services to the user.

A communication middleware supporting the integration of resource-poor with more powerful devices should hide the details of the communication among nodes from the programmer of pervasive computing applications and services. The programmer should be able to read data from nodes in the environment, send out requests and information and also directly control devices without worrying about the inner workings of the communication mechanism. However, the middleware itself should operate in a resource-aware fashion and should be considerate of the capabilities of the devices participating in the communication.

There exists a large number of middleware solutions and middleware research activities for pervasive computing, for example Gaia [170], one.world [69] or BASE [14]. However, these "traditional" middleware solutions mostly start at a higher level than the communication middleware that we envision and tackle problems like providing a uniform abstraction of services or supporting reconfiguration and adaptation. They typically assume that the basic connectivity among nodes is provided by the underlying systems. Consequently, a low-level communication middleware managing such connectivity among a heterogeneous set of devices would not replace other pervasive computing middleware solutions but would rather complement them.

In order to better illustrate our idea of a communication middleware for heterogeneous pervasive computing environments, let us now discuss a few examples of possible services provided by such a middleware. One example relates to the sleep cycles of wireless sensor nodes: While mobile client devices might start a query or send a message at any time, wireless sensor nodes are usually only activated periodically for short time periods in order to conserve energy. In this case, the middleware would have to manage such sleep cycles, trigger inactive nodes to wake up if necessary and buffer messages until the next hop node can be reached. Another example is the selection of routes between a mobile device and wireless sensor nodes providing data. In general, the middleware should prefer routes over less resource-constrained nodes but should also take the requirements of the application (e.g., the maximum acceptable delay) into account.

As discussed in the related work section of chapter 4, there has already been some effort on supporting communication among mobile devices and between mobile devices and resource-constrained wireless sensor nodes, for example using broadcasts, geographic routing or routes generated and maintained in an ad hoc fashion. One exemplary project where such a routing solution has already been integrated in a communication middleware is the AWARE project [7]. The AWARE middleware provides for a communication among mobile devices and between mobile devices and static wireless sensor nodes based on the publish/subscribe paradigm. The communication between mobile devices and the wireless sensor nodes is done using dedicated gateway nodes that support the exchange of messages between the relatively static sensor network part and the highly dynamic network of the mobile devices. The communication among mobile devices including the realization of the publish/subscribe paradigm is done with the help of flooding.

Looking at the AWARE example and our routing solution based on symbolic coordinates raises an interesting research question that must be solved as part of developing a communication middleware for pervasive computing: What is the right abstraction for communicating with wireless sensor nodes in pervasive computing scenarios? One aspect of such an abstraction relates to the question of how individual sensor nodes or groups of sensor nodes are addressed by mobile devices. Examples of possible address types include node identifiers, geographic location identifiers and symbolic coordinates. Alternative addressing schemes like service-based or data-centric addressing might also be useful. The second important aspect of the communication abstraction used pertains to the communication paradigm used. Examples of possible approaches include publish/subscribe systems as used by AWARE, query-based systems or approaches based on a database abstraction.

While the communication among heterogeneous sets of nodes is probably the primary area of application for a middleware supporting the integration of sensor networks and pervasive computing, we expect that it could also deal with other tasks related to an integration. One example are the areas of security and privacy where the middleware could help in hiding the peculiarities of resource-constrained nodes and provide a consistent overall security service.

Another area where the middleware could provide support is data management and data storage. This is a classic issue and area of research in wireless sensor networks dealing with questions like "Where to store a specific piece of data?" (e.g., centralized, local, distributed) or "How to find and access data?". By adding mobile devices and by entering the pervasive computing application domain, the data management problem gets additional aspects. For example, mobile devices can proactively collect data from neighboring nodes while moving through the network area and buffer this data for later use or to make it available to other pervasive computing devices. Moreover, there are several tradeoffs that must be considered like requesting fresh data from the network versus using older data already buffered on the device or contacting sensor nodes directly versus going through the infrastructure. Such data management tasks are hard to implement within individual applications but definitely require input from the application level which makes them a prime candidate for applying middleware support.

Looking at the exemplary goals of the middleware described in the paragraphs above, one can detect similarities to the goals of distributed operating systems which manage several independent computers and aim to make them appear as a single computer. In our context the distributed operating system would aim to provide the illusion of having the complete pervasive computing application running locally on the client device with access to all functionality provided by the individual devices. For this purpose, it would have to manage both the data storage and the data access thereby providing location transparency (with respect to accessing the data sources) to the upper layers. We prefer speaking of a middleware instead of a distributed operating system as we see some areas where the distribution of the participating devices and their location should be explicit and not hidden by the operating system. We perceive the middleware concept as more flexible in this regard.

10.2.2 Mutual Support of Mobile Devices and Sensor Nodes

One basic idea underlying the work presented in this thesis was to look for solutions where mobile devices and wireless sensor nodes support each other's operations in order to fulfill the common goal of providing pervasive computing services to the user in an effective and efficient manner. The six solution approaches illustrate this principle in different areas with some prevalence of solutions where mobile devices support the wireless sensor nodes.

We see considerable potential for more solutions that build upon a mutual support between mobile devices and wireless sensor nodes. In particular, we expect more approaches where the operation of wireless sensor nodes or the complete wireless sensor network is supported by mobile devices providing additional resources for special tasks. The application scenarios for such solutions do not necessarily have to come from the area of pervasive computing. They can also be "classic" sensor network scenarios monitoring certain aspects of the environment where mobile devices are used as client devices to collect data or to investigate specific parts of the environment.

One example of a possible future application with mobile devices supporting the operation of a wireless sensor network that we have been thinking of targets the localization of wireless sensor nodes. The idea is to let mobile devices collect network topology information while they are moving through the network. The aggregation and analysis of this information can then produce information on the relative position of nodes with respect to each other without the mobile devices having any location information by themselves. For example, this could be done by analyzing how the set of neighboring nodes of a mobile device varies over time.

10.2.3 Self-Organization of Wireless Sensor Networks

The self-organization of sensor nodes and sensor networks remains a very interesting albeit difficult topic. The idea of being able to deploy a large set of nodes and these nodes then autonomously organizing themselves is particularly appealing in pervasive computing scenarios and in smart environments, because it would simplify the creation of large-scale pervasive computing scenarios and would also allow non-expert users to deploy nodes.

As part of this thesis, we have provided several solutions to facilitate the manual configuration of nodes and a solution to group nodes based on the area they reside in as one specific type of context information. For approaching the ultimate vision of a fully self-organizing network, an important goal for future research is to find additional ways for nodes to learn about their context relevant to pervasive computing applications using as little external input as possible. At the same time, such solutions must take the resource limitations of the sensor nodes into account.

Based on our experience with the approaches developed as part of this thesis, we perceive the relation to context as a major challenge for self-organization in pervasive computing with wireless sensor networks. Unlike for many existing, often network-centric self-organization solutions for wireless sensor networks (e.g., node clustering, time synchronization, creation of routing trees), context-based self-organization usually requires input on the relation of the nodes to the real world they operate in. Such information is difficult to capture autonomously.

10.2.4 Heterogeneity of Sensing Devices

An interesting recent development is the integration of sensors and sensing capabilities in all kinds of everyday devices. For example, many of today's mobile phones come equipped with a variety of integrated sensors like accelerometers or magnetometers. Sensor data collected with such devices can be used locally on the device but also in the context of a large-scale sensing task with many nodes cooperating and contributing their respective sensor information. Campbell et al. [29] use the term "people-centric sensing" for such scenarios to emphasize the involvement of people carrying mobile devices in recording sensor data.

In some sense, using sensors from different static and mobile devices to contribute to wireless sensor network scenarios inverts the approach of this thesis and a work in this area could be called "Integrating pervasive computing in sensor network scenarios".

An interesting research question resulting from this development is how a more diverse set of sensors and a contribution of mobile devices to sensing tasks changes the sensing problem and wireless sensor networks. We expect that some of the classic sensor network problems will have a smaller importance in these scenarios (e.g., energy consumption) whereas other problems will become more critical and new problems will emerge (e.g., privacy of users contributing sensor data).

Looking back at the pervasive computing scenarios that are the focus of this thesis, an interesting aspect of this development is the diversity of devices participating in the overall task. Instead of only considering mobile client devices on the one hand and resource-poor, static wireless sensor nodes on the other hand, these scenarios might consist of many different types of nodes with different levels of capabilities, constraints and requirements. We expect that the overall performance of the network of devices and sensor nodes can be greatly optimized by considering the capabilities of the individual nodes and adapting the allocation of tasks accordingly.

10.3 Conclusions

The areas of wireless sensor networks and pervasive computing have been developing in a similar direction: More and more sensor network application scenarios integrate dynamic and mobile elements. On top of that, many sensor network scenarios have been starting to include actuators that have a direct impact on the environment monitored by the sensors. Advanced pervasive computing scenarios, in turn, rely on a large amount of context data whose capturing requires a variety of sensor information. A lot of this context information can be recorded with the help of wireless sensor nodes and wireless sensor networks or devices underlying similar constraints.

The common direction of development and the significant overlap of application scenarios motivate examining the two research areas together. In particular, it is worth considering wireless sensor nodes and wireless sensor networks operating as part of pervasive computing applications as such a setup allows to cover many novel pervasive computing and wireless sensor network application scenarios. However, so far the two research areas have largely been considered separately from each other.

In this thesis, we have considered the integration of wireless sensor networks in pervasive computing scenarios. One important contribution of our work was to highlight the importance of such an integration. With our work we have also provided better insights on the problems and challenges associated with such an integration.

With the six solution approaches presented in this thesis, we have covered many important problems related to integrating resource-poor wireless sensor networks and pervasive computing scenarios and have achieved our goal of facilitating such an integration. However, since pervasive computing, wireless sensor networks and scenarios integrating the two types of systems are extremely wide and diverse fields, there are still many areas for future improvements and future research left. We have listed some of them in the previous section.

Another important insight from our work is that there will not be one definite solution for supporting integrated pervasive computing scenarios, because there exist significant differences in the applications and the scenarios to support. Instead, we see a great need for application-specific and scenario-specific integration solutions. We perceive that our solution approaches constitute a good foundation for such developments.

10 Conclusions and Future Work

Bibliography

[1] The network simulator - ns-2. URL: http://nsnam.isi.edu/nsnam/.

[2] Department of defense world geodetic system 1984, its definition and relationships with local geodetic systems. Technical Report TR8350.2, National Imagery and Mapping Agency (NIMA), 1997.

[3] H. Abrach, S. Bhatti, J. Carlson, H. Dai, J. Rose, A. Sheth, B. Shucker, J. Deng, and R. Han. Mantis: system support for multimodal networks of in-situ sensors. In *WSNA '03: Proceedings of the 2nd ACM International Conference on Wireless sensor networks and applications*, pages 50–59, New York, NY, USA, 2003. ACM.

[4] Kemal Akkaya and Mohamed F. Younis. A survey on routing protocols for wireless sensor networks. *Ad Hoc Networks*, 3(3):325–349, 2005.

[5] Ian F. Akyildiz, Su Weilian, Yogesh Sankarasubramaniam, and Erdal Cayirci. A survey on sensor networks. *IEEE Communications Magazine*, 40(8):102–114, 2002.

[6] K.J. Austin, M.A. Calder, and P.R. McAree. Machine monitoring with wireless sensor networks. In *Proceedings of the 2005 Australian Mining Technology Conference*, 2005.

[7] AWARE Project. Platform for autonomous self-deploying and operation of wireless sensor-actuator networks cooperating with aerial objects. http://grvc.us.es/aware/.

[8] Chris R. Baker, Kenneth Armijo, Simon Belka, Merwan Benhabib, Vikas Bhargava, Nathan Burkhart, Artin Der Minassians, Gunes Dervisoglu, Lilia Gutnik, M. Brent Haick, Christine Ho, Mike Koplow, Jennifer Mangold, Stefanie Robinson, Matt Rosa, Miclas Schwartz, Christo Sims, Hanns Stoffregen, Andrew Waterbury, Eli S. Leland, Trevor Pering, and Paul K. Wright. Wireless sensor networks for home health care. In *AINAW '07: Proceedings of the 21st International Conference on Advanced Information Networking and Applications Workshops*, pages 832–837, Washington, DC, USA, 2007. IEEE Computer Society.

[9] Dennis J. Baker and Anthony Ephremides. The architectural organization of a mobile radio network via a distributed algorithm. *IEEE Transactions on Communications*, 29(11):1694–1701, November 1981.

[10] Dirk Balfanz, D.K. Smetters, Paul Stewart, and H. Chi Wong. Talking to strangers: Authentication in ad-hoc wireless networks. In *Proceedings of the Network and Distributed System Security Symposium*, 2002.

[11] Jakob E. Bardram and Henrik B. Christensen. Pervasive computing support for hospitals: An overview of the activity-based computing project. *IEEE Pervasive Computing*, 6(1):44–51, 2007.

[12] Stefano Basagni. Distributed clustering for ad hoc networks. In *Proceedings of the 1999 International Symposium on Parallel Architectures, Algorithms and Networks (ISPAN '99)*, page 310, Washington, DC, USA, 1999. IEEE Computer Society.

[13] Christian Becker and Frank Dürr. On location models for ubiquitous computing. *Personal Ubiquitous Computing*, 9(1):20–31, 2005.

[14] Christian Becker, Gregor Schiele, Holger Gubbels, and Kurt Rothermel. Base – a micro-broker-based middleware for pervasive computing. In *Proceedings of the First IEEE International Conference on Pervasive Computing and Communications (PerCom 03)*, 2003.

[15] Pavel Berkhin. Survey of clustering data mining techniques. Technical report, Accrue Software, San Jose, CA, 2002.

[16] Pratik K. Biswas and Shashi Phoha. Self-organizing sensor networks for integrated target surveillance. *IEEE Transactions on Computers*, 55(8):1033–1047, 2006.

[17] Ljubica Blazevic, Silvia Giordano, and Jean-Yves Le Boudec. Self Organized Terminode Routing. *J. of Cluster Computing,*, 5, 2002.

[18] Jan Blumenthal, Dirk Timmermann, Carsten Buschmann, Stefan Fischer, Jochen Koberstein, and Norbert Luttenberger. Minimal transmission power as distance estimation for precise localization in sensor networks. In *IWCMC '06: Proceeding of the 2006 international conference on Communications and mobile computing*, pages 1331–1336, New York, NY, USA, 2006. ACM Press.

[19] Prosenjit Bose, Pat Morin, Ivan Stojmenović, and Jorge Urrutia. Routing with guaranteed delivery in ad hoc wireless networks. In *DIALM '99: Proceedings of the 3rd international workshop on Discrete algorithms and methods for mobile computing and communications*, pages 48–55, New York, NY, USA, 1999. ACM Press.

[20] Azzedine Boukerche, Horacio A. B. F. Oliveira, Eduardo F. Nakamura, and Antonio A. F. Loureiro. Localization systems for wireless sensor networks. *Wireless Communications, IEEE*, 14(6):6–12, December 2007.

[21] David Braginsky and Deborah Estrin. Rumor routing algorithm for sensor networks. In *WSNA '02: Proceedings of the 1st ACM international workshop on Wireless sensor networks and applications*, pages 22–31, New York, NY, USA, 2002. ACM Press.

[22] R. A. Brooks. The intelligent room project. In *CT '97: Proceedings of the 2nd International Conference on Cognitive Technology (CT '97)*, page 271, Washington, DC, USA, 1997. IEEE Computer Society.

[23] Barry Brumitt and Steven Shafer. Topological world modeling using semantic spaces. In *Workshop Proceedings of Ubicomp 2001: Location Modeling for Ubiquitous Computing*, 2001.

[24] Nirupama Bulusu, John Heidemann, and Deborah Estrin. Gps-less low cost outdoor localization for very small devices. *IEEE Personal Communications Magazine*, 7(5):28–34, October 2000.

[25] C. Buschmann, H. Hellbrück, S. Fischer, A. Kröller, and S.P. Fekete. Radio propagation-aware distance estimation based on neighborhood comparison. In *Proceedings of the European Conference on Wireless Sensor Networks (EWSN 2007)*, volume 4373 of *Springer Lecture Notes in Computer Science*, pages 325–340, 2007.

[26] Zack Butler, Peter Corke, Ron Peterson, and Daniela Rus. Networked cows: Virtual fences for controlling cows. In *MobiSys 2004 Workshop on Applications of Mobile Embedded Systems (WAMES 2004)*, June 2004.

[27] Matthew Caesar, Miguel Castro, Edmund Nightingale, Greg O'Shea, and Antony Rowstron. Virtual ring routing: Network routing inspired by DHTs. In *Proceedings of the ACM SIGCOMM 2006*, 2006.

[28] Mario Cagalj, Srdjan Capkun, and Jean-Pierre Hubaux. Key agreement in peer-to-peer wireless networks. *Proceedings of the IEEE*, 94(2):467–478, Feb. 2006.

[29] Andrew T. Campbell, Shane B. Eisenman, Nicholas D. Lane, Emiliano Miluzzo, Ronald A. Peterson, Hong Lu, Xiao Zheng, Mirco Musolesi, Kristóf Fodor, and Gahng-Seop Ahn. The rise of people-centric sensing. *IEEE Internet Computing*, 12(4):12–21, 2008.

[30] S. Capkun and J. Hubaux. Secure positioning in wireless networks. *IEEE Journal on Selected Areas in Communications*, 24:221–232, 2006.

[31] Claude Castelluccia and Pars Mutaf. Shake them up!: A movement-based pairing protocol for cpu-constrained devices. In *MobiSys '05: Proceedings of the 3rd International Conference on Mobile Systems, Applications, and Services*, pages 51–64, New York, NY, USA, 2005. ACM.

[32] Haowen Chan and Adrian Perrig. Pike: peer intermediaries for key establishment in sensor networks. In *Proceedings of the 24th Annual Joint Conference of the IEEE Computer and Communications Societies*, 2005.

[33] Haowen Chan, Adrian Perrig, and Dawn Song. Random key predistribution schemes for sensor networks. In *Proceedings of the 2003 IEEE Symposium on Security and Privacy*, 2003.

[34] J. Clatworthy, D. Buick, M. Hankins, J. Weinman, and R. Horne. The use and reporting of cluster analysis in health psychology: A review. *British Journal of Health Psychology*, 10(Part 3):329–358, 2005.

[35] T. Clausen and P. Jacquet. RFC 3626: Optimized link state routing protocol (OLSR). http://tools.ietf.org/html/rfc3626, October 2003.

[36] Diane Cook and Sajal Das, editors. *Smart Environments: Technology, Protocols and Applications*. Wiley, 2005.

[37] Peter Corke, Ronald Peterson, and Daniela Rus. Networked robots: Flying robot navigation using a sensor net. In *Proceedings of the Eleventh International Symposium of Robotics Research (ISRR)*, 2003.

[38] Crossbow Technology Inc. http://www.xbow.com/.

[39] David E. Culler and Hans Mulder. Smart sensors to network the world. *Scientific American*, (June):85–91, 2004.

[40] Fei Dai and Jie Wu. An extended localized algorithm for connected dominating set formation in ad hoc wireless networks. *IEEE Transactions on Parallel and Distributed Systems*, 15(10):908–920, 2004.

[41] Anind K. Dey. Understanding and using context. *Personal and Ubiquitous Computing*, 5(1):4–7, 2001.

[42] Falko Dressler. *Self-Organization in Sensor and Actor Networks*. John Wiley & Sons, December 2007.

[43] Adam Dunkels, Björn Grönvall, and Thiemo Voigt. Contiki - a lightweight and flexible operating system for tiny networked sensors. In *Proceedings of the 1st Workshop on Embedded Networked Sensors*, 2004.

[44] Adam Dunkels, Oliver Schmidt, Thiemo Voigt, and Muneeb Ali. Protothreads: simplifying event-driven programming of memory-constrained embedded systems. In *SenSys '06: Proceedings of the 4th international conference on Embedded networked sensor systems*, pages 29–42, New York, NY, USA, 2006. ACM.

[45] Carl Ellison and Steve Dohrmann. Public-key support for group collaboration. *ACM Transactions on Information and System Security (TISSEC)*, 6(4):547–565, 2003.

[46] Eiman Elnahrawy, Xiaoyan Li, and Richard P. Martin. The limits of localization using signal strength: A comparative study. In *Proceedings of The First IEEE International Conference on Sensor and Ad hoc Communications and Networks (SECON 2004)*, 2004.

[47] Alois Ferscha and Stefan Resmerita. Gestural interaction in the pervasive computing landscape. *Elektrotechnik und Informationstechnik*, 124:17–25, 2007.

[48] Luca Filipponi, Silvia Santini, and Andrea Vitaletti. Data collection in wireless sensor networks for noise pollution monitoring. In *Proceedings of the 4th IEEE/ACM International Conference on Distributed Computing in Sensor Systems (DCOSS'08)*, Santorini Island, Greece, June 2008.

[49] Paul Föckler, Thomas Zeidler, Benjamin Brombach, Erich Bruns, and Oliver Bimber. Phoneguide: museum guidance supported by on-device object recognition on mobile phones. In *Proceedings of the 4th International Conference on Mobile and Ubiquitous Multimedia*, 2005.

[50] Rodrigo Fonseca, Sylvia Ratnasamy, Jerry Zhao, Cheng Tien Ee, David Culler, Scott Shenker, and Ion Stoica. Beacon vector routing: scalable point-to-point routing in wireless sensornets. In *NSDI'05: Proceedings of the 2nd conference on Symposium on Networked Systems Design & Implementation*, pages 329–342, Berkeley, CA, USA, 2005. USENIX Association.

[51] Christian Frank and Kay Römer. Algorithms for generic role assignment in wireless sensor networks. In *Proc. of the 3rd Int. Conf. on Embedded Networked Sensor Systems*, 2005.

[52] Thomas Fuhrmann. Scalable routing for networked sensors and actuators. In *Proceedings of the Second Annual IEEE Communications Society Conference on Sensor and Ad Hoc Communications and Networks*, pages 240–251, 2005.

[53] Thomas Fuhrmann, Pengfei Di, Kendy Kutzner, and Curt Cramer. Pushing chord into the underlay: Scalable routing for hybrid manets. Interner Bericht 2006-12, Fakultät für Informatik, Universität Karlsruhe, 2006.

[54] Matthias Gauger. Dynamischer Austausch von Komponenten in TinyOS. Diplomarbeit, Universität Stuttgart, Fakultät Informatik, Elektrotechnik und Informationstechnik, Germany, April 2005.

[55] Matthias Gauger, Pedro José Marrón, Marcus Handte, and Kurt Rothermel. Routing in sensor networks based on symbolic coordinates. In *Proceedings of the 5th GI/ITG KuVS Fachgespräch Drahtlose Sensornetze, Technical Report 2006/07, Universität Stuttgart*, July 2006.

[56] Matthias Gauger, Pedro José Marrón, Marcus Handte, Olga Saukh, Daniel Minder, Andreas Lachenmann, and Kurt Rothermel. Integrating sensor networks in

pervasive computing environments using symbolic coordinates. In *Proceedings of the Third International Conference on Communication System Software and Middleware (COMSWARE 2008)*, 2008.

[57] Matthias Gauger, Pedro José Marrón, Daniel Kauker, and Kurt Rothermel. Low overhead assignment of symbolic coordinates in sensor networks. In *Proceedings of the IFIP International Conference on Wireless Sensor and Actor Networks (WSAN 2007)*, pages 179–190. Springer, September 2007.

[58] Matthias Gauger, Pedro José Marrón, Daniel Kauker, and Kurt Rothermel. Low overhead assignment of symbolic coordinates in sensor networks. *Telecommunication Systems*, 40(3-4):117–128, April 2009.

[59] Matthias Gauger, Pedro José Marrón, and Christoph Niedermeier. TinyModules: Code module exchange in TinyOS. In *Proceedings of the Sixth International Conference on Networked Sensing Systems (INSS 2009)*, June 2009.

[60] Matthias Gauger, Daniel Minder, Pedro José Marrón, Arno Wacker, and Andreas Lachenmann. Prototyping sensor-actuator networks for home automation. In *Proceedings of the 3rd Workshop on Real-World Wireless Sensor Networks (REALWSN 2008)*, 2008.

[61] Matthias Gauger, Olga Saukh, Marcus Handte, Pedro José Marrón, Andreas Heydlauff, and Kurt Rothermel. Sensor-based clustering for indoor applications. In *Proceedings of the European Conference on Wireless Sensor Networks (EWSN 2008), Poster/Demo session*, 2008.

[62] Matthias Gauger, Olga Saukh, Marcus Handte, Pedro José Marrón, Andreas Heydlauff, and Kurt Rothermel. Sensor-based clustering for indoor applications. In *Proceedings of the 5th IEEE Communications Society Conference on Sensor, Mesh and Ad Hoc Communications and Networks (SECON 2008)*, 2008.

[63] Matthias Gauger, Olga Saukh, and Pedro José Marrón. Enlighten me! Secure key assignment in wireless sensor networks. In *Proceedings of the 6th IEEE International Conference on Mobile Ad-hoc and Sensor Systems (MASS 2009)*, 2009.

[64] Matthias Gauger, Olga Saukh, and Pedro José Marrón. Talk to me! On interacting with wireless sensor nodes. In *Proceedings of the Seventh Annual IEEE International Conference on Pervasive Computing and Communications (PerCom 2009)*, 2009.

[65] David Gay, Philip Levis, Robert von Behren, Matt Welsh, Eric Brewer, and David Culler. The nesc language: A holistic approach to networked embedded systems. In *Proceedings of the Conference on Programming language design and implementation*, 2003.

[66] Sinan Gezici. A survey on wireless position estimation. *Wireless Personal Communications*, 44(3):263–282, 2008.

[67] Ahmed Ghali, Steve Benford, Sahar Bayoumi, Jonathan Green, and Tony P. Pridmore. Visually-tracked flashlights as interaction devices. In *Proceedings of the IFIP TC13 International Conference on Human-Computer Interaction (INTERACT 03)*, 2003.

[68] Tj Giuli, David Watson, and K. Venkatesh Prasad. The last inch at 70 miles per hour. *IEEE Pervasive Computing*, 5(4):20–27, 2006.

[69] Robert Grimm, Janet Davis, Eric Lemar, Adam Macbeth, Steven Swanson, Thomas Anderson, Brian Bershad, Gaetano Borriello, Steven Gribble, and David Wetherall. System support for pervasive applications. *ACM Transactions on Computer Systems*, 22(4):421–486, 2004.

[70] Zygmunt J. Haas. A new routing protocol for the reconfigurable wireless networks. In *Proceedings of the IEEE International Conference on Universal Personal Communications*, 1997.

[71] Zygmunt J. Haas, Joseph Y. Halpern, and Li Li. Gossip-based ad hoc routing. *IEEE/ACM Transactions on Networking*, 14(3):479–491, 2006.

[72] Chih-Chieh Han, Ram Kumar, Roy Shea, Eddie Kohler, and Mani Srivastava. A dynamic operating system for sensor nodes. In *MobiSys '05: Proceedings of the 3rd international conference on Mobile systems, applications, and services*, pages 163–176, New York, NY, USA, 2005. ACM.

[73] Chih-Chieh Han, Ram Kumar, Roy Shea, and Mani Srivastava. Sensor network software update management: a survey. *International Journal of Network Management*, 15:283–294, 2005.

[74] Paul Havinga, Sandro Etalle, Holger Karl, Chiara Petrioli, Michele Zorzi, Harry Kip, and Thomas Lentsch. EYES energy efficient sensor networks. In *Proceedings of the 8th International Conference on Personal Wireless Communications (PWC 2003)*, 2003.

[75] Tian He, Pascal Vicaire, Ting Yan, Liqian Luo, Lin Gu, Gang Zhou, Radu Stoleru, Qing Cao, John A. Stankovic, and Tarek Abdelzaher. Achieving real-time target tracking using wireless sensor networks. In *Proceedings of the 12th IEEE Real-Time and Embedded Technology and Applications Symposium (RTAS 06)*, 2006.

[76] Wendi Rabiner Heinzelman, Anantha Chandrakasan, and Hari Balakrishnan. Energy-efficient communication protocol for wireless microsensor networks. In *HICSS '00: Proceedings of the 33rd Hawaii International Conference on System Sciences-Volume 8*, page 8020, Washington, DC, USA, 2000. IEEE Computer Society.

[77] Sumi Helal, William Mann, Hicham El-Zabadani, Jeffrey King, Youssef Kaddoura, and Erwin Jansen. The gator tech smart house: A programmable pervasive space. *Computer*, 38(3):50–60, 2005.

[78] Jason Hill, Mike Horton, Ralph Kling, and Lakshman Krishnamurthy. The platforms enabling wireless sensor networks. *Commun. ACM*, 47(6):41–46, 2004.

[79] Jason Hill, Robert Szewczyk, Alec Woo, Seth Hollar, David Culler, and Kristofer Pister. System architecture directions for networked sensors. *SIGPLAN Not.*, 35(11):93–104, 2000.

[80] Loc Ho, Melody Moh, Zachary Walker, Takeo Hamada, and Ching-Fong Su. A prototype on rfid and sensor networks for elder healthcare: progress report. In *E-WIND '05: Proceedings of the 2005 ACM SIGCOMM workshop on Experimental approaches to wireless network design and analysis*, pages 70–75, New York, NY, USA, 2005. ACM.

[81] Lars Erik Holmquist, Friedemann Mattern, Bernt Schiele, Petteri Alahuhta, Michael Beigl, and Hans-Werner Gellersen. Smart-its friends: A technique for users to easily establish connections between smart artefacts. In *UbiComp '01: Proceedings of the 3rd International Conference on Ubiquitous Computing*, 2001.

[82] Jonathan W. Hui and David Culler. The dynamic behavior of a data dissemination protocol for network programming at scale. In *Proceedings of the 2nd International Conference on Embedded Networked Sensor Systems*, 2004.

[83] Joengmin Hwang and Yongdae Kim. Revisiting random key pre-distribution schemes for wireless sensor networks. In *SASN '04: Proceedings of the 2nd ACM Workshop on Security of Ad Hoc and Sensor Networks*, pages 43–52, New York, NY, USA, 2004. ACM.

[84] IEEE. IEEE 802.15 wireless personal area networks standards. http://standards.ieee.org/getieee802/802.15.html.

[85] A. K. Jain, M. N. Murty, and P. J. Flynn. Data clustering: a review. *ACM Computing Surveys*, 31(3):264–323, September 1999.

[86] Jaein Jeong and David Culler. Incremental network programming for wireless sensors. In *Proceedings of the Conference on Sensor and Ad Hoc Communications and Networks*, 2004.

[87] D. Johnson, Y. Hu, and D. Maltz. RFC 4728: The dynamic source routing protocol (DSR) for mobile ad hoc networks for ipv4. http://tools.ietf.org/html/rfc4728, February 2007.

[88] David B. Johnson and David A. Maltz. Dynamic source routing in ad hoc wireless networks. In *Mobile Computing*. Kluwer Academic Publishers, 1996.

[89] Joseph M Kahn, Randy Howard Katz, and Kristofer S. J. Pister. Emerging challenges: Mobile networking for smart dust. *Journal of Communications and Networks*, 2(3):188–196, September 2000.

[90] Elliott Kaplan and Christopher Hegarty, editors. *Understanding GPS: Principles and Applications*. Artech House, 2005.

[91] Tufan C. Karalar and Jan Rabaey. An rf tof based ranging implementation for sensor networks. In *Proceedings of the IEEE International Conference on Communications (ICC 2006)*, 2006.

[92] Chris Karlof and David Wagner. Secure routing in wireless sensor networks: Attacks and counter- measures. In *Proceedings of the 1st International Workshop on Sensor Network Protocols and Applications*, 2003.

[93] Brad Karp and H. T. Kung. Gpsr: greedy perimeter stateless routing for wireless networks. In *MobiCom '00: Proceedings of the 6th annual international conference on Mobile computing and networking*, pages 243–254, New York, NY, USA, 2000. ACM Press.

[94] Cory D. Kidd, Robert Orr, Gregory D. Abowd, Christopher G. Atkeson, Irfan A. Essa, Blair MacIntyre, Elizabeth D. Mynatt, Thad Starner, and Wendy Newstetter. The aware home: A living laboratory for ubiquitous computing research. In *CoBuild '99: Proceedings of the Second International Workshop on Cooperative Buildings, Integrating Information, Organization, and Architecture*, pages 191–198, London, UK, 1999. Springer-Verlag.

[95] Sung Woo Kim, Min Chul Kim, Sang Hyun Park, Young Kyu Jin, and Woo Sik Choi. Gate reminder: a design case of a smart reminder. In *DIS '04: Proceedings of the 5th conference on Designing interactive systems*, pages 81–90, New York, NY, USA, 2004. ACM.

[96] Young-Jin Kim, Ramesh Govindan, Brad Karp, and Scott Shenker. Geographic routing made practical. In *Proceedings of the USENIX Symposium on Networked Systems Design and Implementation*, 2005.

[97] Young-Jin Kim, Ramesh Govindan, Brad Karp, and Scott Shenker. On the pitfalls of geographic face routing. In *DIALM-POMC '05: Proceedings of the 2005 joint workshop on Foundations of mobile computing*, pages 34–43, New York, NY, USA, 2005. ACM Press.

[98] Young-Jin Kim, Ramesh Govindan, Brad Karp, and Scott Shenker. Lazy cross-link removal for geographic routing. In *SenSys '06: Proceedings of the 4th international conference on Embedded networked sensor systems*, pages 112–124, New York, NY, USA, 2006. ACM Press.

[99] Joel Koshy and Raju Pandey. Remote incremental linking for energy-efficient reprogramming of sensor networks. In *Proceedings of the 2nd European Workshop on Wireless Sensor Networks (EWSN 2005)*, pages 354–365, 2005.

[100] Joel Koshy and Raju Pandey. Vmstar: synthesizing scalable runtime environments for sensor networks. In *Proceedings of the 3rd International Conference on Embedded Networked Sensor Systems*, 2005.

[101] Lakshman Krishnamurthy, Robert Adler, Phil Buonadonna, Jasmeet Chhabra, Mick Flanigan, Nandakishore Kushalnagar, Lama Nachman, and Mark Yarvis. Design and deployment of industrial sensor networks: experiences from a semiconductor plant and the north sea. In *SenSys '05: Proceedings of the 3rd international conference on Embedded networked sensor systems*, pages 64–75, New York, NY, USA, 2005. ACM.

[102] Fabian Kuhn, Thomas Moscibroda, and Roger Wattenhofer. Initializing newly deployed ad hoc and sensor networks. In *MobiCom '04: Proceedings of the 10th annual international conference on Mobile computing and networking*, pages 260–274, New York, NY, USA, 2004. ACM.

[103] Fabian Kuhn, Roger Wattenhofer, Yan Zhang, and Aaron Zollinger. Geometric ad-hoc routing: of theory and practice. In *PODC '03: Proceedings of the twenty-second annual symposium on Principles of distributed computing*, pages 63–72, New York, NY, USA, 2003. ACM Press.

[104] Sandeep S. Kulkarni and Limin Wang. Mnp: Multihop network reprogramming service for sensor networks. In *Proceedings of the 25th International Conference on Distributed Computing Systems*, 2005.

[105] Cynthia Kuo, Mark Luk, Rohit Negi, and Adrian Perrig. Message-in-a-bottle: user-friendly and secure key deployment for sensor nodes. In *SenSys '07: Proceedings of the 5th International Conference on Embedded Networked Sensor Systems*, pages 233–246, New York, NY, USA, 2007. ACM.

[106] Branislav Kusy, Akos Ledeczi, Miklos Maroti, and Lambert Meertens. Node density independent localization. In *IPSN '06: Proceedings of the fifth international conference on Information processing in sensor networks*, pages 441–448, New York, NY, USA, 2006. ACM Press.

[107] YoungMin Kwon and Gul Agha. Passive localization: Large size sensor network localization based on environmental events. In *Proceedings of the 2008 International Conference on Information Processing in Sensor Networks (IPSN 2008)*, pages 3–14, Washington, DC, USA, 2008. IEEE Computer Society.

[108] Anthony LaMarca, Waylon Brunette, David Koizumi, Matthew Lease, Stefan B. Sigurdsson, Kevin Sikorski, Dieter Fox, and Gaetano Borriello. Plantcare: An investigation in practical ubiquitous systems. In *UbiComp '02: Proceedings of the*

4th international conference on Ubiquitous Computing, pages 316–332, London, UK, 2002. Springer-Verlag.

[109] Koen Langendoen and Niels Reijers. Distributed localization in wireless sensor networks: a quantitative comparison. *Computer Networks*, 43(4):499–518, 2003.

[110] Marc Langheinrich. Privacy by design - principles of privacy-aware ubiquitous systems. In *UbiComp '01: Proceedings of the 3rd international conference on Ubiquitous Computing*, pages 273–291, London, UK, 2001. Springer-Verlag.

[111] Steven Lanzisera, David T. Lin, and Kristofer S. J. Pister. Rf time of flight ranging for wireless sensor network localization. In *Proceedings of the Workshop on Intelligent Solutions in Embedded Systems*, 2006.

[112] François-Joseph Lapointe and Guy Cucumel. The average consensus procedure: Combination of weighted trees containing identical or overlapping sets of taxa. *Systematic Biology*, 46, 1997.

[113] Deirdre Lee and Rene Meier. Primary-context model and ontology: A combined approach for pervasive transportation services. In *PERCOMW '07: Proceedings of the Fifth IEEE International Conference on Pervasive Computing and Communications Workshops*, pages 419–424, Washington, DC, USA, 2007. IEEE Computer Society.

[114] Seungjoon Lee, Bobby Bhattacharjee, and Suman Banerjee. Efficient geographic routing in multihop wireless networks. In *MobiHoc '05: Proceedings of the 6th ACM international symposium on Mobile ad hoc networking and computing*, pages 230–241, New York, NY, USA, 2005. ACM Press.

[115] Ben Leong, Barbara Liskov, and Robert Morris. Geographic routing without planarization. In *Proceedings of the Third Symposium on Networked Systems Design and Implementation (NSDI 06)*, 2006.

[116] Jonathan Lester, Blake Hannaford, and Gaetano Borriello. Are you with me? using accelerometers to determine if two devices are carried by the same person. In *Proceedings of the 2nd International Conference on Pervasive Computing*, 2004.

[117] Philip Levis and David Culler. Maté: a tiny virtual machine for sensor networks. In *Proceedings of the 10th International Conference on Architectural support for programming languages and operating systems*, 2002.

[118] Philip Levis, Neil Patel, David Culler, and Scott Shenker. Trickle: a self-regulating algorithm for code propagation and maintenance in wireless sensor networks. In *NSDI'04: Proceedings of the 1st conference on Symposium on Networked Systems Design and Implementation*, Berkeley, CA, USA, 2004. USENIX Association.

[119] Weijia Li, Youtao Zhang, Jun Yang, and Jiang Zheng. Ucc: update-conscious compilation for energy efficiency in wireless sensor networks. *ACM SIGPLAN Notices*, 42:383–393, 2007.

[120] Ben Liang and Zygmunt J. Haas. Virtual backbone generation and maintenance in ad hoc network mobility management. In *Proceedings of the 19th Annual Joint Conference of the IEEE Computer and Communications Societies (INFOCOM 2000)*, 2000.

[121] Chieh-Jan Mike Liang, Razvan Musaloiu-E., and Andreas Terzis. Typhoon: A reliable data dissemination protocol for wireless sensor networks. In *Proceedings of the 5th European Conference on Wireless Sensor Networks*, 2008.

[122] Joshua Lifton, Manas Mittal, Michael Lapinski, and Joseph A. Paradiso. Tricorder: A mobile sensor network browser. In *Proceedings of the ACM CHI 2007 Conference - Mobile Spatial Interaction Workshop*, April 2007.

[123] Chunhung Richard Lin and Mario Gerla. Adaptive clustering for mobile wireless networks. *IEEE Journal on Selected Areas in Communications*, 15(7):1265–1275, September 1997.

[124] J. P. Lynch, A. Sundararajan, H. Sohn, G. Park, C. Farrar, and K. H. Law. Embedding actuation functionalities in a wireless structural health monitoring system. In *Proceedings of the International Workshop on Smart Materials and Structures Technology*, January 2004.

[125] Hongshen Ma and Joseph A. Paradiso. The FindIT Flashlight: Responsive tagging based on optically triggered microprocessor wakeup. In *Proceedings of the 4th International Conference on Ubiquitous Computing*, 2002.

[126] Samuel R. Madden, Michael J. Franklin, Joseph M. Hellerstein, and Wei Hong. Tinydb: an acquisitional query processing system for sensor networks. *ACM Transactions on Database Systems (TODS)*, 30(1):122–173, 2005.

[127] Kaj Mäkelä, Sara Belt, Dan Greenblatt, and Jonna Häkkilä. Mobile interaction with visual and rfid tags: a field study on user perceptions. In *Proceedings of the SIGCHI Conference on Human Factors in Computing Systems*, 2007.

[128] Guoqiang Mao, Barış Fidan, and Brian D. O. Anderson. Wireless sensor network localization techniques. *Computer Networks*, 51(10):2529–2553, 2007.

[129] Miklós Maróti, Branislav Kusy, Gyula Simon, and Ákos Lédeczi. The flooding time synchronization protocol. In *Proc. of the 2nd Int. Conf. on Embedded Networked Sensor Systems*, 2004.

[130] Miklós Maróti, Péter Völgyesi, Sebestyén Dóra, Branislav Kusý, András Nádas, Ákos Lédeczi, György Balogh, and Károly Molnár. Radio interferometric geolocation. In *SenSys '05: Proceedings of the 3rd international conference on*

Embedded networked sensor systems, pages 1–12, New York, NY, USA, 2005. ACM Press.

[131] Pedro José Marrón, Matthias Gauger, Andreas Lachenmann, Daniel Minder, Olga Saukh, and Kurt Rothermel. Flexcup: A flexible and efficient code update mechanism for sensor networks. In *Proceedings of the 3rd European Workshop on Wireless Sensor Networks*, 2006.

[132] Pedro José Marrón, Olga Saukh, Markus Krüger, and Christian Große. Sensor network issues in the Sustainable Bridges project. In *European Projects Session of the Second European Workshop on Wireless Sensor Networks (EWSN 2005)*, January 2005.

[133] Michele Mastrogiovanni and Alessandro Panconesi. Localized protocols for ad hoc clustering and backbone formation: A performance comparison. *IEEE Transactions on Parallel and Distributed Systems*, 17(4):292–306, 2006. Member-Stefano Basagni and Member-Chiara Petrioli.

[134] Friedemann Mattern. Pervasive / ubiquitous computing. *Informatik Spektrum*, 24(3):145–147, 2001.

[135] John McCulloch, Paul McCarthy, Siddeswara Mayura Guru, Wei Peng, Daniel Hugo, and Andrew Terhorst. Wireless sensor network deployment for water use efficiency in irrigation. In *REALWSN '08: Proceedings of the workshop on Real-world wireless sensor networks*, pages 46–50, New York, NY, USA, 2008. ACM.

[136] Ren Meier, Anthony Harrington, and Vinny Cahill. A distributed framework for intelligent transportation systems. In *Proceedings of 12th World Congress on Intelligent Transport Systems (ITSWC 2005)*, 2005.

[137] Anand Meka and Ambuj K. Singh. Distributed spatial clustering in sensor networks. In *Proceedings of the 10th International Conference on Extending Database Technology (EDBT 2006)*, pages 980–1000, 2006.

[138] David Merrill and Pattie Maes. Augmenting looking, pointing and reaching gestures to enhance the searching and browsing of physical objects. In *Proceedings of the 5th International Conference on Pervasive Computing*, 2007.

[139] Christian Metzger, Matt Anderson, and Thad Starner. Freedigiter: A contact-free device for gesture control. In *Proceedings of the 8th International Symposium on Wearable Computers*, 2004.

[140] Jonas Meyer, Reinhard Bischoff, Olga Saukh, and Glauco Feltrin. A low power wireless sensor network for structural health monitoring. In *Proceedings of the 3rd International Conference on Bridge Maintenance (IABMAS 06)*, 2006.

[141] Daniel Minder, Pedro José Marrón, Andreas Lachenmann, and Kurt Rothermel. Experimental construction of a meeting model for smart office environments. In *Proceedings of the First Workshop on Real-World Wireless Sensor Networks (REALWSN 2005), SICS Technical Report T2005:09*, June 2005.

[142] David Moore, John Leonard, Daniela Rus, and Seth Teller. Robust distributed network localization with noisy range measurements. In *SenSys '04: Proceedings of the 2nd international conference on Embedded networked sensor systems*, pages 50–61, New York, NY, USA, 2004. ACM Press.

[143] Michael C. Mozer. *Smart Environments*, chapter Lessons from an Adaptive Home. Wiley, 2005.

[144] Tomohiro Nagata, Hisashi Oguma, and Kenichit Yamazaki. A sensor networking middleware for clustering similar things. In *Proceedings of the Workshop on Smart Object Systems*, September 2005.

[145] Asis Nasipuri and Kai Li. A directionality based location discovery scheme for wireless sensor networks. In *WSNA '02: Proceedings of the 1st ACM international workshop on Wireless sensor networks and applications*, pages 105–111, New York, NY, USA, 2002. ACM Press.

[146] Mats Näslund (Edt.). ECRYPT yearly report on algorithms and keysizes (2007-2008). Technical report, ECRYPT European Network of Excellence in Cryptology, 2008.

[147] Tomasz Naumowicz, Robin Freeman, Andreas Heil, Martin Calsyn, Eric Hellmich, Alexander Brändle, Tim Guilford, and Jochen Schiller. Autonomous monitoring of vulnerable habitats using a wireless sensor network. In *REALWSN '08: Proceedings of the workshop on Real-world wireless sensor networks*, pages 51–55, New York, NY, USA, 2008. ACM.

[148] Dragos Niculescu and Badri Nath. Ad hoc positioning system (aps) using aoa. In *Proceedings of the 22nd Annual Joint Conference of the IEEE Computer and Communications Societies (INFOCOM 2003)*, 2003.

[149] Dragos Niculescu and Badri Nath. Dv based positioning in ad hoc networks. *Journal of Telecommunication Systems*, 22(1-4):267–280, 2003.

[150] Carsten Orwat, Andreas Graefe, and Timm Faulwasser. Towards pervasive computing in health care a literature review. *BMC Medical Informatics and Decision Making*, 8(26), 2008.

[151] Rajesh Krishna Panta, Issa Khalil, and Saurabh Bagchi. Stream: Low overhead wireless reprogramming for sensor networks. In *Proceedings of the 26th International Conference on Computer Communications*, 2007.

[152] Vincent D. Park and M. Scott Corson. A highly adaptive distributed routing algorithm for mobile wireless networks. In *INFOCOM '97: Proceedings of the Sixteenth Annual Joint Conference of the IEEE Computer and Communications Societies. Driving the Information Revolution*, 1997.

[153] Shwetak N. Patel, Jeffrey S. Pierce, and Gregory D. Abowd. A gesture-based authentication scheme for untrusted public terminals. In *UIST '04: Proceedings of the 17th Symposium on User Interface Software and Technology*, 2004.

[154] Chunyi Peng, Guobin Shen, Yongguang Zhang, Yanlin Li, and Kun Tan. Beep-beep: a high accuracy acoustic ranging system using cots mobile devices. In *SenSys '07: Proceedings of the 5th international conference on Embedded networked sensor systems*, pages 1–14, New York, NY, USA, 2007. ACM.

[155] Rong Peng and Mihail L. Sichitiu. Angle of arrival localization for wireless sensor networks. In *Proceedings of the Third Annual IEEE Communications Society Conference on Sensor and Ad Hoc Communications and Networks (SECON 2006)*, 2006.

[156] C. Perkins, E. Belding-Royer, and S. Das. RFC 3561: Ad hoc on-demand distance vector (AODV) routing. http://tools.ietf.org/html/rfc3561, July 2003.

[157] Charles E. Perkins and Pravin Bhagwat. Highly dynamic destination-sequenced distance-vector routing (dsdv) for mobile computers. In *SIGCOMM '94: Proceedings of the conference on Communications architectures, protocols and applications*, 1994.

[158] Charles E. Perkins and Elizabeth M. Royer. Ad-hoc on-demand distance vector routing. In *Proceedings of the Second IEEE Workshop on Mobile Computer Systems and Applications*, 1999.

[159] Adrian Perrig, John Stankovic, and David Wagner. Security in wireless sensor networks. *Commun. ACM*, 47(6):53–57, 2004.

[160] Adrian Perrig, Robert Szewczyk, J. D. Tygar, Victor Wen, and David E. Culler. Spins: security protocols for sensor networks. *Wireless Networks*, 8:521–534, 2002.

[161] Ronald Peterson and Daniela Rus. Interacting with sensor networks. In *Proceedings of the IEEE 2004 International Conference on Robotics and Automation*, 2004.

[162] Joseph Polastre, Robert Szewczyk, and David Culler. Telos: enabling ultra-low power wireless research. In *IPSN '05: Proceedings of the 4th international symposium on Information processing in sensor networks*, page 48, Piscataway, NJ, USA, 2005. IEEE Press.

[163] Salil Pradhan. Semantic location. *Personal and Ubiquitous Computing*, 4(4):213–216, 2000.

[164] Ramesh Rajagopalan and Pramod K. Varshney. Data-aggregation techniques in sensor networks: a survey. *IEEE Communications Surveys & Tutorials*, 8(4):48–63, 2006.

[165] David R. Raymond and Scott F. Midkiff. Denial-of-service in wireless sensor networks: Attacks and defenses. *IEEE Pervasive Computing*, 7(1):74–81, 2008.

[166] Niels Reijers and Koen Langendoen. Efficient code distribution in wireless sensor networks. In *Proceedings of the 2nd International Conference on Wireless sensor networks and applications*, 2003.

[167] Jun Rekimoto. Gesturewrist and gesturepad: Unobtrusive wearable interaction devices. In *Proceedings of the 5th International Symposium on Wearable Computers*, 2001.

[168] Jun Rekimoto and Katashi Nagao. The world through the computer: computer augmented interaction with real world environments. In *Proceedings of the 8th annual ACM symposium on User interface and software technology (UIST 1995)*, pages 29–36, New York, NY, USA, 1995. ACM.

[169] Michael Rohs and Beat Gfeller. Using camera-equipped mobile phones for interacting with real-world objects. In Alois Ferscha, Horst Hoertner, and Gabriele Kotsis, editors, *Advances in Pervasive Computing*, pages 265–271, Vienna, Austria, April 2004. Austrian Computer Society (OCG).

[170] Manuel Román, Christopher K. Hess, Renato Cerqueira, Anand Ranganathan, Roy H. Campbell, and Klara Nahrstedt. Gaia: A middleware infrastructure to enable active spaces. *IEEE Pervasive Computing*, 1:74–83, 2002.

[171] Kay Römer. The lighthouse location system for smart dust. In *MobiSys '03: Proceedings of the 1st international conference on Mobile systems, applications and services*, pages 15–30, New York, NY, USA, 2003. ACM Press.

[172] Enrico Rukzio, Gregor Broll, Karin Leichtenstern, and Albrecht Schmidt. Mobile interaction with the real world: An evaluation and comparison of physical mobile interaction techniques. In *Proceedings of the European Conference on Ambient Intelligence (AmI-07)*, 2007.

[173] Enrico Rukzio, Karin Leichtenstern, Victor Callaghan, Paul Holleis, Albrecht Schmidt, and Jeannette Shiaw-Yuan Chin. An experimental comparison of physical mobile interaction techniques: Touching, pointing and scanning. In *Proceedings of the 8th International Conference on Ubiquitous Computing*, 2006.

[174] Debashis Saha and Amitava Mukherjee. Pervasive computing: A paradigm for the 21st century. *IEEE Computer*, 36(3):25–31, 2003.

[175] Paolo Santi. Topology control in wireless ad hoc and sensor networks. *ACM Comput. Surv.*, 37(2):164–194, 2005.

[176] Mahadev Satyanarayanan. Pervasive computing: Vision and challenges. *IEEE Personal Communications*, 8:10–17, 2001.

[177] Olga Saukh, Pedro José Marrón, Andreas Lachenmann, Matthias Gauger, Daniel Minder, and Kurt Rothermel. Generic routing metric and policies for WSNs. In *Proceedings of the Third European Workshop on Wireless Sensor Networks (EWSN 2006)*, pages 99–114, February 2006.

[178] Olga Saukh, Robert Sauter, Matthias Gauger, Pedro José Marrón, and Kurt Rothermel. On boundary recognition without location information in wireless sensor networks. In *Proceedings of the 7th IEEE/ACM International Conference on Information Processing in Sensor Networks (IPSN 2008)*, 2008.

[179] Olga Saukh, Robert Sauter, Jonas Meyer, and Pedro José Marrón. Motefinder: A deployment tool for sensor networks. In *Proceedings of the ACM Workshop on Real-World Wireless Sensor Networks (REALWSN'08)*, 2008.

[180] Andreas Savvides, Wendy L. Garber, Sachin Adlakha, Randolph L. Moses, and Mani B. Srivastava. On the error characteristics of multihop node localization in ad-hoc sensor networks. In *Proceedings of the Second International Workshop on Information Processing in Sensor Networks*, pages 317–332, 2003.

[181] Andreas Savvides, Chih-Chieh Han, and Mani B. Strivastava. Dynamic fine-grained localization in ad-hoc networks of sensors. In *MobiCom '01: Proceedings of the 7th annual international conference on Mobile computing and networking*, pages 166–179, New York, NY, USA, 2001. ACM Press.

[182] Edward Sazonov, Kerop Janoyan, and Ratan Jha. Wireless intelligent sensor network for autonomous structural health monitoring. In *Smart Structures/NDE 2004*, 2004.

[183] Curt Schurgers and Mani B. Srivastava. Energy efficient routing in wireless sensor networks. In *Proceedings of the 2001 Military Communications Conference (MILCOM 2001). Communications for Network-Centric Operations: Creating the Information Force.*, pages 357–361, 2001.

[184] Yi Shang, Wheeler Ruml, Ying Zhang, and Markus Fromherz. Localization from connectivity in sensor networks. *IEEE Transactions on Parallel and Distributed Systems*, 15(11):961–974, 2004.

[185] Yi Shang, Wheeler Ruml, Ying Zhang, and Markus P. J. Fromherz. Localization from mere connectivity. In *MobiHoc '03: Proceedings of the 4th ACM international symposium on Mobile ad hoc networking & computing*, pages 201–212, New York, NY, USA, 2003. ACM Press.

[186] Pavan Sikka, Peter Corke, Leslie Overs, Philip Valencia, and Tim Wark. Fleck – a platform for real-world outdoor sensor networks. In *Proceedings of the Third International Conference on Intelligent Sensors, Sensor Networks and Information Processing (ISSNIP 2007)*, 2007.

[187] Frank Stajano and Ross J. Anderson. The resurrecting duckling: Security issues for ad-hoc wireless networks. In *Proceedings of the 7th International Workshop on Security Protocols*, 2000.

[188] William Stallings. *Data and Computer Communications*. Prentice Hall, 2004.

[189] Vince Stanford. Pervasive health care applications face tough security challenges. *IEEE Pervasive Computing*, 1(2):8–12, 2002.

[190] Thad Starner, Jake Auxier, Daniel Ashbrook, and Maribeth Gandy. The gesture pendant: A self-illuminating, wearable, infrared computer vision system for home automation control and medical monitoring. In *Proceedings of the 4th International Symposium on Wearable Computers*, 2000.

[191] Thanos Stathopoulos, John Heidemann, and Deborah Estrin. A remote code update mechanism for wireless sensor networks. Technical Report CENS-TR-30, University of California, L.A., November 2003.

[192] Dimitar H. Stefanov, Zeungnam Bien, and Won-Chul Bang. The smart house for older persons and persons with physical disabilities: Structure, technology arrangements, and perspectives. *IEEE Transactions on Neural Systems and Rehabilitation Engineering*, 12(2):228–240, June 2004.

[193] Ivan Stojmenovic, Mahtab Seddigh, and Jovisa Zunic. Dominating sets and neighbor elimination-based broadcasting algorithms in wireless networks. *IEEE Transactions on Parallel and Distributed Systems*, 13(1):14–25, 2002.

[194] Radu Stoleru, Tian He, John A. Stankovic, and David Luebke. A high-accuracy, low-cost localization system for wireless sensor networks. In *SenSys '05: Proceedings of the 3rd international conference on Embedded networked sensor systems*, pages 13–26, New York, NY, USA, 2005. ACM Press.

[195] Radu Stoleru, Pascal Vicaire, Tian He, and John A. Stankovic. Stardust: a flexible architecture for passive localization in wireless sensor networks. In *SenSys '06: Proceedings of the 4th international conference on Embedded networked sensor systems*, pages 57–70, New York, NY, USA, 2006. ACM Press.

[196] Robert Szewczyk, Alan Mainwaring, Joseph Polastre, John Anderson, and David Culler. An analysis of a large scale habitat monitoring application. In *SenSys '04: Proceedings of the 2nd international conference on Embedded networked sensor systems*, pages 214–226, New York, NY, USA, 2004. ACM Press.

[197] Robert Szewczyk, Eric Osterweil, Joseph Polastre, Michael Hamilton, Alan Mainwaring, and Deborah Estrin. Habitat monitoring with sensor networks. *Communications of the ACM*, 47(6):34–40, 2004.

[198] Quan T. Tran, Gina Calcaterra, and Elizabeth D. Mynatt. Cook's collage: Deja vu display for a home kitchen. In *Proceedings of Home Oriented Informatics and Telematics (HOIT 2005)*, 2005.

[199] Andrew Tridgell. *Efficient Algorithms for Sorting and Synchronization*. PhD thesis, The Australian National University, 1999.

[200] Yu-Chee Tseng, Meng-Shiuan Pan, and Yuen-Yung Tsai. Wireless sensor networks for emergency navigation. *IEEE Computer*, 39(7):55–62, 2006.

[201] Koji Tsukada and Michiaki Yasumura. Ubi-finger: Gesture input device for mobile use. *IPSJ SIG Notes*, 2001(72):9–14, 2001.

[202] Upkar Varshney. Pervasive healthcare and wireless health monitoring. *Mobile Networks and Applications*, 12(2-3):113–127, 2007.

[203] N. Villar, G. Kortuem, K. Van Laerhoven, and A. Schmidt. The pendle: A personal mediator for mixed initiative environments. In *Proceedings of the IEE International Workshop on Intelligent Environments*, 2005.

[204] Arno Wacker, Mirko Knoll, Timo Heiber, and Kurt Rothermel. A new approach for establishing pairwise keys for securing wireless sensor networks. In *SenSys '05: Proceedings of the 3rd International Conference on Embedded Networked Sensor Systems*, pages 27–38, New York, NY, USA, 2005. ACM.

[205] Qiang Wang, Yaoyao Zhu, and Liang Cheng. Reprogramming wireless sensor networks: challenges and approaches. *IEEE Network*, 20:48–55, 2006.

[206] Xi Wang, Fabio Silva, and John Heidemann. Infrastructureless location aware configuration for sensor networks. In *WMCSA '04: Proceedings of the Sixth IEEE Workshop on Mobile Computing Systems and Applications (WMCSA'04)*, pages 174–183, Washington, DC, USA, 2004. IEEE Computer Society.

[207] Roy Want, Kenneth P. Fishkin, Anuj Gujar, and Beverly L. Harrison. Bridging physical and virtual worlds with electronic tags. In *Proceedings of the SIGCHI Conference on Human factors in Computing Systems*, 1999.

[208] Brett Warneke, Matt Last, Brian Liebowitz, and Kristofer S. J. Pister. Smart dust: Communicating with a cubic-millimeter computer. *IEEE Computer*, 34(1):44–51, 2001.

[209] Mark Weiser. The computer for the 21st century. *Scientific American*, 265(3):94–104, September 1991.

[210] Mark Weiser. Some computer science issues in ubiquitous computing. *Communications of the ACM*, 36(7):75–84, 1993.

[211] Chih-Yu Wen and William A. Sethares. Automatic decentralized clustering for wireless sensor networks. *EURASIP J. Wirel. Commun. Netw.*, 5(5):686–697, 2005.

[212] Geoffrey Werner-Allen, Konrad Lorincz, Matt Welsh, Omar Marcillo, Jeff Johnson, Mario Ruiz, and Jonathan Lees. Deploying a wireless sensor network on an active volcano. *IEEE Internet Computing*, 10(2):18–25, 2006.

[213] Tracy Westeyn, Helene Brashear, Amin Atrash, and Thad Starner. Georgia tech gesture toolkit: Supporting experiments in gesture recognition. In *Proceedings of the 5th International Conference on Multimodal Interfaces*, 2003.

[214] E. Westkaemper, L. Jendoubi, M. Eissele, and T. Ertl. Smart factory - bridging the gap between digital planning and reality. In *Proceedings of the 38th CIRP International Seminar on Manufacturing Systems*. CIRP, May 2005.

[215] Kamin Whitehouse, Chris Karlof, and David Culler. A practical evaluation of radio signal strength for ranging-based localization. *SIGMOBILE Mobile Computing and Communications Review*, 11(1):41–52, 2007.

[216] Alec Woo, Terence Tong, and David Culler. Taming the underlying challenges of reliable multihop routing in sensor networks. In *SenSys '03: Proceedings of the 1st international conference on Embedded networked sensor systems*, pages 14–27, New York, NY, USA, 2003. ACM Press.

[217] Anthony D. Wood and John A. Stankovic. Denial of service in sensor networks. *Computer*, 35:54–62, 2002.

[218] Jie Wu. Extended dominating-set-based routing in ad hoc wireless networks with unidirectional links. *IEEE Transactions on Parallel and Distributed Systems*, 13(9):866–881, 2002.

[219] Jie Wu and Hailan Li. On calculating connected dominating set for efficient routing in ad hoc wireless networks. In *DIALM '99: Proceedings of the 3rd international workshop on Discrete algorithms and methods for mobile computing and communications*, pages 7–14, New York, NY, USA, 1999. ACM Press.

[220] Jennifer Yick, Biswanath Mukherjee, and Dipak Ghosal. Wireless sensor network survey. *Computer Networks*, 52(12):2292 – 2330, 2008.

[221] Sunhee Yoon and Cyrus Shahabi. The clustered aggregation (cag) technique leveraging spatial and temporal correlations in wireless sensor networks. *ACM Transactions on Sensor Networks*, 3(1):3, 2007.

[222] Ossama Younis and Sonia Fahmy. Heed: A hybrid, energy-efficient, distributed clustering approach for ad hoc sensor networks. *IEEE Transactions on Mobile Computing*, 3(4):366–379, 2004.

[223] Ossama Younis, Marwan Krunz, and Srinivasan Ramasubramanian. Node clustering in wireless sensor networks: recent developments and deployment challenges. *IEEE Network*, 20(3):20–25, 2006.

[224] Wei Zhang, George Kantor, and Sanjiv Singh. Integrated wireless sensor/actuator networks in an agricultural application. In *SenSys '04: Proceedings of the 2nd international conference on Embedded networked sensor systems*, pages 317–317, New York, NY, USA, 2004. ACM Press.

[225] Ziguo Zhong and Tian He. Msp: multi-sequence positioning of wireless sensor nodes. In *SenSys '07: Proceedings of the 5th international conference on Embedded networked sensor systems*, pages 15–28, New York, NY, USA, 2007. ACM.

Bibliography

Index